BLACK MEN/WHITE MEN

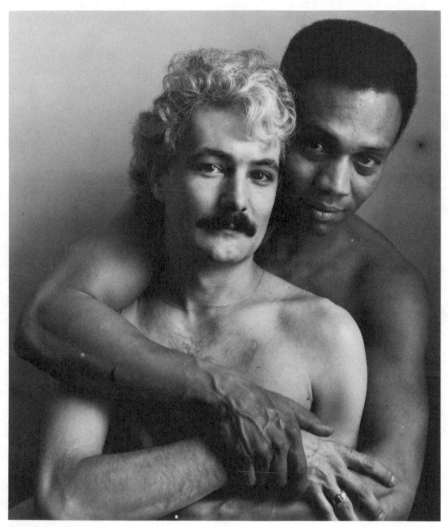

Photo: David Greene

BLACK MEN/WHITE MEN

A Gay Anthology

Edited by Michael J. Smith

Gay Sunshine Press
San Francisco

Cover design by Lois Grimm
Cover and frontispiece photos by David Greene

Library of Congress Cataloging in Publication Data
  Main entry under title:

  Black men/white men.

    1. Homosexuals, Male—Literary collections.   2. American literature—
Men authors.   3. American literature—20th century.   4. Homosexuality,
Male—United   States—Addresses,   essays,   lectures.   5.   Afro-American
men—Addresses, essays, lectures.   I. Smith, Michael J., 1944-

  PS509.H57B55   1983   810'.8'0353   83-16497
  ISBN 0-917342-28-3
  ISBN 0-917342-27-5 (pbk.)

Gay Sunshine Press
P.O. Box 40397
San Francisco, CA 94140
Illustrated catalog of titles available for $1 postage.

CONTENTS

PHOTOS AND DRAWINGS

All Sierra Domino photos are by photographer Calvin Anderson

T'AIN'T NOBODY'S BIZNESS
Homosexuality in 1920's Harlem

Eric Garber

FLAPPERS, RACCOON COATS, cars with running boards, pocket flasks, bathtub gin and jazz bands—all these images spring quickly to mind whenever the Roaring '20s are mentioned. But other images that were just as much a part of that time have slipped out of memory and out of the popular imagination. These are the images of Harlem in the '20s, when a renaissance of Black culture made this poor and crowded neighborhood a vital, busy hub of creativity. Many of the key figures who made the renaissance possible were lesbians and gay men. Then, as now, sexual minorities played an important role in the formation of urban minority culture.

Harlem was largely the creation of the thousands of Black Americans who migrated north after the turn of the century. They came in search of a better life and to escape the racist violence of the South. When the United States entered World War I, a freeze was put on all immigration, and hundreds of openings in northern factories were immediately available for Blacks. Within two decades, large metropolitan communities of Black Americans had sprung up. So significant was this shift of population that historians refer to it as the "Great Migration." Black communities developed in Chicago, Detroit and San Francisco, but the largest and most spectacular was Harlem.

Harlem became the mecca for Afro-Americans all over the country. Nowhere else could you find so large an area, really a city within a city, populated entirely by Blacks. The lure was particularly enticing to young, unmarried, transient Blacks, and Harlem's streets became filled with energetic, often gifted, youth.

Following the war, the United States, yearning in vain for a return to simpler times, took a decided swing to the right. The most conspicuous manifestation of this conservative trend was the prohibi-

7

tion of alcohol, mandated by passage of the 18th Amendment. Hand in hand with this reactionary political climate was the frightening resurgence of White racism. In 1918 alone, 78 Blacks were murdered by White lynch mobs.

The Afro-American community quickly countered with a self-conscious pride and militancy. Marcus Garvey, the charismatic West Indian orator, had thousands of followers in his Black nationalistic "Back to Africa" movement. Black servicemen had been treated with a degree of respect and been given a taste of near equality while in Europe; their wartime experiences influenced their expectations when they returned home. Participation in the war effort had given the Black community a sense of involvement in the American process, and there was a new feeling in the air that demanded participation in the mainstream of American life. W.E.B. Dubois and his National Association for the Advancement of Colored People (NAACP) usually appealed to a more educated crowd than Garvey's followers but were just as powerful and influential. Though different, both of these popular movements offered Black pride and racial unity as a means to help their people.

This rise in Black militancy coincided with a nationwide surge of White interest in aspects of Afro-American culture. Some Whites, in reaction to the nation's new conservatism, had adopted a devil-may-care attitude, tweaking their noses at authority and devoting themselves to the discovery of new thrills. They began to listen to the jazz of Duke Ellington, Fletcher Henderson and Fats Waller. The Charleston and the Black Bottom, dances previously limited to the jazz halls, became national crazes. *Shuffle Along*, an all-Black musical, was a smash success on Broadway and rocketed Florence Mills to stardom. White authors and playwrights began to use race and racial prejudice as serious subject matter.

In Harlem this vogue for the Negro manifested itself primarily in the huge influx of Whites slumming in the district's nightclubs. The Cotton Club, Connie's Inn, Small's Paradise and Pod and Jerry's were packed nightly with Whites drinking bootleg liquor and watching talented Black entertainers.

It came as no surprise to most of Harlem that many of these fancy clubs were exclusively for Whites. The majority of those slumming had little concern for social equality or justice. Americans had recently been exposed to popular versions of the shocking theories of Sigmund Freud. Spotting neuroses, latent homosexual tendencies and other discomfitting evidence of the unconscious at work became a sort of parlor game. Harlem and its inhabitants became a symbol of the "natural" human consciousness, unrestrained and uncontaminated by civilization. A trip to Harlem represented an escape to a primitive, exotic community where the natives were uninhibited, passionate and animalistic. And how convenient—only a taxi ride away!

One of the people primarily responsible for this influx of White tourists to Harlem was the tall, blond, Iowa-born author Carl Van Vechten.

Van Vechten was everything a sophisticated Manhattan dilettante should have been: witty, talented and homosexual. He had written for years as a music critic before achieving acclaim as an author. There was hardly an avant-garde intellectual movement or artistic form that Van Vechten was not on top of. He introduced Gertrude Stein and Ronald Firbank to American audiences and rediscovered Herman Melville. Throughout the '20s he produced a series of novels that were sparkling, frothy and exceedingly camp, including *Peter Whiffle, The Tattooed Countess, The Blind Bow Boy* and *Parties*. Though rarely overtly homosexual, Van Vechten's novels became very popular with the gay set, who sensed a kindred spirit in his preciousness.

In 1924 Van Vechten turned his attention to the Afro-American community, in what was to become, for him, almost an addiction. He began to frequent the nightclubs and saloons, quickly becoming a regular, and his circle of friends included most of educated Harlem. As an influential critic, he helped launch the careers of numerous talented Blacks, but he is notorious for his 1926 novel, naively titled *Nigger Heaven*.

Nigger Heaven told the story of the tragic love between a young Black writer and his Harlem girlfriend and was intended to impart a sympathetic understanding of Harlem and its people. Some of Van Vechten's Black friends, appreciated it, but the majority of Harlem was outraged. The few who could get beyond the title were put off by the author's affectations, which had become a Van Vechten trademark.

The White reading public had the opposite reaction, and the novel quickly became a best seller. After reading the novel, many Whites hurried to Harlem to see the real thing.

But for Van Vechten, and for the other White homosexuals who followed him, Harlem offered deeper rewards than it did to the slumming parties of Flaming Youths. Prior to the '20s, homosexual social life had been limited to private gatherings, annonymous situations such as parks and bathhouses, or to socially disreputable places such as red-light districts or Bowery-like areas. The Jazz Age was a time when lesbians and gay men began to acquire new territories for themselves. These new territories provided greater freedom and made secrecy less crucial. One place where sexual minorities were beginning to meet and socialize was in the bohemian circles of radicals, feminists, artists and free-thinkers that were developing in places such as New York's Greenwich Village and London's Bloomsbury district. Another such place was Harlem.

Many White lesbians and gay men felt a kinship with Harlem's residents, a kinship White heterosexuals were less able to feel. Blair Niles' 1931 novel *Strange Brother* describes a young, White, gay man who frequents the nightclubs and speakeasies of Harlem. He comes to Harlem not to find adventure or make assignations but because he identifies with those he believes are also outcasts from American life. Niles was a heterosexual journalist who was personally involved with uptown gay life, and she modeled the characters of her novel on real individuals. There is no reason to doubt that her fictional portrait was often mirrored in real life.

If White homosexuals found sanctuary and a sense of camaraderie uptown in Harlem, Black lesbians and gay men found a comfortable home. Black homosexuals could be found on the street corners, in the cabarets, at church on Sundays and attending parties. Their bemused, nongay neighbors referred to them as "pansies," "sissies," "bulldykes" (or its variation, "bulldaggers") or people with "freakish ways." Harlem homosexuals, when speaking to each other about themselves, preferred the terms "*the* people" or "*the* life." And as new settlers always do, they quickly developed territories and social institutions all their own.

Speakeasies and nightclubs provided part of this new Black gay territory, and many lesbians and gay men could be found dancing at The Garden of Joy or listening to the bands at Rockland Palace. Entertainer Ethel Waters would later remember loaning her gowns to the "drags" who patronized Edmond's, the club in which she was discovered.

Usually gays were forced to hide their sexual preferences at such clubs and to blend in with the heterosexuals, but there were several Harlem speakeasies, actually little more than dives, that catered specifically to the pansy trade. One such place, an "open" speakeasy, since there was no doorman to keep the uninvited away, was located on the northwest corner of 126th Street and 7th Avenue. It was a large, dimly lit bar where gay men could go to pick up rough trade. Artist Bruce Nugent, who occasionally went there, remembers it catering to "rough" queers ... the kind that fought better than truckdrivers and swished better than Mae West." The rowdy atmosphere and the frequent fights limited the speakeasy's patronage.

Within the Black entertainment milieu, composed of the singers, dancers, musicians and actors who provided much of the excitement of the nightlife of Harlem, homosexuality was not a liability. Female impersonators Charles Anderson and "Gloria Swanson" were well known and well respected within the community. George Hanna could sing of his "freakish ways" without fear of censure. The debonair Porter Grainger, composer of the blues classic "T'ain't Nobody's Bizness" and an intimate of Van Vechten's, was not judged on his private life.

For lesbians, whose social options were even more limited, the Black entertainment field also offered support for non-traditional lifestyles. Harlem lesbian Mabel Hampton left her family home in Winston-Salem, N.C. to migrate to the North. She worked with her lover as a dancer in a Coney Island show before landing a position at the famed Lafayette Theatre. Being a dancer gave Hampton a good income, limited her social contact with heterosexual men, and provided her with a predominantly lesbian social group of similarly inclined chorus girls.

Many bixexual and lesbian Black women sought the advantages of the show-business life, including Ma Rainey, Bessie Smith, Jackie "Moms" Mabley and Josephine Baker. But undoubtedly the most celebrated lesbian to find her home in the Harlem nightlife was Gladys Bentley. She was born into a poor Pennsylvania family in 1907. Even as a youngster her boyish ways were noticeable, and eventually the unhappy girl, tormented by family and schoolmates alike, ran away from home to try and earn her living. She got her first job at The Mad House on 133rd Street, after convincing the owner that a girl could play piano just as well as a boy. Her exceptional musical abilities and her habit of wearing male attire not only got her the job, they made her famous. During the '20s, Bentley played most of the fashionable clubs in Harlem. She was the featured entertainer at the popular after-hours eatery The Clam House, where she entertained guests with the risque lyrics she wrote to popular melodies. For a time, she owned and operated The Exclusive Club.

Bentley was always open about her lesbianism. She would parade daily down 7th Avenue in men's clothing and even married her girlfriend in an Atlantic City civil ceremony in the early 1930s. Bentley, of course, wore the tuxedo. A friend remembers her as being genuinely happy about her homosexuality.

"Buffet flats" were another social institution that tolerated, and frequently encouraged, homosexual patronage. Apartments where rooms could be rented by the night, buffet flats had sprung up during the late 1800s to provide overnight accommodations to Black travelers, who were often refused service in White-owned hotels. By the 1920s, buffet flats ranged from genteel apartments offering food and lodging; to more raucous establishments where numerous illegal activities such as drinking, gambling, and prostitution were available; to riotous sex circuses where a wide variety of sexual pleasures were provided cafeteria-style. Hazel Valentine ran such a circus on 140th Street. It catered to homosexuals as well as heterosexuals and became so notorious that both Fats Waller and Count Basie composed tunes commemorating it.

A homosexual relative of Al Capone financed another buffet flat in Chicago. More sedate than Hazel Valentine's, this flat would sometimes hold racially mixed parties for gay men. The proceedings were festive, with couples discreetly meandering into the back rooms when they wished to be alone.

Even though the Harlem nightlife and the buffet flats offered Black lesbians and gay men certain benefits, they were, at least technically, illegal. But the frequent drag balls, where both women and men could dress as they pleased and dance with whom they wished, were not only socially acceptable, they were officially sanctioned.

Drag balls, part of the American homosexual underground for decades, had developed from clandestine private events into lavish formal affairs attended by thousands. The Harlem balls in particular were anticipated with great excitement by both Blacks and Whites. The largest were annual events at the regal Rockland Palace, which held up to 6,000 people. Only slightly smaller were the ones given irregularly at the dazzling Savoy Ballroom, with its crystal chandeliers and elegant marble staircase. The organizers would obtain a police permit making the ball, and its participants, legal for the evening. The highlight of the event was the beauty contest, in which the fashionably dressed drags would vie for the title Queen of the Ball. Julian, the White protagonist of the classic 1933 gay novel by Charles Henri Ford and Parker Tyler, *The Young and Evil*, dons a little make-up (just enough to be "considered in costume and so get in for a dollar less") and sets off to a Harlem ball. Once there he greets his friends, dances to the jazz music, gets exceedingly drunk, flirts with the band leader and eventually exchanges phone numbers with a handsome stranger.

But drag balls had their disadvantages. A large percentage of those who attended the balls were heterosexual, there to observe rather than participate. It was not unusual to see the cream of Harlem society, as well as much of the White avant-garde set, on the ballroom's bandstand, straining their necks to view the drags. Many gays didn't like being gawked at.

Private parties were the best place for Black lesbians and gay men to socialize. "We used to go to parties every other night . . . . The girls all had the parties," remembers Mabel Hampton.

Like much in Harlem, parties were extremely varied. The commonest kind was the "rent party." Few of Harlem's residents had much money, and sometimes rent was hard to come by. To raise funds, people would throw an enormous party, inviting the public and charging admission. There would be dancing and jazz, and bootleg liquor for sale in the kitchen. It is about just such a party that Bessie Smith sang her famous "Gimmie a pigfoot and a bottle of beer." On any given Saturday night, there would be scores of these parties throughout Harlem. Those in attendance rarely knew their hosts. The dancing and merriment would continue until dawn, and by morning the landlord could be paid.

One such party was satirically described by Wallace Thurman in his 1932 novel *Infants of the Spring*. To raise supplies, the residents of a Harlem boarding house decide to throw a donation party; the price of admission is a sack of groceries. By 11 p.m. a crowd has assembled and the party is under way. Among the multitude of schoolteachers, intellectuals and artists is a flamboyant bisexual painter, Paul Arbian, who proudly displays his new protege, a handsome bootblack, to the "fanciful aggregation of Greenwich Village uranians" he has invited. Apparently, anything was likely to ocur at rent parties.

One gay Harlemite whose parties were more exclusive was Alexander Gumby. Gumby, who had arrived in Harlem near the turn of the century, immediately became entranced with the theatrical set and decided to open a salon to attract them. He saved the money he earned as a postal clerk and rented a large studio on 5th Avenue between 131st and 132nd streets. Known as Gumby's Bookstore because of the hundreds of books that lined the walls, the salon drew many theatrical and artistic luminaries. White author Samuel Steward remembers being taken to Gumby's one evening by a lesbian friend and enjoying a delightful evening of "reefer," bathtub gin, a game of truth and homosexual carrying on.

Certainly the most opulent parties in Harlem were thrown by the heiress A'Lelia Walker. A'Lelia was a striking, tall, dark-skinned woman who was rarely seen without her riding crop and her imposing, jeweled turban. She was the only daughter of Madame C.J. Walker, a former washerwoman who had made millions marketing her own hair-straightening process. When she died, Madame Walker left virtually her entire fortune to A'Lelia.

Whereas Madame Walker had been civic minded, donating thousands of dollars to charity, A-Lelia used most of her inheritance to throw lavish parties in her palatial Hudson River estate, Villa Lewaro, and at her Manhattan dwelling on 136th Street. Because A'Lelia adored the company of lesbians and gay men, her parties had a distinctly gay ambiance. Elegant homosexuals Edward Perry, Caska Bonds and Van Vechten became her closest friends and were regulars at her affairs. Everyone from chorus girls to artists to socialites to visiting royalty would come at least once to enjoy her hospitality.

A'Lelia took particular pleasure from the Black poets, artists and writers of Harlem. This should not be surprising. Just as White bohemia served as a refuge for sexual nonconformists, so too did Black bohemia. Many of the writers, intellectuals and artists of what we now call the Harlem Renaissance were homosexual, bisexual or otherwise sexually unorthodox. Their status as artists, part of the "talented tenth" who were thought by DuBois to be the saviors of their race, protected them from public disapproval of their private lives. Alain Locke, the Howard University professor who heralded the renaissance in 1925 with his seminal anthology *The New Negro*, received no censure for never marrying, nor for his predilection for intelligent, male students.

That poet Langston Hughes never married was seen as peculiar, but the motives behind his bachelorhood were never questioned. The community was certainly aware of poet Countee Cullen's lifelong relationship with Harlem schoolteacher Harold Jackman, but people remained tactfully silent. Arna Bontemps would later remember Cullen and Jackman as the "Jonathan and David of the Harlem Renaissance."

But the most bohemian of them all was Richard Bruce Nugent.

Raised in a proper Washington, D.C., family, Nugent dabbled successfully in painting, drawing, poetry and dancing. He was self-consciously avant-garde and often had no permanent address, preferring to drift from place to place. Nugent spent much of his time drawing erotic, often phallic, drawings.

Bruce Nugent (left) & Philander Thomas, with a deck steward on the *Bremen,* on their way to London (*Porgy* tour, ca. 1927)
Photo courtesy of Bruce Nugent

Nugent was openly homosexual throughout the renaissance period but was seldom rebuffed because of it. He is credited with writing the first fictional portrayal of Black male homosexuality: In 1926 in the Harlem little magazine *Fire!!*, he published "Smoke, Lilies and Jade" (under the pseudonym "Richard Bruce" to avoid parental disapproval). The story concerned a Harlem homosexual who falls in love with a stunningly beautiful Latin male. A good portion of Harlem society found the story shocking. Nevertheless, Nugent was ostracized for no more than a few days.

The editor of *Fire!!*, Wallace Thurman, was a close friend of Nugent's. Thurman was an iconoclast: cynical, sarcastic, alcoholic and deeply ambivalent about his bisexuality. After the demise of *Fire!!*, which in fact ran for only one issue, Thurman published a novel that has since become a classic of the Harlem Renaissance, *The Blacker the Berry . . .* (1929). The novel concerns the attempts of a dark-skinned woman to overcome the color prejudices of her own culture. Thurman brings homosexual situations into the plot twice: once in the form of a lesbian boarding-house manager, and again in the form of the protagonist's bisexual boyfriend.

But it is in *Infants of the Spring* that Thurman deals most explicitly with homosexuality. Published in 1932, this obvious *roman a clef* retrospectively satirizes the Harlem Renaissance movement and its participants. It focuses on two Black bohemians: Paul, the flamboyant bisexual artist mentioned earlier, and Raymond, a dark-skinned writer who develops a quasi-homosexual relationship with a White youth. One would have to overlook much of the novel's commentary to categorize *Infants of the Spring* as exclusively homosexual in nature; Thurman was writing about more than that. But there is no mistaking the importance of homosexuality to the novel's plot: a point often ignored by heterosexual critics.

The stock market crash of 1929 brought the glittering Jazz Age to an abrupt halt. Without the money of the White pleasure seekers, the buoyant spirit of Harlem gave way to the far more insistent reality of the worldwide Depression. But gifts from this generation of lesbians and gay men still survive for us, 60 years later. Ma Rainey's "Prove It on Me Blues" still speaks to the pride and strength of lesbians. The work of Bruce Nugent and Wallace Thurman reminds us that much of gay male life and thought has remained the same. These pioneer lesbians and gay men have left us a legacy that speaks to the wide diversity of our evolving gay culture. It is a legacy we should not forget.

SMOKE, LILIES AND JADE
A Short Story

Bruce Nugent

This story is believed to be the first fictional portrait of Black gay male life in the United States. It was published in the Harlem Renaissance magazine, Fire!! *(1926). For more on Bruce Nugent see the preceding article by Eric Garber (with accompanying photo) and the biographical note at the end of this volume.*

H E WANTED TO DO SOMETHING ... to write or draw ... or something ... but it was so comfortable just to lay there on the bed ... his shoes off ... and think ... think of everything ... short disconnected thoughts—to wonder ... to remember ... to think and smoke ... why wasn't he worried that he had no money ... he *had* had five cents ... but he had been hungry ... he *was* hungry and still ... all he wanted to do was ... lay there comfortably smoking ... think ... wishing he were writing ... or drawing ... or something ... something about the things he felt and thought ... but what did he think ... he remembered how his mother had awakened him one night ... ages ago ... six years ago ... Alex ... he had always wondered at the strangeness of it ... she had seemed so ... so ... so just the same ... Alex ... I think your father is dead ... and it hadn't seemed so strange ... yet ... one's mother didn't say that ... didn't wake one at midnight every night to say ... feel him ... put your hand on his head ... then whisper with a catch in her voice ... I'm afraid ... sh don't wake Lam ... yet it hadn't seemed as it should have seemed ... even when he had felt his father's cool wet forehead ... it hadn't been tragic ... the light had been turned very low ... and flickered ... yet it hadn't been tragic ... or weird ... not at all as one should feel when one's father died ... even his reply of ... yes he is dead ... had been commonplace

. . . hadn't been dramatic . . . there had been no tears . . . no sobs
. . . not even a sorrow . . . and yet he must have realized that one's
father couldn't smile . . . or sing any more . . . after he had died . . .
every one remembered his father's voice . . . it had been a lush voice
. . . a promise . . . then that dressing together . . . his mother and
himself . . . in the bathroom . . . why was the bathroom always the
warmest room in the winter . . . as they had put on their clothes . . .
his mother had been telling him what he must do . . . and cried softly . . . and that had made him cry too but you mustn't cry Alex . . .
remember you have to be a little man now . . . and that was all . . .
didn't other wives and sons cry more for their dead than that . . .
anyway people never cried for beautiful sunsets . . . or music . . .
and those were the things that hurt . . . the things to sympathize
with . . . then out into the snow and dark of the morning . . . first
to the undertaker's . . . no first to Uncle Frank's . . . why did Aunt
Lula have to act like that . . . to ask again and again . . . but when
did he die . . . when did he die . . . I just can't believe it . . . poor
Minerva . . . then out into the snow and dark again . . . how had his
mother expected him to know where to find the night bell at the
undertaker's . . . he was the most sensible of them all tho . . . all he
had said was . . . what . . . Harry Francis . . . too bad . . . tell
mamma I'll be there first thing in the morning . . . then down the
deserted streets again . . . to grandmother's . . . it was growing light
now . . . it must be terrible to die in daylight . . . grandpa had been
sweeping the snow off the yard . . . he had been glad of that because
. . . well he could tell him better than grandma . . . grandpa . . .
father's dead . . . and he hadn't acted strange either . . . books lied
. . . he had just looked at Alex a moment then continued sweeping
. . . all he said was . . . what time did he die . . . she'll want to know
. . . then passing thru the lonesome street toward home . . . Mrs.
Mamie Grant was closing a window and spied him . . . hallow Alex
. . . an' how's your father this mornin' . . . dead . . . get out . . . tch
tch tch an' I was just around there with a cup a' custard yesterday
. . . Alex puffed contentedly on his cigarette . . . he was hungry and
comfortable . . . and he had an ivory holder inlaid with red jade and
green . . . funny how the smoke seemed to climb up that ray of sunlight . . . went up the slant just like imagination . . . was imagination blue . . . or was it because he had spent his last five cents and
couldn't worry . . . anyway it was nice to lay there and wonder . . .
and remember. . . why was he so different from other people . . .
the only things he remembered of his father's funeral were the
crowded church and the ride in the hack . . . so many people there
in the church . . . and ladies with tears in their eyes . . . and on their

cheeks . . . and some men too . . . why did people cry . . . vanity that
was all . . . yet they weren't exactly hypocrites . . . but why . . . it
had made him furious . . . all these people crying . . . it wasn't *their*
father . . . and he wasn't crying . . . couldn't cry for sorrow altho he
had loved his father more than . . . than . . . it had made him so
angry that tears had come to his eyes . . . and he had been ashamed
of his mother . . . crying into a handkerchief . . . so ashamed that
tears had run down his cheeks and he had frowned . . . and some
one . . . a woman . . . had said . . . look at that poor little dear . . .
Alex is just like his father . . . and the tears had run fast . . . because
he *wasn't* like his father . . . he couldn't sing . . . he didn't want to
sing . . . he didn't want to sing . . . Alex blew a cloud of smoke . . .
blue smoke . . . when they had taken his father from the vault three
weeks later . . . he had grown beautiful . . . his nose had become
perfect and clear . . . his hair had turned jet black and glossy and
silky . . . and his skin was a transparent green . . . like the sea only
not so deep . . . and where it was drawn over the cheek bones a pale
beautiful red appeared . . . like a blush . . . why hadn't his father
looked like that always . . . but no . . . to have sung would have
broken the wondrous repose of his lips and maybe that was his
beauty . . . maybe it was wrong to think thoughts like these . . . but
they were nice and pleasant and comfortable . . . when one was
smoking a cigarette thru an ivory holder . . . inlaid with red jade
and green . . . . .

he wondered why he couldn't find work . . . a job . . . when he had
first come to New York he had . . . and he had only been fourteen
then was it because he was nineteen now that he felt so idle . . . and
contented . . . or because he was an artist . . . but was he an artist
. . . was one an artist until one became known . . . of course he was
an artist . . . and strangely enough so were all his friends . . . he
should be ashamed that he didn't work . . . but . . . was it five years
in New York . . . or the fact that he was an artist . . . when his
mother said she couldn't understand him . . . why did he vaguely
pity her instead of being ashamed . . . he should be . . . his mother
and all his relatives said so . . . his brother was three years younger
than he and yet he had already been away from home a year . . . on
the stage . . . making thirty-five dollars a week . . . had three suits
and many clothes and was going to help his mother . . . while he . . .
Alex . . . was content to lay and smoke and meet friends at night . . .
to argue and read Wilde . . . Freud . . . Boccaccio and Schnitzler . . .
to attend Gurdjieff meetings and know things . . . Why did they
scoff at him for knowing such people as Carl . . . Mencken . . .
Toomer . . . Hughes . . . Cullen . . . Wood . . . Cabell . . . oh the

whole lot of them[†] . . . was it because it seemed incongruous that
he . . . who was so little known . . . should call by first names people they would like to know . . . were they jealous . . . no mothers
aren't jealous of their sons . . . they are proud of them . . . why then
. . . when these friends accepted and liked him . . . no matter how
he dressed . . . why did mother ask . . . and you went looking like
that . . . Langston was a fine fellow . . . he knew there was
something in Alex . . . and so did Rene and Borgia . . . and Zora and
Clement and Miguel . . . and . . . and . . . and all of them . . . if he
went to see mother she would ask . . . how do you feel Alex with
nothing in your pockets . . . I don't see how you can be satisfied . . .
Really you're a mystery to me . . . and who you take after . . . I'm
sure I don't know . . . none of my brothers were lazy and shiftless
. . . I can never remember the time when they weren't sending
money home and your father was your age he was supporting a
family . . . where you get your nerve I don't know . . . just because
you've tried to write one or two little poems and stories that no one
understands . . . you seem to think the world owes you a living . . .
you should see by now how much is thought of them . . . you can't
sell anything . . . and you won't do anything to make money . . .
wake up Alex . . . I don't know what will become of you . . . . .
    it was hard to believe in one's self after that . . . did Wilde's
parents or Shelly's or Goya's talk to them like that . . . but it was
depressing to think in that vein . . . Alex stretched and yawned . . .
Max had died . . . Margaret had died . . . so had Sonia . . . Cynthia
. . . Juan-Jose and Harry . . . all people he had loved . . . loved one
by one and together . . . and all had died . . . he never loved a person
long before they died . . . in truth he was tragic . . . that was a lovely
appellation . . . The Tragic Genius . . . think . . . to go thru life
known as The Tragic Genius . . . romantic . . . but it was more or
less true . . . Alex turned over and blew another cloud of smoke . . .
was all life like that . . . smoke . . . blue smoke from an ivory holder
. . . he wished he were in New Bedford . . . New Bedford was a nice
place . . . snug little houses set complacently behind protecting
lawns . . . half open windows showing prim interiors from behind
waving cool curtains . . . inviting . . . like precise courtesans wink-

---

†These friends of Nugent were associated with the Harlem Renaissance:
Carl Van Vechten (1880-1964), music critic, novelist, author of *The Blind
Bow Boy* etc. Henry Louis Mencken (1880-1956), editor, author, critic. Jean
Toomer (1894-1967), author of the poetic novel *Cane*. Langston Hughes
(1902-1967), and Countee Cullen (1904-1946), poets. Clement Wood
(1888-1950), novelist, poet, author of *Deep River*. James Branch Cabell
(1879-1958), experimental novelist, author of *Jurgen*.

ing from behind lace fans . . . and trees . . . many trees . . . casting
lacey patterns of shade on the sun dipped sidewalks . . . small
stores . . . naively proud of their pseudo grandeur . . . banks . . .
called institutions for saving . . . all naive . . . that was it . . . New
Bedford was naive . . . after the sophistication of New York it
would fan one like a refreshing breeze . . . and yet he '
in New York . . . and sophistication . . . was he sophist
because he was seldom bored . . . seldom bored by anyt.
weren't the sophisticated continually suffering from er.
the contrary . . . he was amused . . . amused by the arti
naively and sophistication alike . . . but may be that in l
the essence of sophistication or . . . was it cynicism . . . or \
two identical . . . he blew a cloud of smoke . . . it was groun
now . . . and the smoke no longer had a ladder to climb . . . bu
the moon would rise and then he would clothe the silver mo
blue smoke garments . . . truly smoke was like imagination .

Alex sat up . . . pulled on his shoes and went out . . . it was a be
tiful night . . . and so large . . . the dusky blue hung like a curtain
in an immense arched doorway . . . fastened with silver tacks . . .
to wander in the night was wonderful . . . myriads of inquisitive
lights . . . curiously prying into the dark . . . and fading unsatisfied
. . . he passed a woman . . . she was not beautiful . . . and he was
sad because she did not weep that she would never be beautiful . . .
was it Wilde who had said . . . a cigarette is the most perfect
pleasure because it leaves one unsatisfied . . . the breeze gave to
him a perfume stolen from some wandering lady of the evening . . .
it pleased him . . . why was it that men wouldn't use perfumes . . .
they should . . . each and every one of them liked perfumes . . . the
man who denied that was a liar . . . or a coward . . . but if ever he
were to voice that thought . . . express it . . . he would be misunderstood . . . a fine feeling that . . . to be misunderstood . . . it made
him feel tragic and great . . . but may be it would be nicer to be
understood . . . but no . . . no great artist is . . . then again neither
were fools . . . they were strangely akin these two . . . Alex thought
of a sketch he would make . . . a personality sketch of Fania . . .
straight classic features tinted proud purple . . . sensuous fine lips
. . . gilded for truth . . . eyes . . . half opened and lids colored mysterious green . . . hair black and straight . . . drawn sternly mock-
ing back from the false puritanical forehead . . . maybe he would
make Edith too . . . skin a blue . . . infinite like night . . . and eyes
. . . slant and grey . . . very complacent like a cat's . . . Mona Lisa
lips . . . red and seductive as . . . as pomegranate juice . . . in truth
it was fine to be young and hungry and an artist . . . to blow blue

smoke from an ivory holder . . . . .

here was the cafeteria . . . it was almost as tho it had journeyed
to meet him . . . the night was so blue . . . how does blue feel . . .
or red or gold or any other color . . . if colors could be heard he
could paint most wondrous tunes . . . symphonious . . . think . . .
the dulcet clear tone of a blue like night . . . of a red like pomegranate juice . . . like Edith's lips . . . of the fairy tones to be heard
in a sunset . . . like rubies shaken in a crystal cup . . . of the sym-
phony of Fania . . . and silver . . . and gold . . . he had heard the
sound of gold . . . but they weren't the sounds he wanted to catch
. . . no . . . they must be liquid . . . not so staccato but flowing varia-
tions of the same caliber . . . there was no one in the cafe as yet . . .
he sat and waited . . . that was a clever idea he had had about color
music . . . but after all he was a monstrous clever fellow . . . Jurgen
had said that . . . how does one go about getting an introduction to
a fiction character . . . go up to the brown cover of the book and
knock gently . . . and say hello . . . then timidly . . . is Duke Jurgen
there . . . or . . . no because if entered the book in the beginning
Jurgen would only be a pawn broker . . . and one didn't enter a book
in the center . . . but what foolishness . . . Alex lit a cigarette . . . but
Cabell was a master to have written Jurgen . . . and an artist . . .
and a poet . . . Alex blew a cloud of smoke . . . a few lines of one of
Langston's poems came to describe Jurgen . . . . .

> Somewhat like Ariel
> Somewhat like Puck
> Somewhat like a gutter boy
> Who loves to play in muck.
> Somewhat like Bacchus
> Somewhat like Pan
> And a way with women
> Like a sailor man . . .

Langston must have known Jurgen . . . suppose Jurgen had met
Tonio Kroeger . . . what a vagrant thought . . . Kroeger . . . Kroeger
. . . Kroeger . . . why here was Rene . . . Alex had almost gone to
sleep . . . Alex blew a cone of smoke as he took Rene's hand . . . it
was nice to have friends like Rene . . . so comfortable . . . Rene was
speaking . . . Borgia joined them . . . and de Diego Padro . . . their
talk veered to . . . James Branch Cabell . . . beautiful . . . marvelous
. . . Rene had an enchanting accent . . . said sank for thank and
souse for south . . . but they couldn't know Cabell's greatness . . .
Alex searched the smoke for expression . . . he . . . he . . . well he
has created a phantasy mire . . . that's it . . . from clear rich im-

agery . . . life and silver sands . . . that's nice . . . and silver sands
. . . imagine lilies growing in such a mire . . . when they close at
night their gilded underside would protect . . . but that's not it at
all . . . his thoughts just carried and mingled like . . . like odors . . .
suggested but never definite . . . Rene was leaving . . . they all were
leaving . . . Alex sauntered slowly back . . . the houses all looked
sleepy . . . funny . . . made him feel like writing poetry . . . and
about death too . . . an elevated crashed by overhead scattering all
his thoughts with its noise . . . making them spread . . . in circles
. . . then larger circles . . . just like a splash in a calm pool . . . what
had he been thinking . . . of . . . a poem about death . . . but he no
longer felt that urge . . . just walk and think and wonder . . . think
and remember and smoke . . . blow smoke that mixed with his
thoughts and the night . . . he would like to live in a large white
palace . . . to wear a long black cape . . . very full and lined with ver-
million . . . to have many cushions and to lie there among them . . .
talking to his friends . . . lie there in a yellow silk shirt and black
velvet trousers . . . like music-review artists talking and pouring
strange liquors from curiously beautiful bottles . . . bottles with
long slender necks . . . he climbed the noisy stair of the odorous
tenement . . . smelled of fish . . . of stale fried fish and dirty milk
bottles . . . he rather liked it . . . he liked the acrid smell of horse
manure too . . . strong . . . thoughts . . . yes to lie back among
strangely fashioned cushions and sip eastern wines and talk . . .
Alex threw himself on the bed . . . removed his shoes . . . stretched
and relaxed . . . yes and have music waft softly into the darkened
and incensed room . . . he blew a cloud of smoke . . . oh the joy of
being an artist and of blowing blue smoke thru an ivory holder inlaid with red jade and green . . . . .

the street was so long and narrow . . . so long and narrow . . . and
blue . . . in the distance it reached the stars . . . and if he walked
long enough . . . far enough . . . he could reach the stars too . . . the
narrow blue was so empty . . . quiet . . . Alex walked music . . . it
was nice to walk in the blue after a party . . . Zora had shone again
. . . her stories . . . she always shone . . . and Monty was glad . . .
every one was glad when Zora shone . . . he was glad he had gone
to Monty's party . . . Monty had a nice place in the village . . . nice
lights . . . and friends and wine . . . mother would be scandalized
that he could think of going to a party . . . without a copper to his
name . . . but then mother had never been to Monty's . . . and
mother had never seen the street seem long and narrow and blue
. . . Alex walked music . . . the click of his heels kept time with a

tune in his mind . . . he glanced into a lighted cafe window . . . inside were people sipping coffee . . . men . . . why did they sit there in the loud light . . . didn't they know that outside the street . . . the narrow blue street met the stars . . . that if they walked long enough . . . far enough . . . Alex walked and the click of his heels sounded . . . and had an echo . . . sound being tossed back and forth . . . back and forth . . . some one was approaching . . . and their echoes mingled . . . and gave the sound of castanets . . . Alex liked the sound of the approaching man's footsteps . . . he walked music also . . . he knew the beauty of the narrow blue . . . Alex knew that by the way their echoes mingled . . . he wished he would speak . . . but strangers don't speak at four o'clock in the morning . . . at least if they did he couldn't imagine what would be said . . . maybe . . . pardon me but are you walking toward the stars . . . yes, sir, and if you walk long enough . . . then may I walk with you I want to reach the stars too . . . perdone me señor tiene vd. fosforo . . . Alex was glad he had been addressed in Spanish . . . to have been asked for a match in English . . . or to have been addressed in English at all . . . would have been blasphemy just then . . . Alex handed him a match . . . he glanced at his companion apprehensively in the match glow . . . he was afraid that his appearance would shatter the blue thoughts . . . and stars . . . ah . . . his face was a perfect compliment to his voice . . . and the echo of their steps mingled . . . they walked in silence . . . the castanets of their heels clicking accompaniment . . . the stranger inhaled deeply and with a nod of content and a smile . . . blew a cloud of smoke . . . Alex felt like singing . . . the stranger knew the magic of blue smoke also . . . they continued in silence . . . the castanets of their heels clicking rhythmically . . . Alex turned in his doorway . . . up the stairs and the stranger waited for him to light the room . . . no need for words . . . they had always known each other . . . . . as they undressed by the blue dawn . . . Alex knew he had never seen a more perfect being . . . his body was all symmetry and music . . . and Alex called him Beauty . . . long they lay . . . blowing smoke and exchanging thoughts . . . and Alex swallowed with difficulty . . . he felt a glow of tremor . . . and they talked and . . . slept . . . . .

Alex wondered more and more why he liked Adrian so . . . he liked many people . . . Wallie . . . Zora . . . Clement . . . Gloria . . . Langston . . . John . . . Gwenny . . . oh many people . . . and they were friends . . . but Beauty . . . it was different . . . once Alex had admired Beauty's strength . . . and Beauty's eyes had grown soft and he had said . . . I like you more than any one Dulce . . . Adrian always called him Dulce . . . and Alex had become confused . . . was

it that he was so susceptible to beauty that Alex liked Adrian so
much . . . but no . . . he knew other people who were beautiful . . .
Fania and Gloria . . . Monty and Bunny . . . but he was never confused before them . . . while Beauty . . . Beauty could make him believe in Buddha . . . or imps . . . and no one else could do that . . .
that is no one but Melva . . . but then he was in love with Melva . . .
and that explained that . . . he would like Beauty to know Melva . . .
they were both so perfect . . . such compliments . . . yes he would
like Beauty to know Melva because he loved them both . . . there
. . . he had thought it . . . actually dared to think it . . . but Beauty
must never know . . . Beauty couldn't understand . . . indeed Alex
couldn't understand . . . and it pained him . . . almost physically . . .
and tired his mind . . . Beauty . . . Beauty was in the air . . . the
smoke . . . Beauty . . . Melva . . . Beauty . . . Melva . . . Alex slept . . .
and dreamed . . . . .

he was in a field . . . a field of blue smoke and black poppies and
red calla lilies . . . he was searching . . . on his hands and knees . . .
searching . . . among black poppies and red calla lilies . . . he was
searching pushed aside poppy stems . . . and saw two strong white
legs . . . dancer's legs . . . the contours pleased him . . . his eyes
wandered . . . on past the muscular hocks to the firm white thighs
. . . the rounded buttocks . . . then the lithe narrow waist . . . strong
torso and broad deep chest . . . the heavy shoulders . . . the graceful
muscled neck . . . squared chin and quizzical lips . . . grecian nose
with its temperamental nostrils . . . the brown eyes looking at him
. . . like . . . Monty looked at Zora . . . his hair curly and black and
all tousled . . . and it was Beauty . . . and Beauty smiled and looked
at him and smiled . . . said . . . I'll wait Alex . . . and Alex became
confused and continued his search . . . on his hands and knees . . .
pushing aside poppy stems and lily stems . . . a poppy . . . a black
poppy . . . a lily . . . a red lily . . . and when he looked back he could
no longer see Beauty . . . Alex continued his search . . . thru poppies
. . . lilies . . . poppies and red calla lilies . . . and suddenly he saw
. . . two small feet olive-ivory . . . two well turned legs curving
gracefully from slender ankles . . . and the contours soothed him
. . . he followed them . . . past the narrow rounded hips to the tiny
waist . . . the fragile firm breasts . . . the graceful slender throat . . .
the soft rounded chin . . . slightly parting lips and straight little
nose with its slightly flaring nostrils . . . the black eyes with lights
in them . . . looking at him . . . the forehead and straight cut black
hair . . . and it was Melva . . . and she looked at him and smiled and
said . . . I'll wait Alex . . . and Alex became confused and kissed her
. . . became confused and continued his search . . . on his hands and

knees . . . pushed aside a poppy stem . . . a black-poppy stem . . .
pushed aside a lily stem . . . a red-lily stem . . . a poppy . . . a poppy
. . . a lily . . . and suddenly he stood erect . . . exultant . . . and in
his hand he held . . . an ivory holder . . . inlaid with red jade . . . and
green . . . . .
　　and Alex awoke . . . Beauty's hair ticked his nose . . . Beauty was
smiling in his sleep . . . half his face stained flush color by the sun
. . . the other half in shadow . . . blue shadow . . . his eye lashes
casting cobwebby blue shadows on his cheek . . . his lips were so
beautiful . . . quizzical . . . Alex wondered why he always thought
of that passage from Wilde's *Salome* . . . when he looked at Beauty's
lips . . . I would kiss your lips . . . he *would* like to kiss Beauty's lips
. . . Alex flushed warm . . . with shame . . . or was it shame . . . he
reached across Beauty for a cigarette . . . Beauty's cheek felt cool
to his arm . . . his hair felt soft . . . Alex lay smoking . . . such a
dream . . . red calla lilies . . . red calla lilies . . . and . . . what could
it all mean . . . did dreams have meanings . . . Fania said . . . and
black poppies . . . thousands . . . millions . . . Beauty stirred . . .
Alex put out his cigarette . . . closed his eyes . . . he mustn't see
Beauty yet . . . speak to him . . . his lips were too hot . . . dry . . .
the palms of his hands too cool and moist . . . thru his half closed
eyes he could see Beauty . . . propped . . . cheek in hand . . . on one
elbow . . . looking at him . . . lips smiling quizzically . . . he wished
Beauty wouldn't look so hard . . . Alex was finding it difficult to
breathe . . . breathe normally . . . why *must* Beauty look so long . . .
and smile *that* way . . . his face seemed nearer . . . it was . . . Alex
could feel Beauty's hair on his forehead . . . breathe normally . . .
breathe normally . . . could feel Beauty's breath on his nostrils and
lips . . . and it was clean and faintly colored with tobacco . . .
breathe normally Alex . . . Beauty's lips were nearer . . . Alex closed
his eyes . . . how did one act . . . his pulse was hammering . . . from
wrists to finger tip . . . wrist to finger tip . . . Beauty's lips touched
his . . . his temples throbbed . . . throbbed . . . his pulse hammered
from wrist to finger tip . . . Beauty's breath came short now . . .
softly staccato . . . breathe normally Alex . . . you are asleep . . .
Beauty's lips touched his . . . breathe normally . . . and pressed . . .
pressed hard . . . cool . . . his body trembled . . . breathe normally
Alex . . . Beauty's lips pressed cool . . . cool and hard . . . how much
pressure does it take to waken one . . . Alex sighed . . . moved softly
. . . how does one act . . . Beauty's hair barely touched him now . . .
his breath was faint on . . . Alex's nostrils . . . and lips . . . Alex stretched and opened his eyes . . . Beauty was looking at him . . . propped on one elbow . . . cheek in his palm . . . Beauty spoke . . .

scratch my head please Dulce . . . Alex was breathing normally now . . . propped against the bed head . . . Beauty's head in his lap . . . Beauty spoke . . . I wonder why I like to look at some things Dulce . . . things like smoke and cats . . . and you . . . Alex's pulse no longer hammered from . . . wrist to finger tip . . . wrist to finger tip . . . the rose dusk had become blue night . . . and soon . . . soon they would go out into the blue . . . . .

the little church was crowded . . . warm . . . the rows of benches were brown and sticky . . . Harold was there . . . and Constance and Langston and Bruce and John . . . there was Mr. Robeson . . . how are you Paul . . . a young man was singing . . . Caver . . . Caver was a very self assured young man . . . such a dream . . . poppies . . . black poppies . . . they were applauding . . . Constance and John were exchanging notes . . . the benches were sticky . . . a young lady was playing the piano . . . fair . . . and red calla lilies . . . who had ever heard of red calla lilies . . . they were applauding . . . a young man was playing the viola . . . what could it all mean . . . so many poppies . . . and Beauty looking at him like . . . like Monty looked at Zora . . . another young man was playing a violin . . . he was the first real artist to perform . . . he had a touch of soul . . . or was it only feeling . . . they were hard to differentiate on the violin . . . and Melva standing in the poppies and lilies . . . Mr. Phillips was singing . . . Mr. Phillips was billed as a basso . . . and he had kissed her . . . they were applauding . . . the first young man was singing again . . . Langston's spiritual . . . Fy-ah-fy-ah-Lawd . . . fy-ah's gonna burn ma soul . . . Beauty's hair was so black and curly . . . they were applauding . . . encore . . . Fy-ah Lawd had been a success . . . Langston bowed . . . Langston had written the words . . . Hall bowed . . . Hall had written the music . . . the young man was singing it again . . . Beauty's lips had pressed hard . . . cool . . . cool . . . fy-ah Lawd . . . his breath had trembled . . . fy-ah's gonna burn ma soul . . . they were all leaving . . . first to the roof dance . . . fy-ah Lawd . . . there was Catherine . . . she was beautiful tonight . . . she always was at night . . . Beauty's lips . . . fy-ah Lawd . . . hello Dot . . . why don't you take a boat that sails . . . when are you leaving again . . . and there's Estelle . . . every one was there . . . fy-ah Lawd . . . Beauty's body had pressed close . . . close . . . fy-ah's gonna burn my soul . . . let's leave . . . have to meet some people at the New World . . . then to Augusta's party . . . Harold . . . John . . . Bruce . . . Connie . . . Langston . . . ready . . . down one hundred thirty-fifth street . . . fy-ah . . . meet these people and leave . . . fy-ah Lawd . . . now to Augusta's party . . . fy-ahs gonna burn ma soul . . .

they were at Augusta's . . . Alex half lay . . . half sat on the floor . . .
sipping a cocktail . . . such a dream . . . red calla lilies . . . Alex left
. . . down the narrow streets . . . fy-ah . . . up the long noisy stairs
. . . fy-ahs gonna bu'n ma soul . . . his head felt swollen . . . expanding . . . contracting . . . expanding . . . contracting . . . he had
never been like this before . . . expanding . . . contracting . . . it was
that . . . fy-ah . . . fy-ah Lawd . . . and the cocktails . . . and Beauty
. . . he felt two cool strong hands on his shoulders . . . it was Beauty
. . . lie down Dulce . . . Alex lay down . . . Beauty . . . Alex stopped
. . . no no . . . don't say it . . . Beauty mustn't know . . . Beauty
couldn't understand . . . are you going to lie down too Beauty . . .
the light went out expanding . . . contracting . . . he felt the bed sink
as Beauty lay beside him . . . his lips were dry . . . hot . . . the palms
of his hands so moist and cool . . . Alex partly closed his eyes . . .
from beneath his lashes he could see Beauty's face over his . . .
nearer . . . nearer . . . Beauty's hair touched his forehead now . . .
he could feel his breath on his nostrils and lips . . . Beauty's breath
came short . . . breathe normally Beauty . . . breathe normally . . .
Beauty's lips touched his . . . pressed hard . . . cool . . . opened
slightly . . . Alex opened his eyes . . . into Beauty's . . . parted his
lips . . . Dulce . . . Beauty's breath was hot and short . . . Alex ran
his hand through Beauty's hair . . . Beauty's lips pressed hard
against his teeth . . . Alex trembled . . . could feel Beauty's body . . .
close against his . . . hot . . . tense . . . white . . . and soft . . . soft . . .
soft . . . . .

they were at Forno's . . . every one came to Forno's once maybe
only once . . . but they came . . . see that big fat woman Beauty . . .
Alex pointed to an overly stout and bejeweled lady making her way
thru the maze   . . .   that's Maria Guerrero   . . .   Beauty looked to see a lady guiding almost the whole opera company to an immense table . . . really Dulce . . . for one who appreciates beauty
you do use the most abominable English . . . Alex lit a cigarette . . .
and that florid man with white hair . . . that's Carl . . . Beauty smiled . . . The Blind bow boy . . . he asked . . . Alex wondered . . .
everything seemed to . . . so just the same . . . here they were
laughing and joking about people . . . there's Rene . . . Rene this is
my friend Adrian . . . after that night . . . and he felt so unembar-
rassed . . . Rene and Adrian were talking . . . there was Lucricia
Bori . . . she was bowing at their table . . . oh her cousin was with
them . . . and Peggy Joyce . . . every one came to Forno's . . . Alex
looked toward the door . . . there was Melva . . . Alex beckoned . . .
Melva this is Adrian . . . Beauty held her hand . . . they talked . . .

smoked . . . Alex loved Melva . . . in Forno's . . . every one came
there sooner or later . . . maybe once . . . but . . . . .

. . . up . . . up . . . slow . . . jerk up . . . up . . . not fast . . . not
glorious . . . but slow . . . up . . . up into the sun . . . slow . . . sure
like fate . . . poise on the brim . . . the brim of life . . . two shining
rails straight down . . . Melva's head was on his shoulder . . . his
arm was around her . . . poise . . . the down . . . gasping . . . straight
down . . . straight like sin . . . down . . . the curving shiny rail
rushed up to meet them . . . hit the bottom then . . . shoot up . . .
fast . . . glorious . . . up into the sun . . . Melva gasped . . . Alex's
arm tightened . . . all goes up . . . then down . . . straight like hell
. . . all breath squeezed out of them . . . Melva's head on his
shoulder . . . up . . . up . . . Alex kissed her . . . down . . . they stepped out of the car . . . walking music . . . now over to the Ferris
Wheel . . . out and up . . . Melva's hand was soft in his . . . out and
up . . . over mortals . . . mortals drinking nectar . . . five cents a
glass . . . her cheek was soft on his . . . up . . . up . . . till the world
seemed small . . . tiny . . . the ocean seemed tiny and blue . . . up . . .
up and out . . . over the sun . . . the tiny red sun . . . Alex kissed her
. . . up . . . up . . . their tongues touched . . . up . . . seventh heaven
. . . the sea had swallowed the sun . . . up and out . . . her breath
was perfumed . . . Alex kissed her . . . drift down . . . soft . . . soft
. . . the sun had left the sky flushed . . . drift down . . . soft down
. . . back to earth . . . visit the mortals sipping nectar at five cents
a glass . . . Melva's lips brushed his . . . then out among the mortals
. . . and the sun had left a flush on Melva's cheeks . . . they walked
hand in hand . . . and the moon came out . . . they walked in silence
on the silver strip . . . and the sea sang for them . . . they walked
toward the moon . . . we'll hang our hats on the crook of the moon
Melva . . . softly on the silver strip . . . his hands molded her
features and her cheeks were soft and warm to his touch . . . where
is Adrian . . . Alex . . . Melva trod silver . . . Alex trod sand . . . Alex
trod sand . . . the sea *sang* for her . . . Beauty . . . her hand felt cold
in his . . . Beauty . . . the sea *dinned* . . . Beauty . . . he led the way
to the train . . . and the train dinned . . . Beauty . . . dinned . . . dinned . . . her cheek *had* been soft . . . Beauty . . . Beauty . . . her breath
had been perfumed . . . Beauty . . . Beauty . . . the sands *had* been
silver . . . Beauty . . . Beauty . . . they left the train . . . Melva walked music . . . Melva said . . . don't make me blush again . . . and kissed him . . . Alex stood on the steps after she left him and the night
was black . . . down long streets to . . . Alex lit a cigarette . . . and
his heels clicked . . . Beauty . . . Melva . . . Beauty . . . Melva . . . and

the smoke made the night blue . . . . .
Melva had said . . . don't make me blush again . . . and kissed him
. . . and the street had been blue . . . one *can* love two at the same
time . . . Melva had kissed him . . . one *can* . . . and the street had
been blue . . . one *can* . . . and the room was clouded with blue
smoke . . . drifting vapors of smoke and thoughts . . . Beauty's hair
was so black . . . and soft . . . blue smoke from an ivory holder . . .
was that why he loved Beauty . . . one *can* . . . or because his body
was beautiful . . . and white and warm . . . or because his eyes . . .
one *can* love . . . . .

Two Poems by Langston Hughes

CAFE: 3 A.M.

Detectives from the vice squad
with weary sadistic eyes
spotting fairies.

Degenerates
some folks say.

But God, Nature,
or somebody
made them that way.

Police lady or Lesbian
over there?

Where?

POEM

For F.S.

I loved my friend.
He went away from me.
There's nothing more to say.
The poem ends,
Soft as it began,—
I loved my friend.

The "friend" in this poem has been identified as
Ferdinand Smith (1893-1961), a merchant seaman, born
in Jamaica, who was later a political activist in Harlem.

ASSUMPTION ABOUT THE HARLEM BROWN BABY

Do not assume I came out on Christopher Street
as the piers and tracks began to heat and dance in the night

I came out at fifteen in the streets of Harlem and South Bronx
On rooftop jungles . . . pulling tigers and leopards to my rhythmic past
Spurting . . . spurting fountains . . . and baking bread never laid . . .
    upon the table
Never laid upon the table before any human's hands . . . mouths . . .
    dragon unasleep
It was natural . . . a raw kind of primitive dance . . . it was my
    ritualistic dance
into manhood . . . into the passage of blood sung in Benin
    linguistic breathing patterns

Breathing . . . breathing down my neck . . . breathing in my face
Between the cries of baby this and that . . . and feelings
of being good . . . of ooh I feel good!

And back then I was Eschu . . . the trickster . . . a chameleon
in my identity . . . I played the butch-queen games well
For the period of blood can be a time of confusion . . .
Of direct lines between straight and narrow paths not taken

But the lullabies of nights remembered on roofs . . .
Was knocking at my door . . . and the black and latin men
made love to those nights so long ago were calling

I came . . . and came again to the hallways . . . and Mt. Morris Park
To sing the song of the bushes in black heat . . . black heat rising
rising in my eyes . . . rising in your eyes . . . your eyes piercing my eyes
in unison . . . the stars now fall and shoot themselves . . . .
from our scepters held to the morning sun . . . rising . . . rising . . . rising
. . .

And do not assume . . . you . . . my friend
that the first bars I went to were gay
and had men posing as wax barbie dolls
and twisted g. i. joes

The first bars that I went to find a man
was mixed and three-fourth straight
And the first man I walked out with . . .
had a thirty-eight between his belt

And a road called "sudden paradise"
He was a dope dealer . . . he was a saint
a devil in disguise . . . and he taught me to bleed
at sixteen . . . with the first heart broken

I did go to gay bars later . . . back then . . . the bars
that spoke the words from the outside "Black Only"
Whites who come in . . . come in at your own risk

And in those places . . . the queens and drags were respected
and sometime feared . . . they were the ones that kept the place together
And if someone wanted to play the macho butch and read
they would make sure . . . they could not sow future seeds

They were no slouch these queens
They carried blades and guns filled with lead
Go off wrong with them . . . you were dead!

And when I came out . . . there were no definite gay code of dress
What got you from A to Z with a man was whether you had nice labels
or looked street cool . . . not whether you were a cowboy or leatherman
or even showing half of your can . . . if you did the queens would look
and read you as being a desperate man

So do not assume that I was some Harlem brown baby
that came out in your world . . . your ghetto . . . your constructs
of your reality . . . I came out in my own

Knowing the even flow to life . . . knowing which cards
had been marked and played . . . the sea . . . the sea
is now at rest . . .fill your bowels of passion with my wisdom

Salih Michael Fisher

GROWING UP IN CHICAGO BLACK AND GAY

Ron Vernon

I THINK I FIRST REALIZED I was a homosexual when people started calling me a faggot, and I really became aware of being a homosexual, you know, in school, in Chicago.

I think people started calling me faggot because of the way I acted, like I acted in sort of a way of always being with girls, and never playing around too much with the boys, and they began to associate that in some way with femininity, with being fem, and eventually, the word "sissy" arose, and I was classified. And that's when I really became aware that something was different about me. I was about 7 or 8 years old.

When I was about 10 or 11, I began to get into a couple of arguments, deep arguments, but nobody ever physically attacked me for being gay, you know. Just arguments. At about 13, I transferred to a high school, which was one of the roughest high schools in Chicago. Not knowing that I would be the only overt homosexual at the school, the first day I wore a red shirt down to my knees and a pair of the loudest pants I could find, and went to school. Because at the other school I had been to, there were other homosexuals I associated with, and we sort of stuck together and nobody ever bothered. There was a lot of alienation on our part. We alienated ourselves from the other people.

The first day I transferred, I remember getting off the bus and it was about 8:30 in the morning, and school didn't open till 9. I walked around the corner, and here the whole street was filled with students getting ready for their bell to ring. I turned the corner; it seemed like a hush came over the whole street, all the way down to the end of the next block. I reacted to it, but I didn't turn away, you know, like I went on up to the center door, and the janitor wouldn't let me in. Like people all the way down the street were whistling, and all this kind of shit. So I had to go back out into all these people, and walk down to the other end of the school, through all these people, to another door by the office, where I got in. When I got in, it was a relief, after having struggled past all these people.

I was assigned my classes and sent to a counsellor immediately when I came into the school, because of my overt femininity. I was like flamboyant. She assigned me classes, gave me certain classes I was going to be taking. I was sort of sticking by myself, because there was no other people there that I felt I could relate to. I felt that I should just be by myself, you know, because I felt that it would be a difficult struggle to try to relate to these straight people. I came to school for about the first three days. And the third day I was in the cafeteria at lunch time, and this woman walked up and said, "Hi, my name is Susan, what's yours?" What had happened was, it sounded like they had wrote out everything of how they were going to approach me, and practiced and rehearsed at it, and then came and did this skit on how to relate to me, because no one had ever related to a homosexual, obviously. And they wanted to try to do it as well as they could. I guess the thing was to write up a script and all take part. It sounded like they had read it and memorized it. She says, "My name's Susan, what's yours?", and I said, "My name's Ron." She sat down and we started just talking about what school I had come from. We were sitting there about five minutes and then some more women came into the cafeteria. She called them over, and pretty soon about five women were sitting at the table, and we were all rapping about how did I feel coming into the school, and things like that. So that was my first communication with any straight people at all, and those were women at school. I sort of hung around with them ever since then. We'd always meet during our breaks and at lunch time and get together and rap.

I was there for about a week and assigned a health class. I was sitting in the front of the classroom, and I was really kind of nervous because of being put in the front and not in the back of the classroom where I could keep an eye on everybody instead of everybody keeping an eye on me. The teacher walked out of the room, and this man got up and said, "That's a faggot." At first I didn't know how to react to it, and I had just gotten out of the Illinois Youth Commission—I'd been there for about eight months. I didn't know what to do. I didn't want to fight with him, because I had just come into the situation, and I really didn't want to jeopardize my freedom in any way. I knew that being kicked out of school—all that would happen is I would go right back to the Youth Commission.

Anyway, he did it a couple of times, and I just had a temper which wouldn't wait, at that time, which I still sort of do, and so I jumped up and said a term which was used a lot then, "Can you box?" I jumped up and said, "I can box, and I don't have to go through any shit, either, put 'em up or shut up." And so he got up and come up the front of the class and I knocked him down. And we just beat each other to death, and in a way I guess you could say I won the fight.

He was very offended by this, because this faggot kicked his ass. So he went and organized a campaign to wipe out faggots around the school. I had a gym class with him also. The next day, I came into my gym class—well this was the first gym class I had had—and we had to wear shorts and a T-shirt, and I came into my gym class with a slip for registering. I came in late for some reason, and everyone was seated on bleachers on either side of the gym. And the teacher's desk was all the way at the other end of the gym. I had to walk across in front of all these people, by myself. I was about 10 minutes late. He was giving a lecture about what we were going to do in gym or some shit like that. So anyway, I walked across the floor, and the whole gym went up. I really felt kind of bad about it. They started whistling, and cackling and all this shit. So I turned my slip in and sat down at the end of the class. Well, eventually everything was really up in arms; people were screaming and yelling. So the teacher blew his whistle for everybody to play ball. And so everyone ran out on the floor and started playing ball, and I walked out of the gym. This fellow who attacked me, well, verbally attacked me— because I did hit him first—was in this gym class. It was gym with about five classes, there were about 200 people; it was a huge, huge gymnasium. That day nothing happened, except that incident.

The day after we had this fight, he came up to me in the hall, and said "2:30." That was when we got out of school; he meant that I should meet him at 2:30 outside. I said, "O.K." and I thought I was going to be going out there to meet him, but when I walked out of the school, there were about 15 boys altogether, waiting for me. And he was standing in front of them woofing like a dog. I turned around and went out the back door and ran home. The next day he saw me in the hall and he told me "2:30" again. And I did the same thing again. So the next day was this gym day, and this thing happened. The next gym class that we had he came up to me in the locker room. What they had done is they planned this fight between about three people, where three people would get in the back of the locker room, because I was the only one who went all the way in the back to dress and undress; all the other people were up front. They had fought all the way back along the wall, to where I was. Maybe it was my paranoia, but I had this idea that they were coming back there after me. And I went around the other side and ran up into the crowd. I left school early that day. I went home and told my father what had happened, and he had always been one to tell me to fight my own battles.

So the next day I took half a razor, the handle was broken off. I wrapped it up in a piece of toilet paper and stuck it down into my underwear and went to school. That day I came out of school and this fellow hit me in the face with a chain. When I walked out of the door, he was waiting behind the door and hit me in the face with a chain. I ran and they were chasing me, and they were catching up. All the time I was running I was reaching down in my drawers trying to pull out this razor, and eventually I got it out, and I just did a U-turn, and went blindly into them, cutting everybody who I could, and going after one person in particular who had hit me in the face with a chain. I cut his face up pretty bad, and I ran home.

I came back to school the next day, and he was there with his mother, the police and everybody under the sun to take me to jail. So the school told me they couldn't tolerate any shit like that, and that they were going to send me to Montefiore, a rehabilitation school for boys, which I really wasn't ready for. I told them I'd quit school before I'd go to Montefiore. So I said I'll quit school. So when I quit school, I was returned back to the Illinois Youth Commission for dropping out of school. This all happened in the course of about a month after I had gotten out.

I went back in, and stayed about a year that time. Ever since then I was getting out and staying out for about two weeks and going back in for curfew and shit like that. Then eventually I turned sixteen, and I was old enough to get an independent parole where I would just leave the institution and come out on the street on my own, you know, without going to any relatives or anything, and working a job as a dishwasher or something, trying to make it until I got off parole.

The Illinois Youth Commission is a jail for juveniles. My reason for going was because at 12 I ran away from home to live with another older man. Eventually I was caught up with. My father put out a "missing person" and all this shit. And they caught me. When I went to court, the judge asked my father, "Are you aware that your son is a homosexual?" And my father said "Yes." We had never talked about it before and that was the first time I had ever heard him refer to me as a homosexual. And he did, and he was very hurt having to do it in that way. And I felt the pain that he encountered because it was really a blow to him in so many ways that someone would come out and ask him. "Are you aware that your son is a homosexual," and his son is standing right there next to him, you know. My father is a very honest man, and just said, "Yeah." So they said, "Well, we're going to send him to Galesburg Mental Institution to try to correct his homosexuality." I couldn't understand anything that was happening. I had sort of an idea that I would be going to the Youth Commission, but never really accepted the fact that they'd send me to the Youth Commission for something so stupid. And they did.

When I got there, well, there were other homosexuals there, but we were so outlandish, you know, we ran the institution practically. Anything that went down, we knew about it. We had something to do with it, all kinds of shit.

The first place I was sent was to the Reception Center in Joliet. Then I was sent to St. Charles. I stayed there for about six months and got into a fight with my cottage mother, who was a woman. I stole some cigarettes out of her room. They gave homosexuals jobs like cleaning up, and I was cleaning up her room and took advantage of cleaning up and stole some cigarettes. And she came down to the basement, and grabbed my arm, or something, told me not to be stealing cigarettes from her, and my immediate response was to hit her, which I did. I turned around and slapped her in the face. That same night they came and handcuffed me and took me to Sheridan, because that was outrageous—to slap a cottage parent, you know.

They sent me to the maximum security institution which was Sheridan, Illinois, with two fences with dogs between and guard towers with guns, and all kinds of shit like this. I stayed there for three months, and I got out and went through that change in high school. Then I went back, and they sent me immediately to Sheridan, because I was, you know, always fighting. Whenever a prisoner called me a faggot or a punk, I would try to knock their brains out and shit like that. They thought they knew so much about psychology and about homosexuality that they could just put us in any type of situation and we would just play along with whatever was the set rules. But we really fucked up a lot of things there.

I was in Sheridan the second time for a year, and I was in the hole ten months out of that year. The hole was a small cell with just a light box and a slot underneath where your food came in. And I was let out once every other day for a shower.

At that time you used to get a milk pill and a vitamin pill for breakfast, a full lunch and a milk pill and a vitamin pill for dinner. Now this is where they put murderers, rapists, you know, people they felt they couldn't handle. I was apparently a murderer and a rapist all combined, with my homosexuality, so they put me in the hole.

A lot of shit went down. A lot were committing suicide. An awful lot of gay people were hanging themselves. They eventually gave us a building which was called C-8, and they put us on the fourth gallery, way up at the top. We had all the cells on the top, and even there, people would slice their wrists and shit, refuse to do any work.

There was this guard giving an awful lot of trouble; his name was Ivy, Big Ivy, and he used to really give us a lot of hell, you know, beat us up—and this was a grown-ass man, and we were like 14 or 15 years old. We had planned to get him. First we tried getting him fired by telling lies and saying he was forcing us into homosexual behavior with him, you know, and all kinds of shit. And then we couldn't get him fired because he had been there so long that everybody just wouldn't believe it. So what we did was, this very good friend of mine we used to call Didi, tied a sheet around his neck, and tied it up to the barred window, and was standing on top of his bed. So I walked up to the door and started screaming: "Guard, come here! Somebody's trying to hang themselves!" So he ran up to the door, and when he opened the door, I pushed him in, and about 7 or 8 gay people ran in and threw a blanket over his head and almost beat him to death and left him there. We used to do shit like that. I remember this straight brother who was very close to a lot of us; he always defended us and stuff like this. He was taken to the hole, and they broke both of his arms and both of his legs before they got him there.

My first day in Sheridan I was in the cafeteria. When you first get there, you come into this big mess hall where everybody eats. The intake people, the new people, eat at one table. I came with two other gay brothers. And we were sitting at the table and like my name was known throughout the institution before I got there for all the shit that I'd been doing. This fellow reached over and grabbed my butt, my ass, you know. I turned around and said: "Don't touch me. Don't put your hands on me, 'cause you don't know me." And we went through this big argument. I jumped up and took my tray and threw it in his face. It was just the thing to do. We had to defend ourselves, and we had these reputations to hold. Otherwise we really would have been fucked over. So I threw the tray in his face. They shot tear gas into the mess hall. The first person they run to grab to carry up over all the tear gas while the tear gas was settling— the first person they're carrying out to the hole, my first day there— was me. They just lifted me up and drug me out and threw me in the hole.

Homosexuality in jail works like this: it's true that the straight men forced people into homosexuality; but it was like most of the gay people who were overt about it and let people know were all put into the same area together, or on the same tier. We didn't have as much of that on our tier. First of all, nobody would even dare to attack one gay person without having to fight 30 or 40 who are on the tier, you know. On the other tiers, I remember this one boy was gang-raped 13 times, and like nobody in the institution knew about it, other than the inmates, but like he wouldn't tell the officials because he would really have been in trouble then. You know, finally we got him to admit his homosexuality and come over to our tier so that he wouldn't be gang-raped. Can you imagine being gang-raped by these men 13 times, you know, 13 times, not 13 men, but 13 different times by many men! So there is a lot of that but, you know, I think institutions encourage things like gang rapes, by keeping this tension, first between homosexual and straight people there. They try their damndest by separating us. I don't feel we should be segregated from the other, straight men. If men are straight they won't relate to me sexually anyway, so I won't have any problems with them, right? So I think that they encourage it by keeping us separate, and then keeping all straight men together to do their thing and calling it mass homosexual uprising and shit like that.

Every once in a while you'd hear like someone was raped over on another tier. But as far as our tier was concerned, they put about 40 homosexuals and about as many supposedly liberal heterosexuals, men, you know, with the role of men, and homosexuals with the role of women, on the tier together. All right? It was a thing where we had, I mean, really had it set up. Nobody would even utter "faggot." I mean, the guards were very careful about what they said. I was playing a role. I was playing a passive, feminine role. All right? Had I not played a passive role and went into the institution and been put on a straight tier, and had a homosexual relationship with one person, you see, on that tier, the whole tier would have known about it. I would have had to have homosexual relationships with everyone on that tier, you see, because I was an overt outlet, so to speak. Someone had initiated it. And I think that's how a lot of the gang rapes are caused, by homosexuals going in with these super-man attitudes about how butch they are, and shit. They get up there and have a relationship with one person, and it's NOT with one per-son, and ends up where someone else will come up to him, or prop-osition him or something, and he'll refuse it, and that's when he's gang-raped. I would not advise any homosexual to go in there with a superman attitude, because some of the biggest, muscular, macho masculine-identified men, they go into prison, they're homosexual, and they go through this change. I don't care how big you are, or how tough you are, it just happens that you'll get raped if you don't go along with the program. That's all.

At that time, I didn't identify those people on our tier who played the roles as men as homosexuals. Because I was into a role thing, where I was a homosexual and he was a straight man, you know, and I related to him that way. My consciousness is entirely different now. I think that having to play those roles was extremely oppres-sive for many of us. In fact that's why so many of us kept returning to the institution. We'd get out and sometimes you'd see someone who left two days earlier walking right back in there.

We'd be going out and prostituting, or going out and ripping some-body off or something. A lot of them had intentions of being caught, and intentions of going back to jail. And intentions of being incar-cerated, because of relationships there. That part was oppressive. It was oppressive in the fact that it was locking people up and making them think it was all right. Nobody should be locked up, that's all. No homosexual or straight man, or anybody.

I finally graduated from grammar school in St. Charles. I took a test and somehow I passed it, and they handed me a diploma. When I got out on the independent parole, I went downtown to some General Equivalency Diploma test office, and passed that. I got a high enough score to get a scholarship to college.

I started college. That was another whole trip. That was going in to how to relate to capitalism, how I could come out of one situation and go into another. I feel that's what school did for me, you know, put me in the same type of oppressive situation, but in a more bourgeois sense, so I'd be able to get a half-assed job after I graduated, supporting the system, you see. And in fact, I wouldn't be able to get a job. To show you how oppressed I was, I WOULDN'T be able to get a job because the record I had was tremendous. And just because I had the intelligence to rap through their books and shit like this, I was so oppressed that I couldn't even see that I'd never be able to teach, I'd never be able to go through school and teach high school students or children, or adults or anybody, because of my criminal record. All I was concerned with was getting that diploma because that made me a part of the system, could make me some money.

I met lots of gay people in college. Most gay people in college that I know just stay in their closets and not let anybody know. That's true for the people I knew in school, until gay liberation and Third World gay revolution came out. Those people in school were very closeted people. Like you would know, maybe by talking with them, they'd drop a hint or something, but other people wouldn't. They'd have to hide and shit like that.

Basically, I've always thought of myself as a revolutionary. When I was in Jail I was a revolutionary, all right? In a sense I was a revolutionary because I was rejecting the system, all right? I was rejecting the system in a negative sense, in that I was not using my rejection constructively to turn it against the system, but perpetuating and helping the system, but still in a revolutionary sense, sort of. I've always had ideas of offing repression, I mean, as early as I can remember people have been fucking over my head, and I've always had a desire to stop people from fucking over my head.

There was quite a movement in jail between Black people, around Malcolm X. I was in jail when I first heard about the Black Panther Party, and related to it very positively, but in a Blackness sense and not out of a gayness sense, because they were offing gay people, verbally offing gay people. You know, saying things like this White man who is fucking you over is a faggot, and that was getting to me, because I was a faggot and I wasn't no White man! Finally their consciousness changed somehow. I don't know how, but it did, and they've begun to relate to homosexuals as people, as a part of the people. That's when I really became a revolutionary, began to live my whole life as a revolutionary. And I could never ever consider another. I mean, now that I'm conscious of my oppression I could not consider any other. If there was a movement to restore capitalism in this country and they offed every revolutionary, they'd have to off me, too. If they restore Black capitalism in this country, they'd have to off me, too. That's going to be oppressing me as a Black, gay person.

I'm really struggling right now with developing my own gay consciousness. I think that most of the people in Third World Gay Revolution and in Gay Liberation are developing their own consciousness, and trying to relate to other consciousness-raising issues. I think that more and more Third World and also White people are coming into the movement and just the idea that they know that they'll have a fighting chance somewhere to be gay people, whether they're Third World or White, you know, opportunity for them to get it, so they're going to get in there and struggle for it.

I think the people I still have the most difficulty understanding are White people. I still feel a lot of negative things about White people because of their racism, basically, and the extreme racism which they in turn bring down on the Black community and on Black people. I really feel that White straight people bring about this whole shit. I think that the thing that I'm able to see better is the White gay person's point of view, and I'm able to identify—I have something to identify with in a White gay person, in a revolutionary sense, whereas I'm able to see that they're oppressed as gay people also. I definitely feel that I still don't understand White straight people. I hope that I will, but I don't think that I'll ever be able to understand White straight people. I feel that they've created all this shit—White, straight MEN in particular. Since the women's liberation movement, I've begun to relate more closely to White women, and understand their oppression, because it sort of parallels gay oppression in many ways. I'm sort of able to understand White straight women because they're sort of able to understand Black gay men, to an extent, where they can understand their gayness. I still feel that a lot of White straight women do not understand Black gay men as far as their Blackness is concerned, but I still think that women's liberation has an awful lot of racism to deal with before they can really understand the whole point of view. And I think that Black gay men and White gay men have an awful lot of consciousness raising to do before they can understand women's oppression; as far as dealing with White women are concerned, we have to really deal with sexism, and that's really a strange thing to think about—that you're oppressed in a sexist sort of way, and that you have to raise your own consciousness on sexism. But I can see it, because Black people are consistently raising their own consciousness about their Blackness, and so that's how I relate to it.

Like I've experienced oppression from White gay men. I was into this hustling trip where I used to prostitute. The people who supported me in prostitution and really had a lot to do with the way I'm fucked up in relating sexually now—I don't know if you can understand that, I mean, the way that I relate in bed to people sexually— were white men, you see. My roles were reinforced by White men at that time. And this is the thing I attach to White men. The thing I wasn't looking at at that time was, I was identifying it with White straight men, and in fact they were White gay men that I was having sex with. Most of them married, suburbia with two children, snuck out of the house to turn a trick, you know, down at the Square, which is all brought on by the system. That people have to in fact do shit like that, and lie about themselves, and when they lie about themselves, and when they lie about themselves, in my case that made it a racist thing. Because they lied about themselves, they had to deal with me, and that really turned me off.

Pigs? How do I relate to pigs? Pigs are, well, I don't know what they are. A pig is a pig, all right? Most people are trying to get in this trip of trying to relate to people, and to think that a pig is actually a person in uniform, with an oppression on him, you know, and that he's in turn oppressing everybody, and if you think about it that way, I guess you could sort of work around it somehow. Even in that way, like I can't relate to them. Like my whole life has been centered around pigs busting me for different things.

Like one time we were on the beach around four in the morning. We were walking around the Oak Street Beach in Chicago. There were about four Third World Gay brothers who were walking together. Now this is on Lake Shore Drive in Chicago, which is the exclusive ritzy area. The reason we were there is gay bars are up that way. Anyway, the pigs saw us walking on the beach, and we passed these two White brothers who were playing a guitar and singing out on the beach. So the pigs came, first they drove by, and then they turned around and came back and drove up onto the concrete on the beach and said, "We have received reports that you are out here disturbing the peace, and it's four o'clock in the morning." And I said, "It wasn't us who was disturbing the peace, officer, it was someone else down the way, and all they were doing was playing the guitar." So he says, "Let's see some identification" . . . I says, "Well, I don't have any identification . . . So he said, "Oh, you're one of those smart faggots, huh?" I said, "Why yes, I'm one of those smart faggots, and I still don't want you putting your hands on me." With that, he says, "Well, you're going to the shithouse." And I says, "Well, I don't see why I have to go to the shithouse, because I haven't done anything." He says, "You're going to the shithouse." I says, "I'm not going to the shithouse." So we attacked the police and another squad was passing by and pulled up—well, it wasn't a squad car, it was the paddy wagon, and it pulled up onto the concrete, and helped them, and that was the way that they got us.

J. J. Johnson   Photo: Sierra Domino

THE LONG HARD RUN
A Short Story

Joel Ensana

THE KIND OF SUNDAY Earl loved to see. Perfect for a long, hard run, he thought, as he headed out towards the beach, the fog, still thick and wet in places, the wind blowing, but not so strong that it blocked his way. He made a beautiful picture as he ran for a short distance alongside San Francisco's Golden Gate Park, the light tan of eucalyptus tree trunks and dark green bushes a perfect backdrop for his long black legs, that lean, muscular body, now and then appearing to leap out of nowhere as he would emerge from the greenery to cross an intersection, then re-enter the park like an animal trying to escape the traffic of civilization, but not so fast that people in cars or on sundecks couldn't make out such details as firm thighs, well-developed pectorals and that bulging cock that felt so good pressing against his nylon shorts.

"Red ones today," one gay said to another as he poured his first Bloody Mary. "I like the long, gray flannel pants much better. That looseness shows the movement so much better. All that—flipping and flopping about. . . ."

"Oh, yes," his roommate said, leaning across the breakfast table to see, "and you know, if you don't look at his face, he's really quite a hunk. . . ."

"In the dark, what difference would it make?"

"Well, I'm not that old yet; that I have to go with Blacks—pay hustlers. . . ."

Earl ran past a group of well-dressed Blacks entering an old Baptist church, recalling all the Sundays he had accompanied his mother, until he began to question where God was when it came to Blacks. Something real, he thought, yeah, fine for the old ones almost frightened to death of the unknown hereafter, but not for a young Black out of work or arrested for demonstrating and wanting equal justice for all. And then, after discovering his gayness he had really turned against their minister who had preached against homosexuality, using the Bible to teach the congregation that it was wrong, very wrong, thereby spreading more hate in a world already poisoned by the moral majority, politicians, and fat generals. The real enemy, he thought, yeah, he knew the real enemy.

(Over a path covered with damp leaves, now imagining himself as an escaping slave headed north with the sound of bloodhounds behind him.)

And then something caught his eye — a white runner coming from the opposite direction — and the two of them nodded in recognition as they waited for a traffic light, the other runner changing course after checking Earl out and they entered the park together and soon disappeared in a tangle of berry bushes and giant ferns, being observed only by someone's lost dog and another jogger who had stopped to tie his laces, but who slowly joined them in a threesome. Earl then rid himself of that early morning throbbing so that now he could run with his body devoid of that burning sensation in his groin and his mind clear of constantly interrupting sexual images.

He did a few exercises, then continued, enjoying the sights and sounds of the park such as a squirrel dashing across his path from one tree to another and a giant black crow cawing as it circled above. Yes, right now, he liked his Blackness and the stories that drew certain, curious Whites to him, liked that Black energy racing through his veins and that Black penis pressing, a bit softer now, against his thigh, but still hating all the other things that went along with it, the looks, the having to settle for less — all those years, settling for less, with his mother having to take the bus across the giant city of Los Angeles in order to clean other people's houses, but neither of them ever ashamed of her work; hey, it was honest, he thought, but the pay was so fucking little. Goddamn, here I am again, hating Whitey, liking Whitey.

"A living legend," was what one of the gays had just said, back there in the bushes, after getting up from a kneeling position and then brushing the dirt from his bare knees. He had touched Earl's arm, saying "Thanks, *man*" and ran off at a jogger's pace. Sure, Earl thought, he had to add the "man" because that's the way he thought all Blacks talked and he smiled. "A living legend." Oh, yeah, and nothing more to many. Just a big cock. Right. A great body and a good fuck — with skin like velvet — how many times had he heard that. Personality? Brains? Feelings? They'd never know he had any because they never took the time to find out. But at least the guy had meant well. It wasn't said with hate. Yeah, the gays weren't perfect, but at least most of them know that we minorities are all in the same boat.

Still, it was size. Always size. And the story was so old it probably went went back to the days of ancient Rome. Yeah, and he smiled, picturing some ancient Roman sissy returning from Cleopatra's Egypt and carrying on about the size of a Black slave's cock and how sex was all they thought about. Sexual feelings — all just sexual feelings — and how through the ages, like all stories handed down, it had gotten bigger and bigger as it was told on clipper ships, camel caravans. Yeah, when you get down to it, that was how Whites saw him — an animal — running — like animals — just following their natural instincts. His anger made him push the wind even harder — and still he looked only at White men as he cut through another section of the park — now a young bearded guy practicing karate and even an Irish "pig" on horseback.

I hate myself, he thought, but not this body, this beautiful big cock that was already beginning to stiffen again as a red-haired biker passed him, Earl noting the hard ass. I just hate myself for liking only White tricks and he watched another one beckon and nod towards a rhododendron bush in full bloom that would have hidden them very nicely, but right now he didn't want to break his jogger's pace, so he kept running towards the ocean, occasionally looking at a White family man, some White jocks playing soccer, but never at a Black brother who might pass by.

He thought of some of his Black friends who liked Whites because they said it made them feel superior having a Whitey down there before them on their knees — and he had Black friends who liked inflicting pain on those white-skinned gays who just wanted sex with them, but never a lasting relationship because they could never introduce them to family or friends, would have had a hard time getting an apartment in a good neighborhood and he also had Black friends who would never go with Whites.

And passing a small pool he could hear his mother calling, "Earl, you're coming with me today. Your aunt's not feeling well, so I asked Mrs. Stark and she said I could bring you as long as I didn't make a habit of it. So while I'm cleaning, I want you to be a good boy and stay out of the way." She had hurried off for the bus, dragging him by one hand, the other carrying a shopping bag filled with her special cleaning aids. He liked going with her — the house was in Beverly Hills, as most of them were — and he recalled all the beautiful things: the soft colors of flowers in vases throughout the house, the abundance of food and even the glass bottles on Mrs. Stark's dressing table that had smelled so pretty, everything so different from their two rooms in a housing project. When they had arrived he heard voices from the back yard, and there were some older boys swimming in the pool, their skin so white, as it was just the beginning of the good weather, then later he saw them in the dressing room drying their pink butts and their pale cocks, his staring interrupted by one of the boys saying, "Hey, little Sambo, come on, let's see what you have ... I hear colored boys are hung like horses...."

They had grabbed him and pulled down his pants.

"See, just like I said. Wish it were mine—only White, of course." And then, suddenly, as Earl pulled up his pants, one of the boys started jacking off the other.

"Hey, what about him? You think he'll tell...."

"Who cares. He's only a colored boy. Who'd believe him?"

And it was always that way—in public restrooms, theater balconies—Whites never cared if a Black man watched—they knew they were safe—knew that a Black person was the last one who'd report it to the police—having always to know when to keep their mouths shut where Whites were concerned, keep their eyes closed, besides feeling that there wasn't anything a Black wouldn't stoop to doing—or so the story was told.

But the beginning was really the lily-white interior decorator his mother cleaned house for on Wednesdays. Once when Earl, then thirteen, had gone to help her with the heavy spring cleaning and while his mother was in the kitchen and he was rolling up a rug in the guest room, the man had simply sat on the edge of the bed, eyeing Earl's crotch and warning him about the fragility of that Oriental carpet; then he reached over and had unzipped his fly, took it out, exclaiming over its size and the had locked the bedroom door. From then on he was always begging his mother to take him with her, and then the decorator took to picking him up after school. Earl had enjoyed it all—the satin sheets, the gifts, but most of all, the attention from that blonde, finely-featured man that reminded him of a movie star, until one day, he was suddenly ordered to leave. "Clients are coming from Santa Barbara—and they're also friends and it won't do—well, I mean the cleaning woman's son . . ." The man had realized his mistake as Earl had run angrily from the house.

He had just been trade until he went into the service where the sergeant in the next room—a young southern career guy and already an alcoholic who would never leave the base on the weekends—always stayed in his room with several bottles of gin. One night, when he had a bad case of the D.T.'s, Earl had helped to restrain him; their wrestling and touching arousing Earl, who then stayed with him until it passed, and then with very little resistance Earl had fucked the sergeant as hard as he could for being just what he was—a rednecked southerner. The guy had turned out to be one swell person and they became the best of friends, the two of them soon sixty-nining. Southern or not, the guy was really good-looking: those high cheek bones, that straight, straw-colored hair that kept falling over his eyes, giving him such a boyish look.

Running—it always stirred up old memories and feelings, and just the picture of those White boys by the pool over twenty years ago brought on a hardening in his shorts and he considered running all the way to the baths. Yeah, he liked the baths best of all; and now, stopping at a red light, he saw his reflection in a store window—face, very black and not at all handsome, but the body and that bold outline in his shorts. Yes, he liked the baths best of all. You never had to talk to anyone, except to say, "Sorry, just resting." You just turned them over—rammed it in—angrily, hatefully ramming it in—not particularly liking the fact that you were giving them pleasure, but just getting the satisfaction of letting it all out . . . .

Earl was now running through an all-White neighborhood, stuccoed tract homes from the 1920's, hearing bits and pieces of conversation as he passed people talking in front of their homes, and other bits and pieces came back of White voices at parties—the diction pure, "I didn't know Jim was a dinge queen. With him it's not the color, just the size." Size. Yeah, size. "The name is Earl," he'd say. "Not man. Hey, man . . . ." And if he tried to talk politics, mentioned the economy, they would look at him as if to say, "Oh, come on, we know what you really want to talk about," and they would start groping and measuring, oh- and ahing at its size, pleased that he was proving true all the stories they had heard, and then it was right to bed. Times with certain tricks he had felt he didn't have a brain at all—nothing but a cock, yeah, just one great big Black dick.

Hating them and loving them—and while waiting on another corner, running in place, he saw one watching him from a corner window—the guy looking down at Earl's cock as it bounced up and down, now hardening as Earl saw the blonde hair, the young skin. Later, as Earl pulled his shorts on, after a half-hour of sex, grunts and groans, the young blonde slowly opening his front door, checking to make certain that no one would see Earl, who then hurried down the stairs and started his running again, recalling all the others who had said, "If possible, don't let anyone see you . . . ." There had been times he'd have liked to grab them by their pale throats and choked—and choked—or stuffed his cock down their throats until they couldn't spew forth another word of hate, told another lie, smiled another condescending smile, but still, something drew him to them—something besides the color and the skin. And there were never any lasting relationships. He didn't want any. He liked being alone, running, going to work, brief encounters with strangers.

He had had one affair that lasted several months, but he could still hear his White lover's voice calling after him as he ran from the flat, "You couldn't love if you wanted to. You're so full of hate. Oh, yes, yes, I felt it—everytime you fucked me! It was the world, Earl! It was the White world you were fucking! You couldn't love if you wanted to—your hate—your experiences with Whites—they always got in the way!"

(Past a stadium and feeling like Jesse Owens at the 1936 Olympics.)

As he ran past a renovated Victorian, the Black gays inside watched him, one saying to the other, "He's into Whites only. Met him once at the Pendulum. Pretty young Whites. You'll notice, he's right on schedule. I think that underneath that Black skin lurks a German businessman . . . ."

"Bitch! Too good for us. And so butch. You notice, so very butch."

He'd have liked waking up with someone beside him every morning, sure, but why take chances. Just being Black was asking to be hurt, why ask for more, he thought, yeah, everything was going just great. Healthy as an ox, getting all the fucking he wanted. Money in the bank. Sure, almost hitting forty, but it didn't bother him, there would always be Whiteys wanting to see if it was true and he could see that hand reaching, hesitantly over, to check out the myth—and in my case, it's true, yeah, it's true, alright.

He always loved it when the beach came into view—that broad expanse of green waves tinged with white, framed by sand and sky. He usually ran right to the very edge, as he did today, took many deep breaths, knelt and then splashed water on his face, doing a few knee bends, some twists and turns, kicks and pushups and then he headed back into the park towards the city with the cries of seagulls following him, cursing him for barging in on their serenity, the sound of waves pounding against the shore, all causing him to run faster, just the joy of it all and then to smile as the contrast of this moment and those of the approaching night when he would enter a world of bars with playrooms and private clubs made up of cubicles with glory holes.

(Past a jungle of tropical ferns and trees reminding him of Vietnam, now hearing shots, explosions, screams of former buddies.)

A car passed him, an old man seated in the back, remarking, from force of habit, "Jogging? Yeah, I'll bet. Wonder how many he's mugged today. Sure, hit an old woman then run like hell. . . ."

Now he passed a lake where White teenagers were jumping from rowboats into the water, reminding him of the two that were still in his fantasies. The very beginning once again rearing its ugly, but beautiful head, and it made him angry to know that he was stuck with certain events, moments in his past that had brought him to this point — stuck with them for the rest of his life.

He increased his speed as he passed a group of tourists near the Japanese tea-garden, a pot-bellied man from Omaha admiring Earl's physique, promising himself to take up jogging when he returned home; a shy teenager with a camera aroused by the sight of Earl's full crotch, wishing there were Blacks on the farm back home which he wanted to leave the minute he turned eighteen.

Around the decaying bandstand, some maintenance men harpooning brown-paper bags, and he visualized people of another era listening to the music, women wearing large hats and men with handlebar mustaches, but never a Black face among them, thinking, oh, yeah, the times are better, we Blacks have advanced, but not enough, never enough. . . .

He turned off the path to stop at the graffiti and vine-covered restroom where several gays stood about the entrance — an older, wino type quickly following him in, thinking, "I'll get this one. Hell, Black as the ace of spaces." Earl, recalling all the times he had been hurt when brushed aside like a piece of shit in public places by Whites not wanting other Whites to see them having sex with a Black, gently, but firmly brushed away the man's anxious, but cautiously moving hand, shaking his head, saying, "I just had it, but thanks anyway." Although he wanted some head very much — he was always in the mood towards the end of his run — the man just wasn't his type. The man nodded, but Earl's being nice hadn't changed anything, the man still thinking "Well, fuck you. I wouldn't want anyone seeing me doing you." Still, he couldn't take his eyes off Earl's throbbing cock.

He continued his running, unaware of the man's hateful thoughts and yet very much aware of the fear in his eyes at the point of rejection. He could always spot fear such as when he would pass a White woman jogger who would smile but cautiously veer away from him, the fear of older people at an intersection as he would silently come up behind them; they were so easily startled, mumbling, "Oh, oh, I didn't hear you," and would quickly draw back, so that now he always tried to make some sort of noise. The fear Whites had of Black men. Images, always images. Whites frightened by stories handed down about Blacks—and all races about gays wanting children. Not wanting any more thoughts of bigotry polluting his head while running, he quickly turned to look at a row of gaily painted Victorian houses lit up by the sun which was now burning through the patches of gray fog, thinking, nothing as cheerful as San Francisco drenched in sunlight.

When he reached home he stripped and showered, and then standing before a full-length mirror, he looked at his body—his Black body—and was very satisfied with himself. Running always did that—made him aware of so many fine things in life like the fog and the trees, all combining to make him feel more alive than ever and slightly above it all, able to survive being not only Black, but gay too, in these United States of America.

Running's like a purge, he thought. All those memories and poisonous feelings implanted in him, tossed at him by bigots, now released and torn to shreds by the wind, crushed beneath his and other runners' feet on the cities' pavement, the paths in the park and finally drowned in the tide that would soon cover his prints in the sand. Hey, why wait until tonight. It was a real good time for cruising, not only for a good, hard fuck, but for some nice, tender loving. Yeah, when you're feeling good—and hot—and your Blackness shining—a perfect time for going forth; so he quickly dried himself, put on jeans and a T-shirt, his boots, grabbed a cold bottle of apple juice and left the building, walking proudly towards the Castro.

BLACK ANGEL

(for Dave Dixon)

1. Crotch-busting bluejeans
   are unzipping.
   Long fingers caress
   stiff uncoiled beckoning

   for softer flesh.
   Between cheeks laughing,
   in a throat drunk with desire,
   fire rages.

2. Lines that say
   how much I love you
   are etched like roots
   I surrender each time.

   Images of you in danger,
   alone in a sea of confusion,
   bring hot tears to my eyes,
   burning through this distance
   to see you, as I do, right now.

3. Black angel:
   thin waist, broad chest,
   deep eyes of which
   the world is just a tributary,
   a dream sees you dancing
   and lifts my arms
   to hold you,
   not hold you back.

   Peace is just an interlude
   to jagged steps,
   roots dispersed
   to cut their way.
   The more we can be,
   the more we can believe in,
   the more we surrender
   what does not survive.

Richard Royal

FREDDI

Eyes smoldering like both barrels
of a smoking shotgun   Jaws & lips pregnated
   from anger at being shanghied 400 miles
      to Erie County Correctional Facility—
the middle of No Where
   from Dutchess County Jail   Poughkeepsie:
nine of us Blackies strolled into the cafeteria-like
messhall   Food was the last thing i had a taste for

But there he was
   tall & slender & tipping across the cafeteria   A brown
   wreath of sepian softness—graceful gladness if ever
   i've seen such   My facial muscles relaxed into a smile
   "Hi, there," i said, disbelieving my own tender vocalizing
   "Hello," was the reply, sang from tulip-shaped lips
      that pleaded guilty to having never said a nasty word
"Whatcha name?" i smilingly asked, giving my boldness
      a temporary furlough
Nameless Brown Sunshine was leaving the dumb-waiter
   and, as he glidingly tipped & tilted behind the
      steamtable, he stopped to speak over small
      shoulders
      "Freddi," he cooed, stroking my ears with cashmere
      gloves
"i didn't hear ya!" i lied, a musician who wanted
to be sure the melody lingered on
"Freddi—Freddi!" His eyes were diamonds set
in a cinnamon-hued face

i was
Ecstatic   But i moved along down-the-counter   oblivious
   to the fare on the menu—even passed the coffee: i
   surrendered one habit for another fueled by only the
   very sight of Freddi

When the officer screamed "Chow!" i was usually first
   on line   First to the steamtable
And last to   leave   the cafeteria
My desire to see   rap with   share with Freddi (i spell the
name with an "I" because it seems consistent with what
i saw & enjoyed of Freddi) was not because he was gay

But in spite of his gayness
Freddi was ever pleasant
                              genuinely concerned
willing to listen
and
made no demands whatever
When i had a desperate need for envelopes—i was 400 miles
from home & didn't have a piss to pot in or a throw
to window it out—Freddi showered me with some

Aware that i see beauty where most see ugliness
        or some others are stungout on societal mores and dictates
        i never felt it was necessary to justify my overt joy
        in the surely physically distant relationship between
                Freddi & me
        I just enjoyed him   to the
                        utmost
        a distant promise untouched by the world

In my mind i knew i would someday take Freddi to N. Y. C.
        i owed my hometown at most that much
Freddi

Jamiel Daud Hassin

Two Poems by Jeffery Beam

YOU GO OFF WITH MY LIFE

for Gene

You go off with my life
With the perfume odor from your wrists
a pendant around my neck
you go from me

I have no regrets
If the dark was more handsome
than doors I would forsake one
for the other
But I forsake nothing

Do not breathe sadly
The cactus blooms
odorless as fingers
They unwrap the loneliness
of your distance
You go from me

But the blackness of your skin is a balm
The lamp burns
I commend these works to paper
Every time the clock strikes the hour
your feet come one step closer
to this room
Here already your shadow sleeps

LEAVE-TAKING

The summons comes with the rising of quails
You rise from the bed
pulling your fatigued pants up to your hips
The sad gourds are beating together in the fields
The dead antelope carried by its feet
stops at our hut
her tender legs the goodbye of your kiss
Their shrouded flock of bone
a black mama's big lips
smoothing her child's dark snake hair
When you go
I walk over the ground alone
The sad gourds beating in fields
When you go
your hips carry your spear through cornflower fields
Whatever I remember
is a place without birds
Whatever I remember
you come back
your beard's shadow an army of pale deer
your heart thumping in your hands
The way you lay there in the morning
the straw sensed your going
Whatever I remember
the dark umbrellas of your eyes

RACISM FROM A
BLACK PERSPECTIVE

Thom Beame

We're sitting on a hill in Pacific Heights, enjoying a panoramic view of The City and a sea of men sunbathing in Lafayette Park. A conversation is in progress.

IT'S EASY TO SEE why San Francisco's called a gay mecca," observes Frank, a 45-year-old social worker who's currently unemployed, "but it's not a mecca for gay Blacks. Los Angeles, Atlanta, Chicago and New York are better for Blacks. They have larger and more politically aware Black communities. I say that," he smiles, "because I'm Black first and gay second."

"But larger doesn't necessarily mean more politically aware," counters Clark, a 39-year-old educator. "The gay community here is one of the most visible and politically powerful in the country, even though the city is barely in the top 15 in terms of population. It has all the socioeconomic extremes of any other urban center—with one major difference: nowhere are so many gay people so open about being gay. San Francisco is the last great gay escape left in America. California promises you nothing. But the innuendo—no, the myth of promise and a new beginning—is there."

"And you've got to give White gays credit for taking advantage of their numbers—hence political clout," adds Mark, who, at 28, is a personnel executive. "Blacks in San Francisco have not organized sufficiently to wield political power with credibility."

"Note, however," Frank interjects, "that the base of gay power in San Francisco is the White gay propertied and merchant class. It's White gays who hold elected offices, own small businesses and own the Castro as well as large portions of other areas in the city; who have key management and executive positions. Yet, as a rule, they don't share useful information or interface socially or professionally with other ethnic factions in the gay community."

57

"Yes," I add, "and the irony is that White gays still don't represent a real threat to the 'ruling order' in the city. The corporate board-rooms may be exclusively White, but they're also as anti-gay and conservative as anywhere else—perhaps more so. I don't believe White gays can get what they want without building some viable coalitions with other minority groups—and I don't mean just window-dressing."

"Take employment as an example," Mark points out. "This is my field, so I know what I'm talking about. San Francisco is a profes-sional city, but the incidence of professional and executive-level Blacks with underemployment or no job at all is disproportionately high. The networking and channels of communication through which most middle- and upper-level management positions travel are closed to us. There are plenty of qualified and experienced Black candidates for the jobs, but if we do apply, by and large, we're ignored.

"Well, nobody said it was easy getting established in San Fran-cisco, especially now," I note. "Positions like that are in extreme de-mand here, and competition for them is cutthroat."

"Yeah," Frank adds dryly, "times are hard and jobs are scarce for White folks, and that always means it's twice as hard for Blacks. Let's face it, San Francisco's a large, White country club. It's easier for Whites to hire, sleep with and socialize with other Whites. It's easier for them to exclude us. That includes the White gay community.

"Why should we believe in White middle-class gay liberation when we are as systematically excluded by them as we are by White straights? Gay power means White gay male power," Frank con-tinues. "That's one of the reasons lesbians in this town are so pissed off. It doesn't mean any new freedom or opportunity or even the remotest concern for them or the rest of us. Whites think we com-plain too much. It embarrasses them. But gay hiring policies, rent-ing policies, banking policies, social customs haven't really changed from the status quo."

"We're fine for show during Gay Pride Week," Mark storms, "when a little color is needed, or for a quick fuck in the dark, when none of their friends are looking, but middle-class Whites don't want to pass along any useful job or investment information or include us in their social circles. They don't hire us to work in their bars and businesses, and after a roll in the hay, they just may not speak the next time they see you."

"I agree," adds Clark. "There's a lot of lip service and rhetoric on liberal posture, but there's very little that addresses issues like jobs for minorities in gay establishments or genuine efforts to involve us politically and socially. Many Whites who sit in the liberal camp are primarily concerned with quelling any social uprising before the uprising alters their status quo. We mustn't discount all self-interest, as we mustn't discount all sincerity."

"You know," confides Frank, "I've lived in New York, Chicago and Los Angeles, and San Francisco is the only place I've ever had to file a housing discrimination suit. It was against a prominent gay businessman who rents only to gay male WASPs in their 20s and 30s. He doesn't even rent to Jews. We eventually settled out of court."

"I believe a lot of blatant discrimination goes uncontested in San Francisco because the housing market—like the job market—is so tight and discrimination is hard to prove," Clark suggests. "We have more than our share of White gay speculators too, profiting from forcing Third-World people out of one neighborhood and into another, Gentrification. Most of the change in the Western Addition and Hayes Valley, for example, is White, middle-class and gay. It's no wonder the Black community feels put upon. 'Gay' to them means culturally unaware and often hostile. Whites increasing rents and moving out disadvantaged Blacks. Some landlords presume we don't have the income to rent because we are Black."

"A not-quite-ready-for-gay-ways Black community versus a not-quite ready-for-Black-ways White gay community. Neither wants to be bothered with the other," adds Mark.

"And it's too bad," I interrupt. "San Francisco has a collective minority majority. Unfortunately, each group has its own sphere of influence and objectives. There's no unity. Each jealously protects its own interests. The resulting disunity serves to insure the sovereignty of the White Establishment."

"Right," Clark warns. "The real fault in the city is not the San Andreas, but a fault along ethnic lines. There is no meaningful coalition yet, based on shared interests of the different minority groups. I think the regard with which we all—that includes us—hold cultural and ethnic differences is the problem. We don't yet know how to accept each other as we really are."

"Cultural difference is always suspect," says Clark.

"I know I question interest shown in me by Whites. I have this gnawing suspicion that it's not genuine, that it's self-serving, that they want something other that what they say," Clark continues.

"Men always want something other than what they say," Mark adds, half in earnest. "But, seriously, don't you think Whites feel the same way about us?" he asks with a laugh

"Maybe," Clark responds, "but it hurts finding out. And I am sick of having my credibility questioned. Whites have a real problem accepting Black success and authority.

"They still have that plantation mentality. If you don't behave like a field hand or a clown, they don't know what the fuck to make of you because you've shot all their stereotypes to hell—and most of them don't have any time or room in their lives to deal with anything beyond stereotypes and gorilla fantasies, anyway. If that."

"So we try and avoid nonissues and nonpeople. Look at how the gay community socializes," I offer. "Everything is neatly segregated and commercialized. It's like a supermarket. Black and White men interested in each other meet at The Pendulum or The Ambush. Blacks interested in Blacks go to Different Strokes. Latins? Esta Noche. Asians? The End-Up. There's an assigned place for everybody and everything. If none of it fits your requirements, you don't exist. If you make the mistake of going where you don't fit in, you're studiously ignored."

"We're still superfluous—nonentities—in many of the gay establishments," Mark contends. "With few exceptions, we don't work there and little consideration is given to encouraging our patronage. If anything, it's discouraged. And a lot of Whites don't identify with us as sexual entities any more than they would with a chair. I guess I should also add vice versa to that," he smiles.

"I don't know of anyone breathing who can't get any in San Francisco," Frank quips, "but there seem to be more older White men interested in us than younger ones. After everything they have has sagged, faded or dried up, they decide it's time to share what's left with us. Most of them wouldn't have been seen speaking to us when they were our age. They were too busy chasing other Whites."

"There are plenty of gorgeous, available men in this city, though," Clark concedes, nodding wistfully at the bevy of sunbathers below, "but those of us who are primarily into eligible Black men find there aren't enough career-oriented, self-actualized, butch-acting Black men to go around. Now that I think of it, there aren't enough of any kind of men to go around," he adds with a chuckle.

"Well, they may be gorgeous," Mark muses, "but I think there's definitely too much emphasis on hot, butch, muscular beefcake and too little on character substance, courtesy and manners."

"Oh, Mary, please—your tongue is dragging on the floor just like everybody else's. The real problem is there are more cakes rising in this town than beef," Clark says with a campy wink, "and relationships, interracial or otherwise, are not as easily established and continued as they used to be. The 'A-list' types simply aren't out there in the bars and baths anymore. It's all transients, tourists, con men and ribbon clerks. It's like living in a candy store, and you can't live on all candy and no substance."

"You're right. It's like trying to be romantic at the circus," Frank agrees. "Too many goddamn clowns."

"And another thing," I add. "Not only are the gay areas more gay, but the whole tone of the city has changed. Ten years ago, it seemed friendlier, more liberal and more fun. Today, the problems, the extremes, the divisions seem to be growing. There are Birchers, fundamentalists, Klanners and cultists. There are alternative lifestyles to boggle the most conservative and the most liberal minds — all living in very close proximity. There's bound to be tension and exclusivity."

"Yes," Frank chimes in, "and we minorities are tolerated as long as we seem safe, are accommodating, drop our drawers on cue, smile and shuffle, don't steal the silver or threaten White sensibilities by seeming too militant or different. And because we haven't learned how to unite effectively, we remain separate and powerless. A lot of us don't want to be bothered with Whites, period. Just like most of them would rather not be bothered with us."

"I think we are just as fucked up in dealing with ourselves," Mark adds. "There's a big difference between not dealing with somebody you think you don't like whom you don't know from personal experience, and not dealing with somebody you know from personal experience you don't like. A lot of us, just like a lot of Whites, don't know each other because we've never gone beyond a physical, superficial level in our relationship. Interracial relationships that work can be more complicated and are a particularly courageous undertaking in these unprogressive times."

"And we're still running stupid color-games on each other," Frank points out. "That combination of disrespect and distrust we have for each other keeps us powerless. There is a bottomless reservoir of disrespect we Third-World people have to contend with every day."

"I have a pet theory on part of that," Clark volunteers. "A big part of racism, as I see it, stems from ignorance, fear and jealousy — especially because of what Whites perceive as race privilege. It's all right for us to have the crumbs from a full table after the meal is done. They expect to see us struggling and striving, but they haven't much taste for our success. They still presume — despite our presence and obvious evidence to the contrary—that there is a class difference. Either they specialize in us or they don't understand us at all—and don't want to."

"And the poorer the Whites are in stature and spirit," Frank retorts, the more anxious they are to put us down. By proving us inferior, they reassert their sense of superiority."

"Let's face it," I add, "we're all vying for the same things—housing, power, status, money and, in our case, men. Most Whites think too many special allowances have been made for us already. Nowadays I don't believe they are as concerned with our betterment. The vestiges of White guilt from the '60s and '70s have all but vanished. We're viewed more as a threat, as competition for the security Whites have always assumed is inherent in this society."

"They don't want to hear about our problems anymore, because they've got problems of their own," Mark points out. "They prefer pretending we're the same as they are—almost. Almost assimilated, almost deethnicized, almost deniggerized, but never quite up to snuff.

"Well, no matter how cynical or bitter we become, we must believe in something. There is no other viable choice. All we have is hope, perseverance and ourselves. Violence, alone, seemed to accelerate the last spurt of social change for Blacks. But now that gays are getting their turn at bat, they may turn out to be too segregated or too silly to band together."

"The gay community has got to realize there's a penalty for betraying its Third-World members," I add. "Divided, we're losing ground across the country. If we don't begin to identify with other disenfranchised groups, we will lose even more.

"I think," I continue, "projects involving the various aspects of the community—like the Gay Olympics, the San Francisco Pride Center or other interracial groups—are a step in the right direction. But we all have to do a lot more work in developing coalitions around issues of mutual interest."

"What's the line from *Animal Farm?*" Mark asks. "'Some of us are more equal than others.' Whites, gay and straight, can no longer pretend nothing extraordinary is happening to minorities in America. It's just not true that everybody shares the same opportunities, that there is no difference. That the only acceptable non-Whites are those who are nelly, nonauthoritarian clowns, or have no vestiges of ethnic awareness left."

"And that's the real issue—being different," I conclude. "That's what's not OK. All of us are fastened to one another without intermingling but are unable to separate entirely or to combine comfortable. Belonging is a very frustrating dream for generations of minorities. We believed the story and paid the price, and it didn't come true. Everybody is part of the charm and the curse that is America. If we're going to turn the tide, we've got to aggressively seek out and target areas of mutual need and begin to interact, to know one another, to stop bullshitting one another and to present a united front to our adversaries."

A. R.

you are lighter
than the back walls of mountain caves.
you are not as black. no matter.
you are as deep, therefore, as black.

you are not as dark as night.
no matter. i would call you black
anyway. you have night in your smile.

you are not as black as black.
you are the sun's other side.

as black as you are
you remind me of green.

you are a cello.

Richard Witherspoon

Rick Martann   Photo: Sierra Domino

TRANSIT HOUSE
A Short Story

Mark J. Ameen

H E TRIED TO SEE the back of his head in the mirror, to check again the line of his new haircut, the squared off, close-cropped line midway down his neck. "A Roman Cut," the designer had said, "not quite a Gay Cut." That had sounded appropriate. He fluffed the edges of his shirt collar so that his chest would remain exposed to the halfway mark and slid the jeans a notch farther down his hip. He looked good but he scared himself. He wasn't sure whether a nerve had snapped or he was learning the ropes, but he knew things were moving as he watched himself dress for the BMT Toilets. One thing said: "You're crazy, Seymour," and another said: "Go get 'em, Harry." It was Wednesday.

His new job wasn't going badly although sooner or later he would believe himself ill-used. The atmosphere was relaxed, but the women seemed bent on finding out what he was all about. This was nothing new either. He wasn't about anything.

Often he would go to the toilets after a quiet evening at the movies. Movies always conjured hand-jobs and cock-sucking. His little trips would make him late to bed and cranky in the morning, for, once inside a tearoom, one didn't leave at least until something happened. This could mean a long wait. It wasn't as if he could do just anybody and it wasn't as if anybody would do just him.

Tonight he was getting an early start and it was giving him a headache. Horny, he was proud of the way he looked and wondering if he might ruin his life in some sad invisible way, if he would grow ugly through quick voiceless encounters with people who were always frowning. He would either fluff his hair and stay home or he would leave at once. He slid into his jacket and locked up.

It was easier if the notion overwhelmed you as you rode. He would climb onto a moderately crowded car and would soon be reading the advertisements hung over the heads of the City's work force—they were more colorful than the workers, easier to look at. He would get lost. He would awaken grinning as though engaged in some stimulating activity, so he'd get off and go to the Men's Room.

Tonight the ride was crowded and his heartbeat accelerated throughout rather than at that final, indecisively stimulated moment. Unarticulated waves of regret swept over him along with the occasional grin. He found himself looking at people. He also looked at his shoes. He decided not to stay in the subways but to visit the large commuter terminal in midtown. The bathrooms would remain underground but might somehow feel open and accessible, like he sometimes did. The air might be less thick.

He had begun of late to imagine the world's tees as untapped reservoirs of communal energy beyond athleticism. Tonight he envisioned a public smelly bathroom blown wide open in sexual forthrightness, saw himself initiating the movement by smiling and remaining. Breaking barriers, talking. He laughed at that. Talking was most painful when he wanted to grab somebody's cock, and he knew it. And yet, isn't it the silents who eventually would speak mysteries? He was convinced, and so he continued to see public lovemaking in the public toilets, men on their fours sucking cock, men against walls fucking madly. No longer fed by the tension of discretion, they would no longer retire their passions upon the entrance of an ambiguous stranger, waiting to see if he was "okay." The new visitor must instead examine himself a priori, for the men he walks past are frolicking unashamed. He had allowed himself to forget that some men might want to piss and shit unaccompanied, because he did not believe that men did that in public toilets, people did that at home. He was, then, in high and adventuresome spirits as he descended the stairs into the gay dungeon and posited himself at the urinal.

He was, then, set into immediate relief from his surroundings and, upon raising his eyes, into direct confrontation with the secretive glance to his left. It was very attractive but pierced by some unpleasantness, something he did not wish to investigate this evening, the hero of our story. On his other hand, a horrible internalization of passion has nearly crippled a young man, or that is what it looks like: He is crushing his pelvis against the urinal as if to hide that which he has come to share. He is contorted in face and body. Perhaps he is too young, but then the hero of our story began much earlier. Perhaps he is just mentally imbalanced. Beyond, a large muscular man peers from a black beard, scattered old men wait and a seven-foot oblivious man strokes himself from a tiny bottle.

The hero of our story now pulls away from the urinal remaining hard and unbound and then stands against the facing tile wall and tucks himself slowly into his jeans. He is no hero but he has that way about him. It is when Harry and Seymour come together, merge into some slightly confused personality which is not sure if it is where it wants to be, that our hero becomes the man we see now, that he becomes who he is, he becomes Dick. The girls at work sometimes call him Dickie, but he does not care for that, not at all. He will not think of them now, in any case.

Dick pulls away from the urinal smiling and still unzipped and tucking himself asks a man against the wall for a light. The man smiles and winks as he complies. This is something anyway although it feels dirty some way. Dick moves to the mirrored sinks and pushes at his hair, then moves up the stairs and into the lobby. A breather.

The disturbed blonde has beat him to it and is festering there; he no doubt crawled by as Dick gazed at his own reflection. Prone before the wall in a state Dick recognizes as the feigning of motive, he's looking as if he's looking for somebody. The conspicuously won presence is painful, and Dick wants to tell the kid that it's too late.

This lobby is public, open to women as well as men, and bodies travel through it regularly. Dick seats himself at one of the marble chairs which once served a shoe-shine enterprise, and the cold stone makes him feel like a statesman. He raises one leg to spread wide his groin, and he lies back to watch the passage while keeping a sidelong eye on the boy. For Dick, it is easy to detect a half-self. The boy will not look at Dick although they come from the same mothers and fathers.

As Dick's thighs cramp, he rises and strolls toward the telephones at the opposite end of the mock marble mausoleum. The tempo under which the boy's head searches to and fro grows alarming, the motion furious. He sneers suddenly at Dick and mouths violently two syllables Dick initially believes unintelligible but soon comes to accept as "fuck off." The boy then moves away, leaving Dick to wonder if this has been a "come-on." Dick doubts it and is feeling alone in his optimism and his attire.

Downstairs there is a new lineup. Shall they be prisoners, soldiers, Nazis, models, cars. Dick is wondering, for he does not feel so good. A few of the earlier gathering are stationed at the wall, but the urinal set has evolved. Of particular interest to Dick is the dark young man with large shoulders who, unconcerned that he is flanked by less than attractive older men, looks down with honest interest at their weighty organs. His hair is full and black and wavy. He wears a belted mohair coat and dress pants and is fired by some special sort of energy which excites Dick and leads him to believe that the man is Caribbean or at least Latin. Dick allows himself to forget that the man may also be straight.

The dark man moves from his space already tucked in and motions to Dick for a light, pulling out a Camel. Dick, as he takes the returning book of matches from the stranger's hand, touching fingers in the exchange, mumbles a quiet "Thank you." The stranger smiles. His face is alive. Some subdued sort of blemish freckles his features, certainly not acne, but something permanent. Dick is intrigued, for the unevenness is not to any unattractive or uncreative end. His mouth is most effective, pursed in some congenital pucker, the lips raised above the contours of the face.

"Thank you." He stresses the you in a manner both manly and relaxed and they both laugh.

"Yeah," says Dick, "I always screw up the thank you's."

"Me, too," says the Dark One. "I'm a waiter and often after serving somebody I say thank you. They think I'm schizo."

Upon hearing the voice Dick is losing his headache and thinking Revolution once again.

There is only one urinal unoccupied on the line. This is directly before them, and claimed on either side of its base by attache cases tilted symmetrically inward. Dick asserts that a photo should be snapped of the two brown bags framing the white urinal, a perfect evocation of "Big City Tee." The dark stranger man agrees and they both laugh.

Dick is fidgety during the silences while they both look forward into the formation. He devotes himself to the far end of the floor. The ragged tall man with the popper is being served the silent adulation of one of the bag-owners. Although he sometimes enjoys the attentions, he soon speaks up in a slowly resonating drawl, "That ain't your hair, is it? That a toupee, ain't it? What wrong with your head? Why you wearing a toupee?" and he laughs in a slow ugly manner. The old man makes no reply but undaunted gropes his interrogator. Finally and feeling forced, he mumbles, "What did you say?" Dick wants to laugh but he has other things on his mind.

His besmirked companion, facing toward Dick, suddenly spirals toward him and glances downward at his blue crotch. Dick returns the signal and then, in a gleeful rush, reaches to his companion's mound and clutches it, quickly saying, "Hi," and feeling his heart return to his center. The Dark Man smiles, although taken back by the fast open movement. He looks to the urinals, where now there are two adjacent spaces. Dick feels himself inching forward, then moves back, not certain of his reading.

The Dark Man answers his own cue and takes a space. Dick is about to follow suit when the hostile youth reappears and occupies the proposed target point. Dick begins to think that the stained babe may be selective and not at all disturbed, until he sees the teeth which have remained clenched and the unusual tightness of the shoulders. Dick feels a bit sorry for the kid and doesn't for a moment believe that the Dark Man will pay any lasting attention to the fierce glance. Another urinal is opening, anyway. Dick moves in.

His friend is as beautiful as Dick thought he would be. Dick removes his penis from society and holds it out, away from the porcelain, so that his friend can see. His friend looks down and also looks beyond at the other men whose open flies surround all action. His friend's cock is long and thick, especially thick at the bottom, from which it tapers columnar into a beautiful skin helmet. At the very base a lush outgrowth of hair creeps neatly upward in a delicate pattern along the flesh. His is a gorgeous organ.

The other men don't matter. Dick and his friend have known since they first felt the other's presence in the room that the other men don't matter, and yet it has taken some time for them to declare to each other that the other men don't matter. They are the most beautiful pair in this or any other tee-room, for they know how to be possessed. They might make quite a couple.

In vulnerability they turn toward one another at naturally the last possible moment, angling their bodies and offering. Dick never believes it of himself, and so always believes himself shy and unaggressive, yet he is always the first to reach out. He reaches out and grabs the large cock fully hard and this motion is duplicated by the other. The two feel one another in this same manner for some minutes until the draw gets stronger and spreads outward, as if a magnetic juice is circulating slowly to fill all of Dick with the fluid that attracts all of his companion. Dick's face is now at his neighbor's neck, and he wants to kiss it, but something beyond magnetism warns him that kissing in the tees might not get a huge response from the Dark One. He is nonetheless nuzzling and allowing himself to be in need of this comforting body talk. He nuzzles and nips, and he wants to suck the feeling which is in his hand.

"I want to suck you."

His friend then makes a suggestion in a hushed manner of talking to which Dick has always been attracted.

"What did you say?" asks Dick.

He suggests that the two enter the section of the tee which demands twenty-five cents admission and houses private enclosed toilets, with sinks. They must however be leery of the attendants who are often mindful of young men within. The friend goes first and Dick follows, slipping his quarter into the slot and remembering the subway. Dick is to get a bathroom near his friend, next to his friend.

The attendant, younger of two, is immediately suspicious and eyes Dick with undercurrents.

Entering the stall, Dick inquires into the wall, "What now?"

"Can you crawl under?" comes the reply.

"Oh, Jesus," mumbles Dick, no longer believing in anything, much less his own mock protest, and so he crawls. He checks the space beneath the partition. He examines the air and he has never seen a narrower pass. He's unsure but he will try. Being at bottom the aggressor he will crawl. He is on three of his fours and plotting strategy when the voice comes low and raucous.

"I see, you know?"

Dick angles his face to see there across the aisle on three of his fours the attendant attending to young things not of his concern, or at least Dick is of this belief, and Dick stands.

"What did he say?" asks his friend through the wall.

"Nothing, nothing, he just saw me, that's all . . . but he doesn't really give a shit," Dick assures. And he waits a moment.

Dick opens the door and enters into the aisle in anarchic belief of safety. He's certain he's got much strength held in check that he will no longer take for granted. He taps on the door of the adjacent stall, and his friend in reply unlatches, his face peering out tight with surprise and suggesting, "No, they won't let us."

"Oh, no you don't! Hey, you fucker, upstairs! Get the fuck out! Upstairs you little bastard!" The attendant is screaming from the far end of the hall.

Dick is infuriated above his immediate feelings of embarrassment and shame. He is finding that his immediate feelings will cut no mustard. But, can he act here, he doesn't know what he can do. His response at present is the idiot's grin from that place within which respects the lunacy of the event. He adapts that grin, and he walks to the attendant, hangs a cigarette from his lip and says, "Hey. You gotta match?"

"Upstairs!" shouts the attendant, and Dick allows himself to think that there is no match upstairs either. He doesn't say what he is thinking but he knows that the grin is not enough. There is something, however, here now within him and moving to make its appearance without him, and it is violent and willing to explode. Nothing explodes, but it implodes, and Dick's only defense remains in his remaining, in the uncertain tenacity of his presence. He clings to the red air and remains woodenly standing there. Then he moves to the sink nearby, turning his back to the attendant, and, quite slowly and with great concentration more than ever he remembers possessing, he washes his fingers of some tingle, drying them after moments of thought with toilet paper, while the attendant looks on no longer believing in anything. Dick might have killed him with scarcely a lost breath had he not watched the blood flow instead into the dirty sink.

To be of such clarity of mind at this murky point amazes Dick, now that he is certain that the attendant has accepted his own impotence. His own Black impotence. What belief had this professional shithouse maintenance man adapted as native in order to take command in the chasing down of faggots, Dick is thinking, to have achieved a dominant stance in the public domain, and here is Dick crawling under his walls and not minding terribly the exertion. Nowadays nobody would let themselves be on the bottom, Dick is thinking, they're all becoming White as porcelain. For a moment Dick wishes he isn't White, then he knows he is no longer and he doesn't miss it.

Dick stands before the sink until he can no longer feel the attendant, and then he opens eyes again and allows his body to respond to the cool shaft of air that is traveling the corridor. The attendant is no longer standing in disbelief but has disappeared or melted into a toilet. Dick thinks of his friend now and what his friend may have been thinking as he stood within his stall and listened to the silent rebellion. Dick waits until he hears the door of the nearby stall unlatching and then he walks.

As Dick exits through the turnstile, he sees before him another of the attendants, this one Black but old and tiny. Dick asks for a match. The little man spits a gob of mucus into a bucket and walks away. "You little prick," says Dick, which surprises the old man for its quiet clarity.

The old attendant can only ask, subdued and semi-tough, "What'd you say?"

Dick can only think of the easy access to shock waves, and then he walks away.

The friend follows upstairs out of the tees and into the lobby. They sit together on the shoeshine marbles, enjoying now a silence much different from the earlier uncomfortable one downstairs facing the lineup and the briefcases which always somehow suggested to Dick a heart attack. There is a definitive life travelling now between them — Dick had thought he may have lost him, but this is not so.

He looks up at Dick. "You're not going to leave, are you?"

"No, I don't want to leave."

"It's so fucked up."

"They'll learn."

"It's stupid."

"It's just none of his business and it wouldn't have bothered him and he doesn't really care." Dick grins. "Do you know any alleys around here?"

"Shit, no."

"Any other Men's Rooms?"

"No, but for one in the subways." Dick laughs. "And it's got a front room and a back room." Dick has never found this one. "Do you want to?"

"Yes."

And so they are on the subway walking very slow and close and rubbing as they sit in the small double seat which the Dark Stranger has chosen for the two of them. They are talking of living in the City and ridiculous train journeys into work and out to nightspots. The Dark One loves the City, although it engenders tensions in his otherwise relaxed progression. He once lived west and that's far better for him and he will return one day. Dick loves the City and does not know why, has visited west but would never commit himself unless he had the cash to flee with frequency.

Dick does not have to listen closely for all he enjoys the Dark One's stories. Dick knows more now than the two of them, and he can be here while letting himself go away as well. He knows things about the Dark One now, things the Dark one is no longer saying and may not be saying at all. Dick can see it in him, in the mouth, the eyes. A fierceness, in that mouth, that hair, that cock. The Dark One is fierce in talking, and his eyes open wide and roll to further animate a head that juggles like a bulldog in the back windshield of a sedan.

Dick is looking and believing that the desiring eyes of the Dark One will floor Dick right there on the train, for Dick is thinking now that the Dark One has certainly the face of a cross-country classical stud, the sexual explicitness of sculpted stone. Dick is happy to let him talk and is smiling in wonder, while the Dark One's eyes take on a madness of uncertain friendship.

They move quickly into the large rooms. Both rooms are large, the front of urinals and the back of doorless stalls. They move directly into the back, where all is deserted, for it is late of a working day.

Upon entering the stall they are not long together in it when they both take deep breaths in order to begin and soon choke them back up into the thickness of the room. The entire arena in which they have chosen to stand has been flooded with liquid agents stronger than straight amonia and they are hacking as though on a college campus. No wonder there's nobody here, they are both thinking, and Dick envisions a lowly attendant covering his face with a towel and gassing the toilets as he prepares to punch out.

"The conspiracy against us will not overcome us," they giggle like revolutionaries, and they begin fondling one another through their trousers and then opening zippers and shoveling one another out as their eyes are burning red. Dick caresses not only the pretty cock but lifts up the teeshirt and begins fondling the chest and stomach and nipples. Dick bends from the waist and kisses and sucks the hard brown tips and then kisses down the stomach and groin through the hair and along the shining length of muscle. Dick takes most of the length into his throat, and then the Dark One begins to fuck into him ever so soft, ever so gentle, and Dick is accommodating.

Dick has been told by the Dark One that he has a beautiful cock; the Dark One has even admitted to loving it, has said that he loves Dick's cock. Dick is remembering now as the Dark One fucks all the way into his throat, and his remembering is allowing him to be totally accommodating. They are the most beautiful couple in this or any other tee-room, and if you could only see their youthful enjoyment, you might not ask questions and instead examine yourself.

The Dark One's is such a compact beauty. Dick stands to hold him and is drawn to caress again the tight tanned belly, the small mound of belly as it lifts out of the groin in a perfect curve.

Says the Dark One, "Gee, I would love to fuck you."

"And I would love you to," says Dick, although something is saying not to be fucked here in the tees, for fucking has always felt special. But so does that belly, says Dick, and so something soon passes away again.

They are holding one another in strong arm clenches, and the Dark One says again that he would love to fuck him, the hero Dick. Suddenly, and for the first time since they have been upon one another, their mouths come together. For what seems the first time Dick is feeling soft exquisite lips and a tongue which has learned. They grope one another's asses and they kiss, and Dick is again surprised to find the Dark One's ass so smooth, so silk-like and soft and so like his own, and the Dark One so manly and alive.

The Dark One's asshole is supple to Dick's finger. The Dark One's finger is all the way up Dick's ass. The fumes are at work now on Dick as he kisses, and his nose has begun to run.

Would Dick like the Dark One to fuck him?

"Yes," says Dick, and he turns around, and he means it when he says yes, the hero of our story, or he would say nothing at all and might even become glum.

"Yes," says Dick and he turns around. He turns around and he places his hands upon the wall while the fumes from the toilet directly below him rise to him, and he says it, he says yes, again, and his nose is running.

The Dark One enters him and Dick recoils with the shock to his insides, his pelvis thrusting forward and his head snapping back. The Dark One pushes and is inside Dick, but Dick cannot meet it and can only push it out, using somehow the muscles which he is not sure exist, not certain he can feel.

Dick says that this will take some time. It's hurting.

The Dark One is so certain when he says it will be smooth, smooth, smooth that Dick knows he can believe and he turns again over the toilet.

When he is inside Dick again, all is still hurting, but Dick has taken him farther than before, and the Dark One has licked Dick's asshole wet for them before reentering. He pushes against Dick and in, hitting the inner wall, and Dick is groaning. He accelerates and Dick can meet this now, can meet and transform it and hold it or let it go and then come back to it. He is holding Dick's cock in one hand and massaging Dick's cock to assure mutual enjoyment and Dick's releasing. Dick wants him to let go and so he tells him so, for Dick feels already that he will explode from the chiming of his prostate alone, and he does not want to finish before his friend, and so he tells him so and pushes the hand away.

The Dark One grabs Dick now by the shoulders with both hands, and he pulls Dick roughly into each of his thrusts. Dick is thinking sparks as he groans and helps himself to move into each push, and he says, "Fuck me," and then "—Baby," and it all sounds to Dick's ears like the same first groan.

Dick hears the Dark One sighing deeply and gathering breaths and skipping beats, and so Dick centers himself to make everything smooth and fast again, and he says to the Dark One, "Are you coming, Baby, because I want to come with you," and the Dark One only groans, and even though Dick knows, he says, "Let me know when, Baby," and the Dark One quickens his pace and says, "Now, Baby," and Dick starts to laugh, and he starts pulling at his own cock and coming with the Dark One and forgetting again and letting go and being unsure of any differentiation between his asshole and his cock and the way in which both are now working to capacity under the rhythmic throbbing of some ravaged muscle deep inside, and the clean white juice is shooting over the toilet onto the dim yellow wall.

A body, a third party, appears at the door of the stall just as the Dark One is pulling his length from inside of Dick, and Dick is thinking that his inside is going out, too, but he knows it will not, and they both jump to see his body which could be anybody but is a young man who smiles after a moment and says that one needs a gas mask in order to hang out in that room, and they all three laugh and agree, and Dick and the Dark One pull their pants up and walk out the door together, and the third one walks out momentarily.

Dick and the Dark One stand near the telephones underground, and they talk of the odd lure of the tees and the streets and everything else. The Dark One believes that one has got to be streetwise, and he smiles at Dick for being streetwise and tells Dick that he would like to write a book about it, a book about the bathrooms. Dick is sure that it has been done but not right he is just as sure.

It is very late, of course, by now, and they both must work, of course, in the morning, and the stairway which leads to Dick's line is before him at the end of the long tunnel. The Dark One's line leaves from a ramp close to the phones where they are standing now and talking. The pretty young man who had been in the Men's Room with them is standing nearby and sometimes looking when they are talking, but never when they are pausing for new thought and glancing about.

The Dark One shakes Dick's hand and takes his phone number, and Dick tells the Dark One, and he has never said it before, he tells the Dark One, "We have to remember one another nowadays," and the Dark One says yes.

Dick walks away then, feeling that he must say more, but doesn't know more, and he is feeling somehow sad, and, as he walks through the long tunnel which leads to his subway, he wants very much to turn his head and to watch that the Dark One goes home as does Dick and does not stay out alone.

And then Dick shakes his head as if to forget something, and he makes himself believe that he has just built a friendship with the Dark One, and he is satisfied with it whatever it is and holding it close to himself by holding lovingly and quite consciously his own ass muscles, which threaten now to fall apart at any moment. He shakes his head and he says, "Yes, yes, yes indeed, indeed Dickie, indeed," and he holds on tight so that he can sit down.

INTERVIEW: BLACK HOMOSEXUAL MASOCHIST

Wayne Alexandre

Drawing by Calvin Anderson

The following self-interview with Black homosexual masochist, Wayne Alexandre, was written in San Francisco.

How long have you been into leather? Not an easy question to answer. Fantasies started about five years ago, but I've only been active for three.

How long have you identified as gay? Since I was fourteen. This preacher gave me a coming out party. A preacher, can you believe it?

Were you very religious? When I was a kid, yeah. My mother was a preacher, only hard core in the pulpit though. I was this Bible totin', gospel singin' little faggot always following behind her. One of these holier than-thou PK's, (that's short for preacher's kid). PK's ought to have a union, we go through a lot of shit.

For instance? Well if you're a PK, a lot is expected of you. Children are naturally cruel, and in church (and the more fundamentalist it is) the more you catch shit from your peers.

Tell me something about your life before puberty. What were you like? Up until about five or six everything was normal, with the exception of the circumstances of my birth, (but I didn't know about that yet). We were a nice middle class Black family with a house, a brand new Ford and every major appliance you could think of. Then my father lost it all and everything changed. My mother decided she had a mission from the Lord and went on the road. Eventually she stopped going out on the road and started school to become a practical nurse. She and my father separated, then I got weird. I was weird from the time I was ten, when they separated. I know it sounds as if, "Aha, there's the cause!" Wrong! Cause I have known all my life that I like male bodies better than female ones. By weird, I mean I understood I was not like everybody else, and I would not be treated like everybody else. I'd do really bizarre things, temper tantrums, I was going to have my way or else; otherwise I was this very sweet loving little kid. Too sweet, I think.

How relevant do you feel your upbringing is to your sexuality? Very.

Then how much is psychological and/or sociological, and how much is your imagination? My sexuality is just there. It's a fact. I can remember when I was five or six and there was this older boy who lived across the street who I admired very much. He was very kind to me and very protective and all I wanted was to see him naked. That's all, I just wanted to see him naked. At that time I had no sexuality, or no definition of it. But like I said, all my fantasies have revolved around men, never females, and I believe quite unconsciously. It's just like the color of my skin. I would not think about it if someone outside didn't make it an issue. It's very probable that s/m is psychological and/or sociolcgical; but as long as it's there and I don't get so extreme that I hurt myself or hurt somebody else more than they want to be hurt...

But haven't you ever questioned your involvement in something that offers the potential for serious harm to yourself? Of course, and in questioning that involvement, I do see the potential to do myself great harm. But I take precautions to reduce the possibilities. You don't refuse to cross the street because you might get hit by a car, you just check the traffic before you cross.

There don't seem to be many Black men into leather. And there aren't too many White men either.

But Blacks, South of Market, are fewer and farther between than un Castro. You'd be surprised how many Blacks are closet s/m freaks.

In other words you think there are just as many Blacks into leather in proportion to the rest of the population? Yes.

Have you ever met or been with any of these men? Yeah. It's usually not with any knowledge that they're into it. The times that it's happened were when we got really fucked up and inhibitions loosened, then they'll try anything and are a little surprised when they find they like it. Sometimes the dude will turn off if I request something out of the ordinary...One time I asked a dude to fistfuck me, and he said in total surprise, 'You want me to WHAT!'

Most of your encounters with Blacks are not s/m then? Right. Sometimes I really get horny for a Black man, and whether or not he's into s/m makes no difference.

Why, because there are so few Blacks into it? Touché!

You said s/m when I asked about leather. Is there a difference?
Sure. Anybody can wear leather. Bikers wear it for protection.
Fetishists wear it. And people who are into s/m wear it, sometimes.

Where specifically do you fit into these categories? I'm into s/m.

*You said the fantasies started about five years ago. What were they
like?* That's complicated. My early fantasies were more intense
than anything I've experienced so far. A lot more violent. Much
heavier than anything I'm able to take after three years, getting
progressively heavier. The first fantasies had one thing in common
with what I look for now, a man in control.

Does it make any difference what color he is? Yes and no. The difference is insignificant.

But what is the difference? Public displays. Exhibitionism. Only
another Black man could show me off properly. It's a matter of
pride. But that can have everything or nothing to do with a scene.
That's what makes it significant. It's a plus, understand. I don't
need it, but it would be nice. In the meantime the choices are slim,
and you can't be too particular in s/m.

Are you saying Blacks don't provide quality? Not necessarily. Most
Blacks who are into leather are primarily fetishists; and I tend to
get bored easily if I get stuck on one note. Besides, my fantasies
about Black men are so specific, anything less is a disappointment.
I have this need for "Daddy."

Were the early fantasies about "Daddy"? In a way.

*Do you see the correlation between the fact that you were from a
broken home, bad-tempered as a child, abused by your peers, and
being a masochist?* Yeah. But the things people strive for are usually those things to make up for stuff they missed. The difference
with me is the social unacceptability of my way in making up that
missed opportunity from my past. "Daddy" is my favorite premise,
and I fully recognise the correlation between that and my upbringing; but to make a judgement because of that is beside the point. It,
(the "Daddy" syndrome), is not the only premise for s/m scenes that
I enjoy anyway, it's just my favorite. It's real rare to find someone
who's secure enough about age to do it properly. This is one of the
reasons why you can't be too particular. To be into s/m requires a
certain need for humiliation and pain and control; either one or the
other or all three. The recipe for me depends on the cook.

There's a certain arrogance that goes with s/m. No offence, but s/m appears to be almost a caricature of masculinity. S/M is an expression in extremes. Extreme in every sense of the word. That includes the way we dress. The reason why people into leather, s/m, who wear leather, hang out together. The extremity of it makes us outcasts. There's a lot of attitude, or arrogance among people who wear leather. It's a form of protection, and more than that it's a turn-on.

There seems to be an s/m elite among people who wear leather. Where does that come from? And why do people who wear leather feel so superior to those who don't? Gay—oh I hate that word! I much prefer the word faggot. There is something angry about that word. There is somethng angry about wearing leather, daring to be different. Identification. Wearing leather is almost a political act. It could be said that wearing leather is some kind of statement about individual rights. What it is is an extreme way of dressing, like s/m is an extreme way of sexual expression. S/m is the best and worst of anything sexual, an extremity; it makes complete sense to me that we consider ourselves superior.

You sound like you're on a soapbox. Sadomasochists are more reviled than anybody. Socially, we take more shit than anybody. And if we happen to be different in the context of that difference, then we take even more shit!

You're talking about Blackness? Yeah. Everything about me separates me from another part of me. I am a Black male homosexual sadomasochist. Black straight people generally don't accept homosexuals readily, if at all, and Black faggots don't accept people who are into s/m. White people don't accept Black people, no matter how liberal their politics. And though there are some exceptions to all of that, the taboo with s/m is so mysterious that people shove it to the bottom of the barrel automatically. And when it's complicated by Blackness, you end up having to fight very hard just living.

Do you think of your Blackness as a handicap? No. But the reality of it is that if you are born Black in America, then you suffer for it. But if you are going to survive, that cause for your suffering must also be the source of pride; otherwise you end up hating yourself. Maybe it (Blackness) is a handicap, but if you think of it that way, you're dead and they've won.

Who are they, Whites? They are the reason why poor people are poor and there are enough weapons to destroy this planet ten times over and why everybody hates everybody else. *They* are the bad people.

Is everything good or bad, so cut and dry? I suppose so. No matter how grey the area seems, if you dig deep enough, there is good or evil, not any superficial religious or social evil. What I mean is human justice—right!

Is that the concept of s/m, good and evil, top and bottom? It's sort of a cliche to define s/m as an exchange of power, but that's what it is and somebody has to hold that power. That's the one thing you can count on, somebody's going to be on top, otherwise it's not s/m, just kinky sex.

If the definition of sexuality is an expression of love and caring, or even a purely animalistic urge, then where does s/m fit in? On what premise are you fullfilled? S/M is at once very sexual and then not sexual at all. I can get horny and meet somebody and get off, cum. I have a very good friend that I love very much who is not into s/m, and we have very loving normal sex and I get off. But I have had s/m scenes where I didn't get off (I didn't even have a hard-on) that have been much more satisfying than this hump-hump, cum-cum business. You see, s/m is a mind-fuck. Earlier I said exchange of power, but that's only partly true. There have been scenes where I have taken extreme pain, where I gave complete control to the top, and others where I have put limits to the pain that I will take, where I have not been able to take much of anything. A great deal of that has to do with how much I am attracted to the top, but even more how much the top takes control. In any case nobody is going to make me do anything I don't want to do. You see, I get a lot of pleasure from pain with some kind of force (in fact the domination serves as a stimulus). So what's happening is the top is given a kind of control, but at the same time is manipulated into giving the bottom what he wants. In between all this is fear, intimidation, and humiliation; the end result if it all works properly is pleasure for both of us.

You describe yourself as a Black homosexual masochist. Not as a cook (which you do for a living), or a writer (where you have ambitions), but a Black homosexual masochist. Why is that important? A Black homosexual masochist is somebody who is in for a lot of problems. If not because he's Black, then because he's homosexual;

then it's because he's an extreme homosexual who makes no attempt to hide it. All three of these have something to say about the
so-called normals. Now your guess is as good as mine as to what
normal is. The White suburban nuclear family, the religious poor
Black family (like mine), the fine upstanding professional gay
couple—all normal until juxtaposed against something so totally
abnormal that they are forced to examine their prejudices,
tolerance, and judgment. If you don't follow the rules, and are extremely different, if you are a White male and come from an upper
middle class perfect nuclear family background, but just
different—you're going to suffer for it. Those people in the suburbs, and people in the cities who are their counterparts, are going
to make you suffer for it. If you are strong enough and have thick
skin, you'll get along; you'll probably destroy yourself, but you'll
get along until you do. Or you may survive if you're really strong. If
you're not, then you fall on your face a lot, and usually you get
kicked once you're down. I don't like the fact that you have to
develop a thick skin to survive if you're different! That's what's so
important about identifying myself as a Black homosexual
masochist! I am simply what I am! I once wrote a poem that said
everybody has their nigger. Well I'd always wondered why I bear
such a heavy burden for being what I am, and the reason is nobody
has the *right* to have a nigger...NOBODY!

IMITATION OF ZEBRAS

the natives say the zebra
is the only animal which wears well
the combination of black on white.

in the heated silence of night
the zebras rest while two men
playfully run, side by side, imitating

the strength and naturalness of black on white.

before dawn they lock themselves together
(the color combination blending to perfection)
and they love
defying their country

and its call for separation.

at sun up the zebras stir.
the men withdraw, say goodbye
and smiling, they remember

> the imitation of the zebras
> fierce and proud

> and the force of nature
> calling for survival.

Jim Brewer, Jr.

FAR AWAY
An Interracial Gay Couple
In South Africa

A PARTHEID: a word derived from the Dutch ("apart") meaning the separation of people by race. Apartheid: the separation idea hideously distorted, whereby one race dominates the destiny of another race. Apartheid: the law in South Africa—a custom elsewhere.

Johannesburg. If you're 15 or 16 and beginning to find people of another race sexually attractive, the last place in the world you want to be is South Africa. If you're a White South African who likes Blacks, there's only one thing worse, being a Black liking Whites. Vusi and Peter are a Black and White gay couple living inside the fist of racial oppression in apartheid South Africa. Yet the first words out of their mouths when greeting the visiting American are conciliatory. "Yes," they admit, apartheid is "totally unacceptable." But they're eager to explain that life here isn't as ... black and white as most outsiders believe.

For starters, we see they associate openly in this large metropolis. "We've been lovers since 1979, as a matter of fact." Under some masquerade, such as master and servant? "No. As peers." They have similar educational backgrounds and are both employed professionally, one in architecture, the other, insurance. Such gay interracial relationships are rare—there's no Black middle class here—but not unique. Vusi and Peter know of others, some of whom are close friends. For those familiar with South Africa's ban against interracial sex—people have been jailed for it—this is dramatic news. Peter explains. "The apartheid policy, designed to preserve the 'purity' of the races, isn't that much concerned with gay people—we can't have babies, you see. Actually, there are two pillars of the policy: no sex and the corollary, no interracial cohabitation." The South African Group Areas Act assigns residential territories according to race, with Whites, of course, assigned the choice areas. Vusi does not live with Peter. His address is Soweto, the nearby Black ghetto. But they do manage to spend a good deal of the time together at Peter's. "Only if a neighbor filed a complaint would we have trouble, but there's been no such problem yet — touch wood."

Other conditions for the two of them are surprisingly unrestricted. There are the usual stares in public, but even those seem to be diminishing. "Either that or we're simply getting used to it. Right now, we're denied common access in only two areas: the cinema and public buses. They're still separated by color. But we can go to the theatre, to concerts, and we can travel fairly openly together." Vusi is philosophical. "In some cities color laws have been repealed. It's a local rule situation, and if there's enough of a fuss, things are changed. In fact, since the coming to power of the P. W. Botha government, social restrictions throughout South Africa have been greatly relaxed." Of course, there's an economic element to all this. White South Africans aren't about to see everything go under in a violent revolution if tensions can be eased in small ways.

One remarkable change is the government's current policy toward homosexuals. Prior to 1970, homosexuality was illegal. With the increasing visibility of gays in other Western countries, however, South Africans took a closer look at their own people. A commission of inquiry was established, and once it was determined that the usual surprising number of prominent citizens happened to be gay, the government moved swiftly to revise the law. Today, homosexuality is legal among consenting adults 19 years of age and older. The gay/lesbian movement itself has grown rapidly. A recent "Jamboree" drew more than 5,000 people, and a national organization, the Gay Association of South Africa, has brought together many local and regional advocacy groups. A brochure put out by G.A.S.A. reads progressively, "Gasa is an association of gays from all walks of life, irrespective of sex, race, creed or age, working together for a better understanding of our lifestyles." It also states, however, that "Gasa is *not* a militant organization...," underscoring a certain resolve to appear non-threatening — to gays and non-gays alike.

Vusi and Peter are also careful to stress their deliberate non-involvement in political activities. "It's futile. However I may feel personally," Peter explains, "for me to make the slightest gesture against apartheid would be in essence to commit suicide." And 'murder' he might add. For in addition to fear of being followed, having his phone tapped, his mail opened, ... fear of being detained indefinitely, possibly tortured, and then put under 5-year house arrest—"if I were released"—any activism on Peter's part would dramatically affect the lives of those around him. "It would be ten times worse for Vusi and his friends. When you consider the immensity of the structure you're up against, you can only play by the rules, bending them occasionally to your advantage." Such a compromise wasn't easy. Peter struggled for some ten years with this racial/sexual quandary before realizing that his very sanity was at stake.

Vusi agrees. "Before we could lift one finger, we'd have to arrange to leave the country. And that's a decision one doesn't make lightly. Our roots are here. Our people, our culture. No matter how brutalized. Are we better human beings if we run out— or remain? Besides, in regard to our gay identity, South Africa is infinitely preferable to the repressiveness of surrounding African nations." The anti-gay stories out of Mozambique, Zimbabwe, Lesotho, Swaziland, *etc.* frighten him.

What about the consciousness of gay people in South Africa? Being sensitive to their own status, are they therefore more sensitive to the racial issue. "I'd have to say 'no'," Vusi concedes, "though undoubtedly I'm more acceptable to gay Whites than to non-gay because of our common oppression as homosexuals. To what extent the average gay White would actively oppose apartheid is a question that really hasn't been put to the test, and I'm not optimistic. I will say, however, that gay restaurants were among the first to open their doors to minorities."

"We're able to contribute in other ways," Peter adds. "Gays and non-Gays alike. People can sponsor an education for promising Black youngsters who can't afford one—Vusi was helped that way— and, as private citizens we can organize and support such groups as the Institute for Race Relations, a government-approved body promoting racial harmony."

Gay life among *Black* South Africans is fundamentally different. As in many non-Western cultures, homosexuality is both more integrated, yet less visible. Most Black African families are still separated by harsh—some would call them genocidal—labor codes. The men, assigned to the mines or to menial service in cities, may not bring their families with them. Wives and children are left behind in the territories in a traditional environment of the extended family, or tribe. And, Vusi and Peter claim, homosexuality is greatly frowned upon there. (There have been reports by U.S.

women's groups who've investigated life in South African territories that lesbianism is not so uncommon — after all, the women
live without men for great lengths of time — but Vusi and Peter are
skeptical.) The compounds, where working men are housed, are
another matter entirely.

"Black men who work in the mines together and then return to
dormitories to spend their leisure time together often form
liaisons. And given the fact that these men are away from their
families for periods of nine to twelve months at a time, the relationships can become quite deep. It's not uncommon to find men
who've been lovers for years. Some even go home together to visit
their families. There's a kind of unspoken understanding. The compounds can become flamboyant at times, with heavy cruising, drag
parties — even mock marriages. We received a photograph from a
Black friend in a compound and there he was in a wedding gown,
surrounded by his attentive 'husband' and friends. The Chamber of
Mines is aware of this sort of thing and, though they forbid Gay activity as an assurance to waiting wives, it's all pretty much out in
the open."

What about Johannesburg's infamous Black ghetto, Soweto?
"When gay Black men first emerged as a separate entity, they were
often too open about it. Coming into town on the train, if they were
'dressed,' they'd be harrassed by other Blacks who perceived them
as being too Western, too pansy. Some of them, having access to an
income for the first time, spent their money on clothes and other
appearances. Blacks are not allowed to 'freehold' — own — property
in South Africa, so what else is there? Gay life in Soweto itself is
surprisingly common. There's a kind of 'open city' atmosphere
there. Shabeens, illegal taverns, are the center of social life and
many of them are gay or mixed. They're converted houses and,
depending on size, each accommodates between, say, thirty and
eighty people. Each also has its own distinct ambience and
clientele. It can be difficult, though, to consummate a
rendezvous — there's so little privacy in Soweto. Two or more
families often share a single home. So one usually has to settle for
cruising and dancing unless you have the money to rent a room, or
you have an accommodating friend back in Johannesburg. The
Soweto shabeens are almost exclusively Black, with an occasional
German or Italian tourist wandering in. You have to have a pass to
visit the area, you see. There's one popular shabeen — not Raba's,
but another — which is run by a well-known Black man. He makes
no bones about his Gayness and his preference for young Black

men. His place is a large, nondescript brick house, and he's very careful about who he admits."

And what about attitudes toward Whites? When asked if he feels an undercurrent of hostility when he visits Soweto, Peters replies, "No, not really. Oh, I'll keep my car door locked when I'm driving through, but once inside a shabeen I feel comfortable."

Vusi disagrees somewhat. "The resentment is there whether it's expressed or not. And sometimes it is expressed. I know of an interracial group that was robbed after leaving a shabeen. And too I've had other Blacks wonder openly why I'm associating with 'the oppressor'."

Indeed, the 'why' comes back. Not the why of one Black man sharing love with a White man in the middle of all this, but the bigger 'why.' American activists, hearing the story of South Africa, are often dumbstruck by its sheer incredibility: a country predominantly Black, ruled by a small White minority. A big brother mentality in government. No Black participation in the political process. And above all, the ugly pervasiveness of apartheid, affecting millions of people in untold ways. When Vusi and Peter expressed an interest in visiting America to see how different life could be, I couldn't help but pause. Had this been New York or Boston or San Francisco, might they have noticed some striking similarities? Perhaps they might have questioned me: if South Africa is ruled by a few privileged Whites at the expense of the many Blacks, how does it differ from the United States, with the rule of millions of deprived Afro-Americans—and others—by a few privileged Whites? Are South African security police 'bigger brothers' than the FBI or CIA? And what of the political process? To what extent, practically, can Black voters and elected Black officials influence their lot? —And apartheid. If it no longer exists in theory, doesn't it prevail in fact, the oppression of American ghettos— American Sowetos—bearing witness?

It's winter in South Africa, coming into spring. North of the equator, it's summer, becoming fall. Things are different, yet things are the same.

Drawings: Ross Paxton, 1983

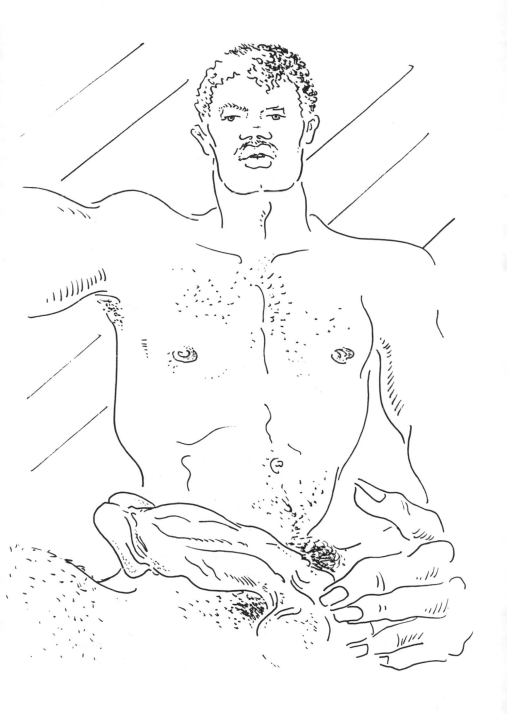

BLACK AND GAY
One Man's Story

Darryl Towles

I AM A BLACK MALE with a sexual preference for White men. It's really no different than preferring vodka to scotch, except that I'm often judged because of it. But the development of my sexual tastes is very logical: When I was growing up, most of the male images I was exposed to were virile, masculine, all-American White types.

I can remember drooling over Bobby Sherman in "Here Come the Brides." "Batman" was my favorite fantasy trip because of the close relationship he had with Robin. I would spend hours imagining myself dressed in green tights and romping through the streets of Gotham with Adam West. That wasn't the only cartoon image I found erotic—I would have gladly drowned to spend an intimate hour submerged with Aquaman, and I'll always remember Jonny Quest and his guardian, Race Bannon, as my favorites. I didn't understand why I felt this way, but I knew what I liked.

My parents, wishing to raise me properly, brought me up in an open environment. I attended the best private schools with the most adorable young men. While I'd always had an inkling about my special tastes, high school gym class was the time when I became quite positive. Gym class was a constant source of anxiety, the dozens of cream-colored bodies heightening my senses. For ninety minutes each week I had my chance to gaze at the objects of my desire in a semi- nude state, but I dreaded the showers. I knew that as soon as I got under the warm stream of water I'd have a hard-on that could be relieved only one way.

I didn't have my first sexual experience, though, until after I'd graduated from high school. I never went through the pains or traumas of "coming out." When I went away to college, I decided that my new friends would accept me on my own terms. That not only made my homosexuality easier for me to deal with, but it made it much easier to meet men who were comfortable with their gayness. My suite mates were able to kid me about a guy down the hall: "Wait till you meet Jim. You even sound like him." Even before I met him, I got the idea that Jim and I might become close.

Jim turned out to be a beautiful specimen of man. He was every one of those boys I'd gone to school with, and more. We were drawn to each other, but because of the roommate situation there was little we could do. One night, when my roommate was home visiting his family, Jim knocked on my door. "My roomie's got a girl in there," he said. "Would it be okay if I slept here?" How could I say no? I wasn't sure if he meant sleeping in the extra bed, or if he had other things in mind. But there was no question as he undressed. His erection stood out stiff in front of him.

There were no words between us as I pulled back my covers and he climbed on top of me. Our lips parted, our tongues met, and our throbbing cocks pulsated as they pressed together. My fist enveloped his shaft, and I knew what I wanted to do with it. I slid down and got my first taste of male meat. It was like nothing I'd ever tasted before. Jim's moans encouraged me and told me I was doing something right. He grasped my ears and drew my mouth almost to the root of his stiff dick. I doubled my efforts, and sucked harder. I knew he was going to cum, and really wanted to taste his seed. But, he pulled away. "Not yet," he whispered. "I want to make this last."

Then he was down on me, giving me the same oral treatment I had given him. Up until then, my only gratification had been with my own hand. The warmth of his mouth, coupled with the tingling sensation of his facial hair, sent me into a frenzy. His head bobbed up and down on my hard cock while his masterful hands kneaded my balls. Years of pent-up passion were unleashed like flood waters. The sensation was so overwhelming that I became oblivious to everything around me. Our bodies, locked into a sixty-nine position, writhed on the small, regulation college mattress. Our thrusting peaked, and then I was shooting a full load all over his face. His tongue swirled around my cock as he smeared my cum across his cheeks. And then I tasted his warm, sticky juice. My cheeks filled, my throat bulged, and I swallowed again and again as he emptied himself into me. We both sighed, and afterward lay wrapped in each other's arms, oblivious to the time, sticky wet, and indescribably happy. We'd each found a new friend. It made the time fly by so much faster.

Jim and I became closer than most friends, but we never quite
became lovers. We each longed to find someone with whom to form
a special bond. That didn't happen for me until I left college and
moved to Boston for a change of scenery. What I was greeted with
were more cute preppies than I knew what to do with. I concentrated on my work, and it was when I least expected it that one of
the most important men in my life happened along.

Greg and I were working on a stage production together and
became friends. He was the cast hunk, and nobody was sure which
way he swung. Since I figured I wasn't even in the running, I never
competed for his affection. That turned out to be one of the things
that attracted him to me.

One night, I went to his apartment with a small token of friendship. Touched, he left the room to give me something he said he'd
been saving, but told me that I had to close my eyes. I waited patiently, not knowing what was in store. "Hold out your hand," he
said. When I did, he took it and placed something solid and warm
in it. "Open your eyes," he ordered. He stood in front of me, clad only in bright red bikini shorts, as I held his erect cock. He stood me
up, slowly unbuttoning my shirt. My clothes fell away, and we were
soon entangled like vines. His long, smooth thighs clasped around
my back and we bucked like broncos.

"Fuck me," he panted. "Put it in me, please!" All I had to rely on
were my impulses, but once again they didn't steer me wrong. He
kept a jar of Vaseline in the nightstand by his bed. He began
lubricating my cock, which throbbed in anticipation. I scooped up
a generous amount to help cut down the friction, but he was
already raring to go. I slid inside him with the ease of a pro. The
glove-tight sensation played on every nerve fiber of my rock hard
cock, and he pushed himself back, forcing me deeper inside him.

The excitement and romance made both of us madmen. He howl-
ed with passion—sex music to my ears. His thrashing became more
frenetic and, as he climaxed, I felt his sphincter contract like a vise,
pulling me past the point of no return. We fell asleep in that position, my cock bathing in its own juices inside his body.

Greg and I were together for almost two years. During that time I
saw an ugly side of prejudice. There were times when people
around us reacted negatively to seeing an interracial couple. The
summer before we split up, we spent some time on the coast of
Maine. This is where we experienced the greatest pressure. We got
stares as though we were from a different planet. We were refused
hotel rooms, and people on the beach actually moved away from

us. So we had a great deal of privacy, as well as a strong sense of what it was like to be outcasts. Though it didn't contribute to our eventual split, it left a strong impression on both of us.

Since then, I've moved to New York. As the saying goes, there are "so many men, so little time." While it's difficult to meet people when you're new, I've been lucky enough to find a select group of friends who either have no racial hang-ups or are specifically attracted to Black men. At a friend's suggestion, I checked out Kellers, a Village bar; the racial mix is evenly balanced, so that this is the place where Black men can go in search of White men and vice versa. It has been there that I've met some of the most important men since my relocation.

I've met one particular man who's helped to fill many of my nights and a few sunny days. He's made New York not such a cold place, and the notion of Black and White men together not such a bizarre idea. For that and more I thank him.

Two Poems by Adrian Stanford

psalm of the visionary

from the quarry of my mind i carried naked through the streets
such burdensome stones as were necessary to build a temple in honor
of lena horne.

and when the work was done and my mental state adjusted to the
heights of her sublimable plane, i washed and oiled myself and
donned the robe of chastity; then went inside and called her name.

i could hear crowds singing and the rhythmic sound of marching
feet. see the white-eyes stone and kill the proud young who dared
to dream of equality.

i heard plantation songs, the cracking of whips (the wet tearing sounds they made pulling flesh from the bone).

I smelled the scent of the breeding houses; listened to the
lustful gurgles of horse-cocked crackers who rammed black virgins
into unconsciousness and pregnancy.

i fell upon my knees and in a loud voice spoke the incantation,
"fuck martin luther coon, fuck martin luther coon."

jasmine blossoms began to fall. a feeling of strength and beauty
enveloped me; i knew she was there.

i turned and saw her, ran to her, kissed her feet and called
her many sacred names—putting to her all the un-answered questions
i longed to know.

her face became a kaleidoscope of suffering. huge tears swelled
in her eyes. she moaned and beat her breast and inflicted upon my
ears one screaming word: NEGRO! N E G R O ! N E G R O !
then she began to fade.

the temple shook. all grew black. something wet fell on me, it
had the odor of vomit and manure; i screamed and tried to run, but
my feet would not move.

i heard singing again—gospel songs of vengeance, and sinister
lullabyes for the redemption of desecrated black skin.

light glimmered in the temple. i found myself crying, wailing
her name, but lena horne had gone.

it was cold outside. i gathered my robe about me. The moon,
moved and far away, was paying court to the greying clouds.

i started down the road to home, my lantern casting shadows on
the path.—
and as i walked, i sang of stormy weather, alone, but somewhat
wiser in the night.

y e a h   b a b y

i've had them roll up in chauffered limousines
swing open the door and beg "please get in."

i've been approached, followed, waited for, hung onto,
and groped by all those staid white queens that
don't like *colored boys.*

and certain nigger fags (who don't want nothin but blonde
hair around the cocks they suck), have more than once pushed
their fat asses my way!

you think all this has gone to my head; made me some kind
of valentino—lena horne queen bitch ? (yeah baby !)

Alex Scott   Photo: Sierra Domino

CHESTER
A Short Story

Lyle Glazier

IN 1947, when I moved to Buffalo to teach at the University, most Black men walked downtown streets with faces lowered, looking out and up through rolled-back lids. In order to piece out their earnings, some of them actively courted gays. I was too naive to comprehend their anger over the pattern of social repression for the advantage of Whites. Although I was romantically turned off by the thought of paying for sex, I soon fell under the spell of their sensuality, seeming to liberate deep wells of sensuality in me.

On a Niagara Falls spur of Grand Central, in the rotting out wooden station on the Terrace, there was an isolated active john with glory holes. It was a shit house of the old-fashioned kind with no plumbing. In late afternoon after school, big Black boys would often be hanging around waiting for well-dressed commuter traffic. I had many casual engagements but don't remember ever paying. I usually picked one of the older men who liked me because in my thirties I still had the face and body of an adolescent.

One afternoon there was a late-teen-age boy in the cabinet next to the one I entered. After he showed himself and got me interested, he leaned and thrust the tip of his tongue through the glory hole. Trembling, I stood facing him, letting him have my cock to tantalize. Then he withdrew his tongue and maneuvered his own generous cock to the hole and I kneeled to tantalize him. Our pleasure in each other grew excruciatingly painful.

Finally he put his lips to the hole and asked, "You got a car? You want to come home with me?" There was no burr to his speech, his voice as elegantly preppy as a boy's from Nichols School.

It was the first time I accepted such an invitation. We drove across Main Street and along Elk, then turned upgrade and across Swan into the warren of back streets with small wooden slum dwellings later torn down to make room for Great Society housing that was never built. Acres of vacant lots festering with crab grass and rubbish now replace the crowded houses. The boy showed me where to park in an alley, then took me into his kitchen. A powerful middle-aged man was playing with a squealing girl, who stood on his thighs pummeling his chest and chin. They exploded with laughter and paid no attention to me.

Having shut the door in a back bedroom, the boy quieted my fear: "You come here any time. If I'm not home, my father will take care of you."

He was scrupulously matter-of-fact, assuring me that my fear was only in my mind. He undressed at once, revealing a cock and balls in their nest of tightcurled hair even more beautiful than they had seemed through the glory hole. He lay on the bed with cock arching.

"Sit on it," he commanded. He pulled me on top facing him and played with me while I guided him inside.

"Take hold of it," he ordered. I tightened my sphincter muscles while he closed his eyes, gripping me with his rhythmically moving hand. He withdrew and had me lie on my belly. He entered from the back, turning me on my side so that he could continue to play.

"Let go now," he ordered. "Don't hold back."

He began stroking me furiously, at the same time plunging full length. He would hold himself still a few seconds and then deliberately withdraw. He was not in the least in a hurry. We pieced out our play a half hour. Then with a final lunge he held himself rigid. I could feel him quiver inside.

Gradually his tension released. Holding me firm with his hand, he renewed the rhythm on my cock.

"Don't be afraid now. I'll whip you off if you'll give me a half dollar."

His passion seemed utterly gone. He sensed my discomfort.

"No kidding. I really want to."

Afterward I gave him the half dollar, hardly looking at him. I held my pocketbook half concealed like a magician performing sleight of hand.

Back in the kitchen, the father was still pummeling his daughter, who squealed and rolled in joy. If he had spoken, I might have been reassured and returned one of the afternoons when I was hard up, remembering the father and son. Very likely not wishing to scare me, he didn't say a word.

One noon in the basement of the Decco Restaurant near the central library, I met a heavy-set, middle-aged skidrow Black and rode the trolley with him a few stops south of Swan Street to one of the decayed brickrow houses. We went silently upstairs to his bedroom, and had leisurely, languid sex for an hour and a half. He was somnolent yet sexually fully alive, like a sensual mountain or a slumbering meadow. Most active about him were his velvety cock and his soft hands that stroked my nipples and thighs. I sank into his mood and lost all thought of time. I was barely conscious of hearing two women come loudly upstairs and into the next room john. Their voices, at first in the background, gradually began to intrude. I lost my feeling of being suspended in time and space. As I became alert to their presence, their voices sank to whispers. I thought they were spying on us through some concealed, half-wallpapered hole.

We lay in full sunlight pouring in from a streaked west window.

"Doan care abou them," my friend whispered when he saw me raising my head. "They ain nothin. They doan amoun to nothin. They ain goan hahm you."

He didn't ask for money. He wanted me to come back. "Doan never mine them women. You come back now. Any time."

He was still lying naked when I dressed and walked to the bed and kissed him. He pulled me down and we lay together for a moment. Then I wrote out my university address.

"Be sure now," he said. "Any time."

I forgot my library book laid on top of his radiator. The next day I returned. The landlady was sitting on the front stoop blocking my way.

"You can't go upstairs."

I told her I came for my book.

She went in and climbed the stairs, her fat legs springless and slow. Back down, she handed me the book.

"Here. You stay away from here. You'll land us all in jail. You ah jailbait fo shuah."

I was sure he was home. I was on fire to see him. Once, later, I walked to the top of Swan Street, but I didn't go on to his house. I thought he had no formal education, no book learning, no academic interest in literature, music, the fine arts. I erased our difference. I was engulfed by his brown warmth. He was pure sexuality—gentle, placid, as open to love as the earth is open to the sun. I loved his brown against my white. His Blackness was male with a difference—just as every cock is different from every other, an infinitude of physical attraction.

I had long-standing friendships with two Blacks, both of them beautifully made. Unresisting to my own sensuality in the presence of one or the other of them, I would undress feverishly and throw myself across him, cramming his cock in my mouth. After a few minutes, when I recovered sanity, we would straighten out on the bed and tamper with each other for hours.

One of them—the younger—was, when I met him, a nurse at Buffalo State Hospital (Insane Asylum) on Elmwood Avenue. He later finished teacher training at the State College just beyond the hospital grounds. He became an elementary school teacher, then an office clerk for the Board of Education. Finally, for reasons I didn't comprehend, he went back to nursing at State Hospital. His body was heavy but not fat, his cock thick and long. He liked to play manually for a half to three-quarters of an hour before moving to oral sex. We would continue at six/nine for a half-hour, rising again and again to the crest, then withdrawing to let the intense feelings subside. Finally—because the hour grew late or we had passed the peak of crescendo—he would enter anally, continuing to handle me. At last he would lengthen his strokes, anal and manual. I could tell when he was about to go off because I could feel the deeper plunge, and the tightening grip on my cock. I would let myself go completely. We hardly had to resort to verbal promptings. I always felt refreshed and morally cleansed when I left him.

Another Black friend was a talented musician, ruined because of his race. He played double bass in a night club and had a moonlight shift as nightwatchman. He was no longer living with his wife, but they would have long, loving talks over the phone. I was often at his house, first on Jefferson Street, then just off Broadway. I passed through his dark living room to reach the bedroom. He had a lovely, longish cock, not so thick but that he could enter without hurting. He loved to lie inside for an hour hardly moving, the tip gently pulsing. From time to time he would make an unexpected sidewise swipe that would take me by surprise (surprise him too) almost driving me mad. I suppose he was on some kind of dope. He was languid, his speech thick.

He and I loved each other with a pragmatic, unsentimental passion. We had no illusions about exclusivity or longevity, claimed no hold on one another. We took what we could on the many, spaced occasions when I could get to see him. He never turned me away but once. That time a young White man was ringing the bell when I came in sight. The stranger had lost patience as if he had been ringing some time. I got there just as he gave a final jab and came off the porch. Since I had a date for that hour, I took my turn at the doorbell, but there was no answer to my ring. The other man was waiting at a streetcorner, spying to see what luck I had where he failed. As horny for Prettyman as I was, he took to me in an instant. We went to his apartment near Delevan/Elmwood and became lovers for more than ten years.

The next time I met Prettyman I accused him of standing me up.

"I was there all the time back of the curtain. I wanted you bad that day. I didn't want him. I saw you two go away. Why didn't you come back after?"

Once in the late '60s his nightclub band had a half hour on Buffalo TV. He sang "Great Big Beautiful Wonderful World" inverting the emotional exuberance so you had the pit-stomach feeling it was the lament of a locked-out, starved soul gazing through an iron fence at a paradise from which he had been banished forever. On the screen his tormented face looked bashed-in as if wasting from inside. Out of this ruin his sorrowful eyes stared like scared ripe olives impaled on toothpicks.

During the '67 war between Egypt and Israel, I was twice caught in a Buffalo speedtrap and sentenced to Driving School, which met in Cheektowaga between 5:30 and 6:30. I would call Prettyman afterward and stop by. One night I got there when he had turned on the news. Things were going bad for Egypt. Prettyman had lost his good manners. He was perfectly indifferent to me. We watched and listened together.

Finally I said, "You want Egypt to win."

He ignored me. I thought he took it for granted I was on the side of Israel. When the news program was over, he switched off the set, and we sat in unbreachable silence. After a half hour I left.

In the last years of our friendship, something got to him, perhaps fatigue with life, perhaps drugs. I would call him and he would say come over, and there was always the same long-jointed Italian there with a tremendous cock, which I loved because it was so gorgeous. He and I had no intellectual rapport, but our physical rapport was unbounded. I would mouth and handle and play with his cock while he agreeably played with mine. Then when we were both broken in, our seminal juices flowing, he would gently and gradually force himself inside, taking plenty of time, delaying if I moaned, till finally I had the whole lubricious ramrod contained. He would slowly and patiently rock back and forth, piecing out sensations for us both. I could never actually come by just internal pressure, but he had a talent to bring me again and again to the brink, in harmony with his own crescendoes. I learned to tighten my muscles driving us both wild. After taking hold, I could feel the length gather itself in a locked-in, violent spasm. Finally he would gently finish off us both.

Gradually racial tensions in Buffalo increased. In the late '50s Blacks were no longer socially passive. At the same time my naivete gave way. As my enlightenment grew, my behavior did not change. Still wild in an instant for sex, I was pragmatic in my relations with Blacks. I abhorred trafficking in money, but continually compromised my principles. By taking chances I paid for my social advantage, risking physical violence if need be.

One night I picked up a wicked-looking, friendly young ruffian across Main Street from the Swan/Seneca Decco and following his directions drove to his neighborhood on the east side near the corner of Burton and Rochevort. Having parked in front of his house, I let him strip down my trousers and fuck me in the front seat of the car. Sometime during the nervous orgasm, I was terrified when a car in back of us turned on headlights illuminating the interior of my car. After a moment the lights were switched off. Having taken leave of my benefactor, who had been relieved without fully satisfying me, I drove back to the Decco to search for another engagement. There, when I took out my wallet to pay for coffee, I found that my friend had neatly fingered out my tenspot, leaving me two ones and the wallet, and a suddenly collapsed carnality.

The Veterans Hospital in Buffalo stands at the edge of the in-city university campus. In the early '50s I volunteered for a program to rehabilitate wounded vets from the second world war.

The one who really got to me was Chester.

Chunky, solid but of small frame, fresh-faced and handsome, he was scarred by tragic experience. For some time he lurked in the background of the crowded and noisy common room where I tutored. One day he brought me some poems, uneven in merit but with phrases that sank like barbs into my spirit. I made suggestions without tampering with his language or rhythms. One entitled "Ode to a Black Beast in Heat" showed familiarity with literary forms in its title, though diction and imagery were his own. In spite of frequent obscurities he was a long way on toward discovering his own tone of voice. He was good enough to be envied.

That spring semester I was teaching a course in creative writing. I told the students about Chester. They were eager to have him visit. I asked Miss O'Grady, in charge of the psycho ward, whether a visit would be possible. At first doubtful, because Chester was "very bad," she soon changed her mind if I would come for him and bring him back. I walked him to and from campus. He sat very quiet listening to the students read and comment on each other's writing. After class they gathered around him. A favorite student asked if she could walk back with us to the hospital. On my next visit when Chester gave me a love lyric, I knew who he had in mind.

He came to class several times. He wouldn't read his poems but asked me to read for him. The girl came to the hospital. It was clear she was deeply attracted but afraid she couldn't seriously help him, but perhaps hurt him by offering affection that would have to be withdrawn. I knew how she felt, for by then my susceptible nature had fallen in love with him, too.

His situation seemed hopeless. In spite of fragments of pure poetry, he couldn't make a whole poem. I was not wise enough to suggest that he let each fragment stand by itself. We both had a false notion of POETRY.

It was late May, the end of the year. His visits from Karen stopped. Her father did not want a good Jewish girl to get deeply involved with a Black man. For a month, till summer school began, I broke off volunteer work.

One afternoon Chester called me at home in Orchard Park south of the city. He was at his sister's in Lackawanna five miles away. He wanted me to come see him—"under the smoke from the steel mill."

I hesitated, then agreed.

I was hardly prepared for the square cement block houses, fenced off from a four-lane highway between the housing development and the steel mills, whose dense smoke was a constant pall. It was company housing. The families were trapped for life.

Chester was watching at the door. He ushered me into a dark living room to an overstuffed chair in the far corner. He sat in another chair between me and the door. We talked about class, about students he had met. Shocked at the poverty in the room, I was happy to show my affection.

Without transition he was saying, "Dr. Glazier, I am sitting on a butcher knife."

My warm spirits, damped in an instant, congealed in the animal self-protectiveness that can come in a moment of terror.

"Oh, you are?" I said, as if mildly curious.

"It's here under the cushion. You want to see?"

"Oh, there," I was careful not to flinch.

"I put it there before I called you."

I held myself back from anxiety, relaxed in my chair. Racing for ideas, I thought of Karen but decided against mentioning her. I asked if he had a new poem.

He said he had a small one.

Then he said, "Dr. Glazier, you are lucky. When we Black people begin to kill White people, you will have me for a friend."

I didn't feel lucky. I kept him talking about poetry. I never knew whether he really sat on a knife. After half an hour of conversation I suggested we could go for hamburgers.

He said, "Will you drive over to your house?"

"Why do you want to go there?"

"I want to see where you live."

I drove him to Orchard Park. When I parked in the driveway, I felt guilty about the size of the house on its acre of lawn, with flowerbeds and vegetable garden. After years of poverty, for me it was a dream realized. To Chester it could look like a mansion.

The entrance hall was bigger than Chester's front room. We walked through to the kitchen, where I poured glasses of milk and got homemade doughnuts from the crock. We were eating when Laura came home and went directly to the piano to practice. I took Chester to introduce him.

For a few minutes we listened. Then I drove back to Lackawanna, where Chester urged me to come in.

"I can't this time. I have to be home for the younger girls when they get there from school."

Driving back, I was engulfed by delayed terror. How could I have taken him in where the children were expected? My hands shook on the wheel as I thought of the knife under the cushion. He could have had a switchblade in his pocket.

I phoned his doctor at the hospital and got a tongue lashing. "You should know better than go to a patient's home. I never do. Chester is paranoid."

A week later in the psycho ward, Miss O'Grady asked me to visit Chester in a recovery room where he had been having electric shock treatment. In bed he was thoroughly tranquilized. His speech was fuzzy as if he were talking under water.

The next time he called from Lackawanna I had my mind made up. I didn't hesitate to go see him. I was utterly fatalistic. If I got hurt, I got hurt. I went many times.

One morning when the girls were in summer school, I took him back to Orchard Park at his request. He wanted to see the whole house, top to bottom.

In one of the upstairs bedrooms he told me, "I'm not any good anymore." He dropped his hand to his groin. "I got hurt. I'm all twisted inside. Nobody can do anything for me."

I put my arm on his shoulder.

Soon we were undressed on the bed. His body was unblemished, but he couldn't raise an erection and expressed no interest in mine. I soon stopped trying.

I saw him again at the hospital. He lost his interest in poems.

The next time he called from his sister's was midsummer. He wanted us to go over on the Canadian shore to an abandoned quarry filled with spring water. That was where he and his friends went swimming.

Though the quarry was isolated, we both wore swim suits. The water was numbingly cold and had the buoyancy of great depth.

"You could drown here," Chester said.

We stretched out on towels in the sun. I tried to interest him in poetry. He had written nothing new in his notebook.

On the way back he wanted to try driving, "just for a couple of miles." He had no sooner turned onto the main road to the Peace Bridge than a car came up behind, nudging our bumper. Chester laughed and gripped the wheel tighter. I looked back into the grinning faces of two Blacks. They kept bumping us, throwing us to the side.

I made Chester pull over. We changed places. The nuisances had gone on. I thought they had followed us from the quarry, probably having parked out of sight, watching. Luckily I hadn't touched him.

I was in trouble of a different kind. I had had run-ins with the Buffalo vice-squad. Not only the police but people I counted on for friendship seemed to be turning on me. I was on my way to the nervous breakdown that set in three years later after I confessed to my wife and two colleagues.

In late August when Chester called, I had made up my mind.

"I can't help you. I want to. There is nothing I can do for you. I don't know enough."

"I need you to come see me."

"I wish I could but I can't."

I dropped out of the VA program to cut Chester out of my life. If he could handle our relationship, I couldn't. I was too cut up by my mix of altruism and sexual heat.

Years later, I was visiting professor in North Yemen. I was invited for 1981-2 but couldn't be gone from home so long. When invited to name a replacement, I named a young Black scholar, my former student, who had written his dissertation on Baldwin.

An American Black in Yemen, he became a lion to his students, many of whom had African roots. Before him, their acquaintance with official America had been limited to men in gray flannel suits. Intelligent, charming, handsome, he was an American such as Yemenese never dreamed of, an American cut to their cloth.

He had no way to know about Chester. He was my surrogate, my atonement. In my relationship with this deserving young man, it seemed important (as for James's Lambert Strether with Mme. de Vionnet) "...not, out of the whole affair, to have got anything for myself."

A MEMORY: SANA'A†

A tiny cock of thatch
threw a shadow across
the sered veld

bearing umbels of small white
and rose flowers
springing from the dried earth

like the ribs of an umbrella

and the gentle breeze
stirred fragrance free
with aromatic cumin

remind me of your eyes
and redolence
the night when moonbeams laced

our path westward to the bend
in Wadi-Dahr; remembering how
we triumphed dawn and rose

forgetting the imprint
of two bodies so closely knit
deserted by the sleeping wind.

Jerome Thornton

†*Sana'a is the capital of the Republic of Yemen in Southern Arabia, where this Black American writer was teaching.*

GAY RACISM

Joe DeMarco

THERE IS A SITUATION that's happened to me every time I've gone out. White men will approach me. They assume I don't know anything. They assume I'm uneducated and stupid," remarks Jimmy J. "They don't expect me to be able to carry on a conversation. But, when they find that I can converse and I do know something, then they're not interested. They walk away. They want *their* images."

Jimmy is 27, well-educated, a salesperson, and a Black man. He is a victim of the vicious stereotypes which all Black people must confront every day.

Negative assumptions, images and stereotypes are at the heart of the matter; they are what racism is built upon and continues to feed on. Such negative beliefs are what people use to bludgeon each other in quiet and simple ways, but the violence inherent in this type of racism is every bit as real as the lynching, burning and maiming that went on in the post-Civil War South. People are scarred psychologically by racism and, because we all participate in this, we are all ruined.

The Philadelphia gay male community has never really come to grips with the problem of racism in its midst. This article attempts to uncover the problem, long buried by uncaring, uninformed and unrealistic attitudes. "They don't want to deal with racism because they don't think it affects them. They don't really dislike Blacks; they just don't think about Black people," comments Charles B., a 32-year-old artist. Charles' observation touches on another facet of racism: what writer Ralph Ellison called the invisibility of Blacks. People disregard what does not immediately concern them. In this way, many problems lose visibility until they impinge upon the world of the non-thinker.

This two-edged, racist sword is evident in the gay male community as well as in America at large. On the one hand, Black gays are largely an invisible minority. They are invisible, that is, until they attempt to mix with the White gay community. Then, all the negative stereotypes leap to the minds of the people involved.

Surprise is not uncommon among black gay men when they find White gays to be racist. "I was surprised. Yes, in a way I was. I thought, 'Here's this group of people, a subculture sharing common interests, looking out for each other.' But it wasn't the case at all," remembers Van, a 33-year-old office worker. His experience is similar to Charles'. As Charles says, "I originally saw gays as a breed unto themselves. I assumed there would be a bond among all gay people. I was naive. Then I realized that the prejudices of society bled into the gay world."

Many Black gays did not have this preconceived notion about gays being more open. Ricardo D., 24, an office manager, declares, "I knew they were racist. People are people, whether they're gay or straight. They will have the same feelings and idiosyncracies." Far more of the men I interviewed echoed Ricardo's thoughts. Racism was no surprise, but it did hurt.

How does gay racism work?

Racism is put into practice through a variety of discriminatory techniques aimed at keeping minority group members from partiating fully in society. The most visible form of discrimination in the gay community is at the bars—our most public and popular gathering places.

Carding is the practice of demanding a Liquor Control Board (LCB) card at the door of a bar before entrance is permitted.

This routine is meant to keep those people under the age of 21 out of the bars. But, as it is most frequently used, the LCB card is a means of keeping Black gays out of White gay bars—because only Black patrons are asked to produce their cards. It has gone on (or is going on) at almost every major gay bar in the city of Philadelphia.

Just going out becomes a real ordeal. "Your heart is in your throat. A block before you come to the bar, you get this awful feeling in your stomach. You wonder what will happen at the door. It makes you feel like trash. You can't even feel like an equal," remembers Stan A., a 27-year-old music student. In reliving the experience he seems almost out of breath.

"It happened to me early this summer at Odyssey II," relates Herb J., a hospital administrator. "We went to the door and were asked for IDs. We are not young looking. I showed my driver's license. The doorman said it was unacceptable." Herb takes a long deep breath—he's obviously trying to control his emotions. "Then, right in front of me, young, White gays were let into the bar. So I asked again if we could go in. We were refused. I would have called the police, but my friends didn't want to press charges."

Almost every bar in town was mentioned by one interviewee or another. There is no set policy—none set down so that you could see it, that is. The only real guide is money. Money talks. Bar owners listen to their patrons and their White patrons do not want to rub elbows with Black customers.

Two bars in town, the Smart Place and the now-defunct Letters, opened with the express purpose of being places where discrimination would not happen. In a short time, both bars became all-Black establishments, due to the refusal of most White gay men to patronize the bars on equal terms with Black gays. As Ed, the White former owner of Letters said some time before his bar closed, "White customers came to me several times and told me, 'It's getting too dark in here. If it doesn't stop, we're not coming back.' I told them that Letters was a bar for everyone."

Robin S., a graduate student in American culture and a Black activist as well as a gay activist, has his own ideas about Black acceptance in White gay bars. "One of the problems that Whites have with Blacks in bars is that they (the Whites) feel overwhelmed by the Blacks. Black men tend to be more social than middle-class, non-ethnic Whites. Also, the music in bars is music derived from Black music. It's okay to listen to Black women singing, but when it comes to having Black folk near you, they can't have it. It's a ripoff of Black culture. They take only what they like from it."

Getting past the door is only the beginning of a racist journey for some Black gays. Once inside, they are subjected to an array of racist emotions and reactions.

The racist ordeal

"Just to walk across the floor of the bar can be an ordeal. The expressions on some people's faces. The questioning looks, the 'why are you here?' expressions are all frightening. It can be mentally challenging, sometimes even physically challenging depending on the people and how hostile they are," according to Alan C., a 24-year old development researcher. Alan shifts uncomfortably in his seat as he talks about his experiences. With a sense of indignation he adds, "It's a very natural part of being a Black person. People have preconceptions. In a gay bar the preconception is: 'You shouldn't be here.' The response I must have is: 'I have every right to be here.' Dealing with this takes a lot of energy."

Like Alan, everyone has developed his own way of dealing with being in a White gay bar. Charles "will not go into a White gay bar alone." He feels strongly that "there are more important places to fight for civil rights."

But David, 32, a government worker, girds himself with feelings of self-worth and plunges ahead. "I don't go into any bar with the feeling that I may encounter discrimination. I've learned that racism is a White problem, not mine. So I go into bars and clubs with that attitude. If they don't respond to me that's their problem. I don't care how they feel or what they think. I can't let that affect my life to the point where I will become withdrawn."

Once over the initial hostile feelings, Black gay men are usually in for a variety of other experiences, all rooted in racist assumptions.

Like Jimmy, Alan has had men walk away because he did not fit their images. "I've had people talk to me, but when they find out you have some brains, they're not interested."

Herb remembers an acquaintance coming up to him in a bar and telling him, "You're too preppy. Where's your ski cap and blue jeans?" He uneasily recalls the incident and the hurt it caused him. "I thought that maybe I wasn't dressing right. I didn't know what to think. But then I decided that I'd dress the way I wanted."

Stan walked into Equus one evening and saw a person he thought was a friend. This "friend," a well-known gay activist, did not notice who Stan was from across the room. The activist did notice, however, that Stan was wearing a Lacoste shirt. Then in a loud voice the activist told the people he was with, "Well, those clothes are sure popular, even the *niggers* (emphasis added) are wearing them." Stan was shocked. "I couldn't believe it. He wasn't joking either. I've never spoken to him since. I thought he was a friend."

Another common occurrence for Black men in bars is described by John. "I'll be standing there and some White man will come up to me and, without saying a word, not even one word, he'll grab me in the crotch and look me in the eye. In front of everyone. I guess I'm expected to follow immediately. I usually tell them what will happen to their arms if they don't move." Wayne A., a college freshman with a similar experience, says, "They assume that Black men have big dicks, and that's all they're interested in. They're size queens, that's all.

Sexual stereotypes

Sexual stereotypes are common and burdensome to Black men, who feel that they are expected to behave in certain ways or meet other arbitrarily imposed standards. Charles thinks for a moment before dealing with the question: "Basically Black people are pictured as being sexually uninhibited and passionate. White men may want to receive this passion and fervor without having to give anything in return."

"They just want their fantasies," Dean interjects bluntly. "They want to be dominated by this dark man with this humongous dick and wonderfully passionate nature."

Surprisingly, with all the resentment this treatment can cause, Jimmy has room to be introspective and philosophical. He tries to cast a positive light on the matter. "I think a lot of White men are attracted to Black men because of the strength we have—not physical strength, but a spiritual strength which comes from putting up with a lot of bullshit." He is aware that this, too, is an image in some men's minds. "We ingest images that allow us to sexually objectify people, consume them, and discard them. It naturally follows that it can be done to Black men."

Sexual stereotyping is rampant, and again, the only reality is the imagery existing in the minds of those possessed of these stereotypes. Alan's anger flashes through his words: "If you don't fit their stereotypes, they become very cold. They don't bother to contact you or to communicate in any way."

Novelist James Baldwin sums up the matter in *A Rap on Race:* "They come to you for the most part, as though you're some extraordinary phallic symbol . . . As if you're nothing but a walking phallus . . . no head, no arms, no nothing . . . actually the act of love becomes an act of murder in which you are also committing suicide."

Donald has experienced another typical approach that some White men have toward Black men. "I will see White men in bars who want nothing to do with me. They're with their White friends and don't want to show their true feelings. They don't even seem to notice me. But, later in the evening, our paths will cross again at the baths. Now they're alone. Their friends are not around to see what they do and who they do it with. They try like hell to get me into bed when no one is around to see. I remind them that they were not interested in me at the bar, and now, I'm not interested in them. If you won't deal with me in the light, you won't get me at night." He smiles as he says this.

Bathhouses also present situations for racism to occur on a variety of levels. The most obvious, of course, is discrimination at the door.

Several years ago, it was rumored that a popular bathhouse would not permit Black men in. A weekly gay newspaper no longer published in Philadelphia, *The Weekly Gayzette*, decided to test the case. Two people were sent, one White, one Black. The White person had a membership, the Black man was seeking one. At the door, the White man said he wanted to sponsor his Black friend. The clerk on duty announced, "I'm sorry, but our membership is full right now. We aren't accepting any more people. But take this card, fill it out and we'll contact you in two weeks." The bathhouse never made contact.

Just this year, a bathhouse which published an ad featuring one-night passes was said to have gone back on its advertised offer. Kenneth C. said, "I was with a friend. It was after we had been in the bars and we decided to go to the baths. We went there and since neither of us had a membership, we asked for their one-night card. The guy at the desk said, 'There isn't any such thing.' I told him it was in their ad. I pointed out the offer to him. Then he told me, 'We don't do that anymore.' I guess it was because we're both Black." *(Editor's note: The one-night pass offer in question, according to the ad in the June 11* Gay News, *was good only for June 14.)*

Inside the baths there are areas which are poorly lit or not lighted at all, places where the most anonymous sex happens. But even here racism finds a way. White patrons will be in these areas when someone comes along—someone they attempt to initiate sexual contact with. They reach out trying to connect. The two men will then come together for sexual contact, but on many occasions Victor B. says the following has happened: "The guy will feel me all over, then he'll reach up and feel my hair. As soon as he does that he figures out that I'm Black and loses all interest. He pushes me away." Victor was not alone in mentioning this phenomenon.

Negative assumptions

The negative assumptions do not stop at the bars and the baths, but follow people into the confines of the bedroom, where one's inhibitions are supposed to be much lower. Jimmy bristles with sexual memories: "I've gone home with White men who are always certain I'm going to steal something. If I say I have to go to the bathroom, I get escorted from the bed to the bathroom and then back again." Herb agrees: "If you meet someone, they're usually afraid to go home with you because they think it won't be safe in your neighborhood. They are also frightened to take you home because they think you'll steal half the house. They walk around the house with you and they check if you're clean."

Others, like John, have experienced relationships in which they are only sex objects. "Once I got to his apartment, I was treated like a toy. I had to do this or that. He wanted to do whatever he wanted, without considering my feelings at all."

Some see racist patterns in the interracial couples they know or observe. Charles says he has noticed "a plantation mentality in the interracial couples I've seen. The Black man is expected to be docile, timid, and often financially dependent on the White man. I maintain that when one man has to degrade himself in order to keep another, I can't see how either will benefit."

Donald sees many of the same features among the interracial couples he knows. "The White man is usually more financially well-to-do than the Black man. This perpetuates many of the stereotypes."

But Alan, who has a White lover, disagrees. "Despite the fact that one may appear dominant, this doesn't mean that this is in fact true. It is easier for them to act this way when the couple is out. A Black man gets a lot more negative attention when he chauffeurs a White man around, buys a drink for a White man, or buys clothes for a White man. You don't always want to deal with that attention. It's a defense."

Dean is quick to point out that interracial couples are subjected to another subtle form of racism built on the assumption that the White man is in control. "In restaurants, the maitre d' will talk to the White man. The waiters always give the check to the White man. Or they assume that the credit card belongs to the White man."

The instances pile up over and over again. The sense of outrage and resentment grows geometrically. Solutions seem unavailable and hope for better relations has never been more elusive. What can be done to change things? If not the world at large, what can be done to make the gay community less racist?

Almost everyone interviewed feels the same way about solving the problem of racism. "Since racism and discrimination are functions of White attitudes and White actions," concludes Robin, "it is White people who have to deal with it." Dale agrees wholeheartedly: "Blacks should stop taking the responsibility for solving the problem of racism. After all, it's not really *our* problem. We, unfortunately, reap the effects of it, though."

From this starting point—White responsibility—people had all manner of suggestions for solving the problem. They ranged from Dale's exhortation for people to "be willing to be wrong because that's where learning starts," to Jimmy who says that White gay men should try to understand what it means to be Black. "It's not fully possible, but there's a way. I ask White gay men to completely 'own' their own gayness and display it constantly, every day as I do my Blackness. This way they can see how pervasive the oppression is out there."

"They've got to acknowledge there is a problem," Robin insists, "and then acknowledge that it should be changed. This doesn't go on. Racism and discrimination exist in bars because they exist on a personal basis. It's not just the carding: it's the White people who see the carding and do nothing about it. They do *nothing*. That perpetuates it. White gays allow it to continue. That's the only way it *can* continue. Racism exists because the majority of White male gays support it."

Can Black gays help?

Not everyone felt that Whites should have to go the distance on their own. Charles, along with others, feels that, although Whites must do the majority of the work in battling racism, Blacks can help.

"There are three ways Black people can react to White racism: a) they can accept the programming and feel inferior; b) they can resent it and respond with hatred; c) they can feel compassion for Whites and work with them and help them. The last way is obviously the most constructive way."

"It's everybody's problem," declares Van animatedly. "If there's a White person who recognizes discrimination or a racist attitude, he or she should say something about it. By the same token, if the incident happens to a Black person, they should say something. It's very difficult for a person to take action if he thinks he's all alone. That's part of the problem. Part of the solution is to let people know that if they feel or think that racism is wrong, then they're not alone."

Alone or not, the problem must be dealt with. The question is: How? Charles Silberman in *Crisis in Black and White*, writes " . . . it is up to Whites to lead the way; the guilt and responsibility are theirs." Again the question is: How?

Unquestionably, a sensible, careful program is needed to begin dealing with racism in the gay male community. The following is a proposal, based on discussion with others, for a program to start with. It must be remembered that these are only suggestions and that these suggestions are merely a starting point. If every facet of this program is followed, racism will still exist and will still present a problem. This program only suggests a starting place. The only certainty is that a start must be made.

One crucial element must be worked at on all levels. Brian, a city planner, hit on this point: "You cannot turn people around unless you first convince them that the change is in their own best interest." The task is ours to work out.

Step One: Recognition and Discussion of the Problem
To deal with the problems of the gay male community they must be recognized and fully explored. Gay men have never really explored themselves or their feelings as have our lesbian sisters. In order to accomplish this, a series of all-male town meetings are required.

Because racism is the foremost problem in our community this should be the topic of, at least, the first of these meetings. Such meetings could consist of:

a) a panel of Black and White men openly and truthfully discussing the problem of racism and methods for ending it;

b) a psychodrama concerning racism (perhaps provided by Plays for Living) and a discussion following;

c) subsequent meetings to deal with racism through role playing, expert lecturers, and problem-solving sessions

Step Two: Action to End Discrimination and Racism
Led by various community groups (the gay religious groups, the Philadelphia Lesbian and Gay Task Force, Black and White Men Together, Philadelphia Black Gays) a plan of action should be formulated to put a stop to discrimination at all public gathering places for gays:

a) open access to bars and baths should be insisted upon. The use of LCB cards to discriminate against Blacks should be stopped;

b) a meeting of bar owners/managers with the leaders of this anti-racist coalition of community groups should be held to discuss the problem of racism and the role bars play in it;

c) a vigilance committee should be set up to ensure that such discrimination does not continue.

This same coalition of groups should set up another vigilance committee to watch gay publications. Robin points out that "positive images of Blacks are necessary to ending racism. The truth must be told about the part that Blacks have played in history. For example, the Black people that were involved in the Stonewall Riots of 1969 which started the modern gay movement."

Step Three: Continuing Communication

In order for racism to be eradicated, anti-racist activity must be continual. Our community must also begin to cooperate with the Black community and support its causes and concerns. As Charles said, "When people show up on picket lines set up by Black people for Black causes, then I'll know they're concerned." To this end, various courses of action can be taken:

a) the anti-racist coalition of groups can meet with groups from the Black community and offer help;

b) a series of rap groups can be set up and run by PBG or BWMT or some other outside agency so that the rap group will have a program and a set procedure;

c) consciousness-raising sessions on the topic of racism should be held at the Gay and Lesbian Community Center and perhaps even in some bars;

d) support groups for those interested in continuing the fight against racism should be set up and managed;

e) cultural sharing sessions to be held at the Community Center could explore Black and White cultures in a positive way, with an emphasis on sharing.

Step Four: Strengthening the Bonds

Gay men have not begun to explore the concept and the comfort of Brotherhood. Our lesbian sisters have long known the joys of Sisterhood. They have, for a long time, drawn on the strengths and supports inherent in Sisterhood.

Gay men have yet to begin the journey on the long road to Brotherhood. Our common bonds as men as well as our strengths, weaknesses, and concerns are still to be explored and exploited.

To this end, a series of Brotherhood meetings should be tried, utilizing the Community Center and all of our community groups. Our community can only gain from such exploration.

THE DOUBLE LIFE OF A
GAY DODGER

Michael J. Smith

THE GAME IS OVER and the baseball player sits in the hotel lobby, his eyes fixed on nothing. He thinks his secret is safe but he is never quite sure, so at midnight in the lobby it is always best to avoid the other eyes. He neither hears the jokes nor notices that a few teammates are starting to wear towels around their waists in the locker room. He does not want to hear or see or know, and neither do they.

The baseball player waits until the lobby empties of teammates and coaches. Some are in the bar, some out on the town, some are in their rooms. Some, of course, have found women. He walks briskly out the door toward the taxicab, never turning his head to look back. He mutters an address to the driver and has one foot in the cab....

"Hey, where you going, man? You said you were staying in tonight."

The baseball player feels his lie running up the back of his neck. "Changed my mind."

"Can I come with you? I got nothing going tonight."

The baseball player pauses. "You don't want to go where I'm going," he says at last. He is leaving a crack there, in case this teammate knows the secret and really *would* like to go with him.

"Okay — have it your way."

The baseball player is in the back seat, the door slams, his heart slams, the cab is pulling away. Fifteen minutes later it stops a block from the place the passenger actually intends to go. He pays the driver. Did the driver look at him sort of funny?

The baseball player steps out and walks back a block, his face turned 90 degrees to his left shoulder, away from the traffic, just in case. What if he meets someone he knows there tonight? There was

119

the ballplayer's brother the one night and the son of a major league manager another. Man, they have to know, don't they? And if he is recognized tonight, should he pretend he is someone else?

Suddenly he is pulling open the door and the men inside smile and the music swallows him and for a few hours in the bar the baseball player does not feel so alone.

At age 22, Glenn Burke was a sexual blank. He grew up attending church six times a week, singing in two choirs and serving as an usher. He bathed two or three times a day and still he never felt clean. He grew up with no father. He grew up with no sex.

He diverted the tension into sports, and there was the scent of animal energy in the way he ran a fastbreak, the way he circled the bases, the way he flogged a line drive. Once, he hit three home runs and two singles in one game, just two days after joining the Merritt College team in midseason. He was 5-11, 193 pounds, he could run 100 yards in 9.7 seconds and bench-press 350 pounds. UCLA and Nevada and Cal all wanted to get him on a basketball court; the Los Angeles Dodgers wanted him to play baseball.

He took the $5,000 Dodger signing bonus and after three seasons as an out-fielder in the minors, his combined average was .303. Three times he led his league in stolen bases.

Still there was a need for more. When NCAA eligibility rules were relaxed, he agreed to play basketball at Nevada in the off-season. He averaged 16 points in six games and then twisted a knee spinning for a layup. The Dodgers said No More and Glenn Burke came home. The void was becoming difficult to ignore. At last, the lidded tension burst.

His younger sister told him that a high school teacher of his had asked how he was doing. Something inside him went *click*. The man had been one of Burke's favorite teachers, so Burke went over to school to see him. He was feeling loose, open. Maybe it was the basketball thing coming to an end, suddenly seeing life as more than just sports.

"The minute he spoke, I knew. I know it sounds a little crazy. Here I was, 22, no sexual experience, nothing. Yet I felt something I'd never felt before, something deep. We went to his place. Funny, he must have known me better than I knew myself. We didn't say much. He fixed dinner and afterwards we lay by the fire and got close. I stayed the night. When I got home the next day, I went into the bathroom and cried. This was who I was, the whole me at last."

He was happy, and yet he felt he was sneaking. He felt guilty. He

knew he never would be accepted in sports. In a profession in which every contest, every movement, every attitude seemed a reassertion of virility, Glenn Burke realized he was gay.

The most famous gay community in the world is a 75-cent bridge toll and a 20-minute freeway ride away from the streets of Oakland where Glenn Burke grew up. In his sexual naivete, he had never known that. He had never known there were bars and entire neighborhoods for homosexuals.

A week after his first experience, he and some friends went to a straight bar in San Francisco. One of the friends pointed to a girl, "Look at that fox," he said. "Look at her boyfriend," Burke thought. They went over to talk and asked if the couple knew a place where they could go dancing. "Try the Cabaret," the girl said, "but watch out—gays go there, too." A *place* for gays? Burke went there and couldn't believe it.

It was a new world and he explored it enthusiastically. He walked Castro Street in San Francisco and felt pulled in two directions. Sports had taught him to keep the fists up and the soft side down and the pants tailor-made and the shirt silk and the walk a powerful strut. This new world was Levi's, and Docksides shoes and Lacoste shirts and handkerchiefs. He wondered if he could be masculine and gay, a baseball player and gay, Glenn Burke and gay.

A few weeks later, he met a man in a bar and the next day he was hanging his clothes in the closet of his first live-in lover. A few more weeks passed and it was time for spring training, time to try to begin living the great untruth.

The trouble with going underground was Burke's personality. He was the guy doing Richard Pryor imitations, the guy leading bench cheers, the guy fiddling with the music box and dancing in the locker room. After games, the guys all wanted to take the party from the locker room to the disco. Burke, the life of the team, started saying no. To explain why not, he had to tame the nervousness in his voice and the muscle formations of his face. These were difficult things for an extrovert to do.

Double A in Waterbury, Connecticut, 1975, was not a good place for a metamorphosis. His friends wanted to share an apartment with him and he groped for an appropriate reason to say no. He ended up rooming at the local YMCA, so they would stop asking. There was one gay bar, but a Black man in a small New England town can feel the eyeballs everywhere he walks. He tried not to go, and went anyway. Sometimes in the bar he would be asked if he had been at the game that night. The team's leading basestealer and home-run hitter would shake his head no. One night he glimpsed a member of the club's front office at the bar. He walked past him and out the door and prayed the man would be too frightened to admit having been there to see him. On the long road trips, he could feel the wall of space he had created between himself and his friends.

He hit .270 and when the season ended, he headed back to San

Francisco. "It was great being back, being myself," he said. "Straight people cannot know what it's like to feel one way and pretend to be another. To watch what you say, how you act, who you're checking out. In San Francisco I opened up again. But I still wasn't sure if I could be gay without being a sissy."

In 1976 the Dodgers summoned him up to play the first and last months of the season. In between, he hit .300 with 63 stolen bases at Albuquerque, but in the major leagues he struggled with the curveball and batted a .239 in 46 at-bats. The Dodgers still saw enough to congratulate themselves.

"Unlimited potential," said second baseman Davey Lopes.

"Once we get him cooled down a little bit," said the late Junior Gilliam, then Dodger coach, "frankly, we think he's going to be another Willie Mays."

The stakes were growing higher now. It was easier to lose himself in the big cities on major league road trips, but in Los Angeles he was becoming a face on the sports pages and a name on the radio. He wanted success, yet he feared it. Half of him wanted to hit .300 and become a superstar and a commodity and then if the secret leaked maybe he could tell them all to go to hell, and half of him said maybe a nice, inconspicuous number like .250 would be better because then he could guard his privacy and they might not find out at all.

He met Dave Kopay, the former 49er and Redskin running back whose book on his homosexuality had become a best seller. The two compared anguish. "He was very nervous about who and what he was," remembers Kopay. "I had compensated for my gayness by going from a player who did not like contact in college to being a super-aggressive player in the pros, as a disguise. It's common among gay athletes, overcompensating for one's sexuality. Glenn might have been doing the same thing, but it doesn't work in baseball. There, you have to be relaxed, not overaggressive. I couldn't really advise him, except to tell him to follow his instincts.

"There is really no one to talk to in sports when you are gay. Who can you really trust? There are so many insecurities, it's tragic. Almost all of them that I know in sports are married and have deep problems. Many of them are heavily into alcohol and drugs."

Burke played on, refusing the ruse of an occasional girlfriend. He caught hepatitis playing winter ball in Mexico and missed most of spring training in 1977. The Dodgers sent him to Albuquerque to open the season and he hit .309. He learned that the Dodgers were recalling him, and that night in his last Albuquerque game, with two outs, runners on first and third with a one-run lead in the ninth inning, he backpedaled to the warning track for a fly ball, switched his glove from his left hand to his right — and squeezed the last out. If there was a metaphor there, the manager was in no mood to admire it. Jim Williams waited for him on the dugout steps, glaring. If you ever do that again...."

"I'm leaving, Skip," chirped Burke. "Now you'll have something to talk about when I'm gone.

He was irrepressible. He bought his first car and celebrated by having his astrological sign, Scorpio, tattooed on his forearm. Within a few months he was stomping into Tommy Lasorda's office, amidst the Hollywood stars who gathered there before games, fixing himself a sandwich from deli tray and shouting, "Hi, Tommy!" He was not a model bench-sitter. He prowled the dugout with a caged hyperactivity, and when a teammate belted a home run he would tweak Lasorda by butting in front of him to be first to hug the returning hero. He would walk back to the dugout imitating Lasorda's big-bellied, bowlegged gait and his teammates would howl.

One day in 1977, a teammate homered and in the heat of his enthusiasm Burke extended his arms and invented a sports ritual. He delivered the first high-five."Most people think I started it," said leftfielder Dusty Baker. "But it wasn't me. I saw Glenn doing it first, and then I started."

On a team preoccupied with presenting the clean-shaven, Dodger-blue front, the street kid from Oakland became one of the behind-the-scenes catalysts. "He always had the music blasting and was saying something silly to keep the team laughing," said Baker. "He'd be playing cards and all of a sudden you would hear this loud voice scream, 'Rack 'em, Ross, the poor boy's just lost!' and then there'd be that crazy laugh of his again."

Burke made them laugh and he made them squirm. In an argument he would swing first and negotiate later. A fastball in a teammate's ear would bring him out of the dugout first. Everybody wanted to keep "Burkey" giggling because when his eyes clouded you could suddenly sense the violence. He wanted that machismo right out there on his skin; it made him feel safer.

"I was like Lou Ferrigno, who kept wanting to get bigger and badder than anybody because he had a speech impediment," Burke said. "I had 17-inch biceps and I made sure everybody knew I wasn't afraid to use them. I wanted to establish that if you found out I was gay, you might not want to start hassling me about it, because I could still kick your ass."

The Dodgers, meanwhile, were in a pennant chase and the double life was becoming more difficult to lead. He was handsome and personable and there was a glut of girls who wanted to walk into a disco next to him. Some nights they grew so insistent he would tell the switchboard operator to reject all calls to his room. He'd go out with girls occasionally, but it would never involve sex. He didn't want to mislead them.

His teammates noticed. In baseball, even married men can be made to feel isolated if they do not join the woman-hunt on the road. "There is a tendency," said A's pitcher Matt Keough, "to achieve the success *off* the field that you are not achieving *on* it."

"I had a really cute cousin that I tried to set up with Glenn," Baker said. "He just ignored her. He'd say, 'Too fat, too ugly.' I'd say, 'Wait a minute. I *know* that one ain't ugly.'"

Without Burke realizing it, word began to seep. "I was eating at a restaurant when someone told me," remembered Lopes, then a teammate on the Dodgers.

"I think some girl from his neighborhood in Oakland had told someone on the team. My fork dropped out of my mouth. He was one of the last guys you would have thought was gay. I still liked him. I don't know how other ballplayers feel, but I believe a man has a right to choose any lifestyle as long as it doesn't infringe on others. It never infringed with Glenn."

"The guys didn't want to believe it," Baker said. "He was built like King Kong. There was no femininity in his voice or his walk. But it all made sense when I thought about it. When we'd go on the road he always went to the YMCA to work out. And he'd never let us take him home. He'd say he had a friend coming later to pick him up and he'd wait at the far end of the parking lot.

"I just made the situation invisible, but some guys began to make jokes. Stuff like, 'Is Glenn waiting in the parking lot for his *girl*friend?' and 'Don't bend over in the shower when he's around.' I know a couple of guys felt uncomfortable in the shower. A few wore towels on their way back and forth in the locker room.

"If you had a team made up of guys from California and New York, I don't think it would bother them as much as guys from the country and small towns. I'm from California and I can get along with priests, prostitutes, pimps and pushers, as long as they don't try to push nothing on me."

Burke didn't push it, as much out of respect as fear of detection.

"I was attracted occasionally by other players," he said, "but I didn't mix business with pleasure. I respected their space. Besides, I always preferred more mature men."

He was a simple man leading a complicated life, and slowly the strain began to break him. He kept one eye on the door when he went in gay bars. He worried about getting in a fight or getting caught high there. There were times he thought the front office had someone following him. He was afraid everybody was whispering about him.

He'd have to plan everything. He'd think, "If they see me leaving the hotel, I'll say I was going to take a walk, or to get something to eat." He was always telling white lies.

Some days he'd sit in a mall and try to meet people, sometimes he would call a friend and ask him to check his directory on where the gay bars were in town. His mind was never clear. Some nights he'd come back to his room sad and smoke a little grass.

The high only interrupted the fears. The Dodgers did a lot of hugging and Burke always worried that they had found out about him and would think he was making a pass. He worried constantly about being blackmailed. The only reason he wasn't, he believed, was that he had gay friends who warned anybody who started to talk too much. He saw a palm reader and she said that he had something inside him that he should let out, or he might have a heart attack in two or three years.

He couldn't sort it all out. "I couldn't understand why people said gays were sick. I wasn't some dizzy queen out trying to make everybody all the time. The bottom line was, I was a man."

There were the good memories mixed with the miseries. There was the night Baker became the fourth Dodger to hit 30 home runs in one season, a major league record, and Burke, the on-deck batter, met him at the plate with a walloping high-five as the people stood and roared, and then before they even had a chance to sit Burke was driving another white speck into the blackness and the festival in the stands went on and on.

He finished the 1977 season hitting .254 in 169 at-bats, the Dodgers made the World Series and his face was on TV screens across the country. He went 1-for 5 in the three games he played, packed after the Yankees had won and headed back for Castro Street. He walked into a gay bar the first night there and was greeted by a party celebrating his World Series appearance.

"I walked out," Burke said. "They weren't my friends there, they were mostly people just making a big deal because I was a gay baseball player."

His insecurity ran rampant. In one world he feared they would *not* like him only because he was gay, and in the other he feared they *did* like him only because he was gay. For the first time since he had picked up a baseball bat, Glenn Burke considered quitting.

"By 1978," said Davey Lopes, "I think everybody knew."

They knew the way parents know their 16-year-old is drinking beer but don't say anything until the bottles are rolling across the floor of the family car. As long as Burke's homosexuality was not official, no one felt compelled to react.

"Then Al Campanis [Dodger vice-president] called me into his office," Burke recalled. "I really liked Al, he was always very nice to me. The whole organization was, for the most part. But Al said, 'Everybody on the team is married but you, Glenn. When players get married on the Dodgers, we help them out financially. We can help you so you can go out and have a real nice honeymoon.'

"I said, 'Al, I don't think I'll be getting married no time soon.'"

The Dodgers, in the words of Junior Gilliam, could not "cool him down." He burned for more playing time and when he did not get it, he did not keep it to himself. "They couldn't con me," he said. "Lasorda would bark an order, and I was supposed to jump like some little kid, grateful for the attention. It bothered him too that I was popular with the guys on the team. Once he got ticked off at some laugh I'd gotten and he said, 'Burke, if I was your age, I'd take you in the bathroom right now and kick your ass.' At first I thought he was kidding, then I realized he wasn't. I think he was trying to get me to explode.

"With one out in the ninth, he'd pull Rick Monday and trot me out to the outfield for the last two outs. I'd stand there waiting for the game to end. Then I'd trot back to the dugout where all the guys are supposed to tell you how great you played. Only I hadn't, and I'd feel like a fool.

"One night I was really ticked and I stared a hole through Lasorda. He took me in the locker room and, in front of Junior Gilliam and Preston Gomez, cussed me to filth. Every other word in his vocabulary was 'mother'. It hurt. Deeply. I didn't really dislike the man, it was just the situation. We probably should have gotten along—we're both hardheaded."

On May 16, 1978, with Glenn Burke in centerfield as the last out was recorded, Vin Scully announced that Burke had been traded to the Oakland A's for Bill North. North had led the American League twice in stolen bases, the last time in 1976, and now he was 30 and his average had dropped 64 points in those two years.

"Lasorda told me, 'We're tired of you walking back and forth in the dugout like a mad tiger in a cage. We're sending you to Oakland, where you can play more.' He was nice about it, but they were being careful so there wouldn't be a scene. I walked out of his office and the whole locker room was dead. Steve Garvey and Don Sutton, two of my best friends on the team, had tears in their eyes. Garvey and me had always gotten along great. He taught me how to tie a tie, he gave me hats and T-shirts, he sat next to me on the team plane and he made me promise to play for him if he ever had a football team.

"Leaving those guys, I was in shock. Players don't come and go on the Dodgers the way they do on other clubs."

Lopes remembers picking up the newspaper the next day and reading a quote from a scout. "I believe it was an American League scout at the Angel game in Anaheim that night," Lopes said. "The guy said, 'Wait until the A's find out what they *really* got in Glenn Burke.' "

The locker room was still silent the next day, and Lopes' reaction was quoted in the Los Angeles *Herald Examiner.* "I knew something was missing when I came in today. It will probably remain like this until somebody comes along with a personality like Glenn's. And I don't think that's going to happen. I've heard a lot of adverse things about him from people, but they didn't know him. He was the life of the team, on the bases, in the clubhouse, everywhere. All of us will miss him."

One Dodger angrily went to the front office and demanded an explanation. Dusty Baker didn't need to go that far. "I was talking with our trainer, Bill Buhler. I said, 'Bill, why'd they trade Glenn? He was one of our top prospects.' He said, 'They don't want any gays on the team.' I said, 'The organization knows?' He said, '*Everybody* knows.' "

Burke sprayed three hits the first night with the A's, and then felt himself becoming absorbed by the damp misery of Charlie Finley's last years in baseball. The Dodgers had not played him as much as he felt he deserved, but the organization had always gone first class. The A's in the late 1970s were a dead thing looking for a box to lie still in. Finley was cutting expenses and players, lopping off fans with them. A man with peace of mind could play on. Glenn Burke could not. In the hush of a baseball stadium with 3,000 people, he could hear a voice urging him to leave and stop living a lie.

Four years of life as a sexual fugitive had passed and his self-esteem was fraying. By now his family had pieced the evidence together and guessed. They still accepted him, removing one weight from his mind, but the weight at the stadium showed no sign of relenting. One day he was playing centerfield in Comiskey Park, and a fan called him a faggot. His first thought was "Damn, if they know, everybody else must know." They probably said it to lots of outfielders, but he didn't think that then, He went to the dugout at the end of the inning and got a felt-tip pen from the trainer. Next inning he went back out and stuck a piece of paper in the back of his pants. It said, "Screw you."

He finished the 1978 season hitting .235. Early in the 1979 season, he was sitting in the A's clubhouse, chatting with outfielder Mitchell Page, a good friend. "Suddenly he got quiet," Burke said. "He said this scout from Pittsburgh—he came up in the Pirate system, and they were interested in me—had come right out and asked him if I was bisexual. *Bisexual.* Me, who'd never been with a woman. They couldn't say *gay,* I guess. It was tough on Mitchell, talking to me like this. I didn't say much and he ended up telling the scout, 'Glenn Burke's sex life is Glenn Burke's business. And if it's any of your business, he's my friend and I'd go anywhere with him.'

"But at that moment, when Mitchell told me, everything stopped. If some joker in Pittsburgh knew, so did a few others. I realized it had all come to an end. They'd stripped me of my innermost thoughts."

Page remembered it as a writer from Oakland who had asked him (Burke still insists it was a scout from Pittsburgh). "The guy told me the word was out," Page said, "and that he didn't know if Glenn would be here next season. I felt I should let Glenn know instead of talking behind his back like the other players were. The guys on the A's never bothered him about it because of the way he handled it. Besides, they were afraid to say anything to his face.

"I liked Glenn, but if I'd seen him walking around making it obvious, I wouldn't have had anything to do with him. I don't want to be labeled and have my career damaged. You make sure you point out that I'm not gay, okay?"

"I roomed with him," said A's pitcher Mike Norris. "Sure, I was worried at first. You came back to your hotel room at midnight, sat around and listened to music, and you wondered if he'd make a move. After awhile you realized he wouldn't, and it wasn't a big problem. Guys would watch out for him, but it wasn't a completely uncomfortable feeling. If it had been out in the open, though, there would have been all kinds of problems. We're all macho, we're all men. Just make sure you put in there that I ain't gay, man."

The walls were beginning to close in. A gay friend, eager to advance the homosexual movement, kept insisting that Burke come out of the closet and tried to arrange a luncheon appointment with San Francisco *Chronicle* columnist Herb Caen. Burke refused to attend, but Caen wrote that there was a rumor out that a local professional ballplayer could be found on Castro Street.

Midway through the 1979 season, Finley learned that Burke was refusing to take a cortisone shot for a pinched neck nerve. "I feel an injury should heal on its own." Burke said. "Once you take the first shot, you take another and another. Charlie came to talk to me on the field before a game. I said no. They sat me for two weeks. Finally, I told them I needed a voluntary retirement and walked out. The whole operation was minor league, with Finley calling the dugout making lineup changes. I probably wouldn't have left if there hadn't been the other problem, the gay thing, but put it all together and it was too much."

It was not that simple to walk away. Baseball had often tortured him, but it still owned a part of him. He returned next spring, attracted by the idea of playing for new manager Billy Martin.

Burke ripped knee cartilage that spring and was sidelined a month. The A's requested he return to the minor leagues, in Ogden, Utah, and Burke reluctantly agreed. To avoid the small-town stares, he drove 56 miles round-trip so he could live in Salt Lake City. He stopped now, and mulled the absurdity of his life. He was 27, getting no closer to the superstar role he knew he must have to declare his homosexuality and knowing that even if he did achieve it, he would likely be afraid to. He was still dodging management, lying to teammates, and now even ducking Mormons, too. Quietly, with the sports world focused on more important things, Glenn Burke quit baseball for good.

"I had finally gotten to the point," he said, "where it was more important to be myself than a baseball player."

Sunshine and shade share the seats in Dodger Stadium and the steady crack of batting practice echoes off the empty concrete. The game is still three hours away. Tommy Lasorda, chipper on this first evening back from the All-Star break, stands in foul territory watching his players re-tune their rhythm at the plate.

A visitor informs him that Glenn Burke is openly discussing his homosexuality. Lasorda's eyes narrow. "He's admitting it?" he says. "I have no comment."

Did he know Burke was gay when he played here? Did it have a bearing on the trade? "I didn't make that trade." Lasorda says. "Go talk to the man who made it. I have no more comment."

The man who made it is just arriving in his office from a trip to assess minor league talent in Hawaii. Al Campanis stands over his desk, looking down at the stack of message slips that has gathered during his absence. He is asked if everybody knew, as Lopes has said, and his eyes stay on his desk, until the length of the silence suggests he is waiting for the subject to crawl out of the room. It does not.

"Quote Davey Lopes then," he says.

He is pressed on the subject. Long pause. "We traded him because of other situations," he says. "We didn't trade him for that. He wasn't hitting enough, and things of that nature. We didn't even know...."

An organization as sharp as the Dodgers did not know? "We thought some things were odd," he allows. "But we didn't *know*. We never saw him with a girl, and when we called his home number a man usually answered. The man said he was his carpenter. But you hear a lot of rumors about players, and just because you see these things, that doesn't mean a guy's a fairy, or gay.

"We're not a watchdog organization, and we're not like an ostrich with our head in the sand. But he was not traded on suspicion. He was traded because we needed a lefthanded hitter in the outfield, one we thought would help us win the pennant. Glenn had problems with the curveball and his attitude was argumentative, but I always liked him. Sure, some people got mad about the trade; one player came to me all worked up, but were they right? Glenn didn't do anything after he left here, did he?"

And what of the offer of financial help if Burke had married?

"That dates way back," he says. "The Dodgers have traditionally liked our players to be married. The player has a wife, children, he gets more serious and settles down. We like our young men to have some responsibilities."

He is reminded that Dodger rightfielder Pedro Guerrero was married in 1980, and received no bonus. Campanis bristles.

"A completely different situation," he says. "Pedro had an agent, he was settled, he was like my son. We treat situations differently. You have to, in this position. The thing with Glenn Burke wasn't a bribe. It was a helpful gesture."

The baseball player swings and meets the ball just beyond the sweet inches of the bat and still he sends the rightfielder staggering up the hill in front of the wire-mesh fence. The ball clears the fence and the baseball player circles the bases with a home plate-sized grin. All his teammates spring from the bench, forming a line to congratulate him.

A few months away from his 30th birthday, Glenn Burke is one of the stars of the Gay Softball League.

There are perhaps 50 people watching from wooden seats that cry for a carpenter. The atmosphere is carefree. A woman in her 50s lifts her blouse to reveal her "Pendulum Pirates" T-shirt and yells, "Take this!" The fans take it, without looking twice.

Burke goes 4-for-4 but bobbles a grounder in the third inning. Disgusted, he straddles the ball with both feet and jumps, launching it up to his hand. The opposing team's fans taunt him good-naturedly. "Queeeeeen!" they shout in chorus.

Burke's team, the Pirates, remains undefeated with a 16-4 victory over On The Mark. The Pirates gather in a huddle at the end and chant, "Two-four-six-eight, who do we appreciate? On The Mark! On The Mark!" On The Mark reciprocates, and both teams stream to their cars for the postgame ritual. The first hour after the game is always spent at the sponsoring bar of the losing team and then all move to the winner's bar for the rest of the afternoon.

At Stables, the bar that sponsors On The Mark, Burke walks out to the sunshine of the patio, where there is enough quiet to reflect. "People say I should still be playing," he says. 'But I didn't want to make other people uncomfortable, so I faded away. My teammates' wives might have been threatened by a gay man in the locker room. I could have been a superstar, but I was too worried about protecting everybody else from knowing. If I thought I could be accepted, I'd be there now. It is the first thing in my life I ever backed down from. No, I'm not disappointed in myself, I'm disappointed in the system. Your sex should be private, and I always kept it that way. Deep inside, I know the Dodgers traded me because I was gay.

"It's harder to be a gay in sports than anywhere else, except maybe President. Baseball is probably the hardest sport of all. Every man in America wants his son to be a baseball player. The first thing every father buys for his son is a ball and glove. It's all-American. Only a superstar could come out and admit he was gay and hope to stay around, and still the fans probably would call the stadium and say they weren't going to bring their kids. Instead of understanding, they blackball you.

"Sure, there are other gays in baseball, the same per cent as there are in society. Word travels fast in baseball. Guys come home from road trips and tell their wives and they tell other player's wives. As soon as a player comes to bat, you'll hear a biography of him in the dugout. I've never heard anybody verbally get on a player from the bench about being gay, though."

He does not want to name names. The relationships, he says, are never between two baseball players. That would be too dangerous.

"There are even more gays in football," he says. "In football they are like a family, there is so much closeness down there in the trenches, and they can really get off on the body chemistry. But most of the gays I know of in sports fake it. They go out with girls and they get married, so their careers won't get ruined. They suffer even more than I did."

Glenn Burke still searches for himself. He plays in five softball leagues and has not worked regularly since leaving baseball. He hopes to finish his college education and become a high school basketball coach, and he hopes that speaking out on the issue will begin to chip at the barriers that marooned him between two cultures. He participates in BWMT (Black and White Men Together), a group fighting racial discrimination within the gay community. "I feel like a representative of the community," he says. "If I can make friends honestly, it may be a step toward gays and straight people understanding each other. Maybe they'll say, 'He's all right, there's got to be a few more all right.' Maybe it will begin to make it easier for other young gays to go into sports."

As he talks, muscles move on both sides of his forehead, and one can sense that half of his energies still seethe in a person just beneath the skin. It may be a different half there now, but it is still a half.

"Sure, I miss baseball," he says, "but I wouldn't change a thing. It's been a test and it has made me mentally stronger."

It has created a hollowness and a happiness and an image that lingers, of Glenn Burke walking a gauntlet of high-fives after his home run over the wire-mesh fence and laughing that crazy laugh once again. There might have been more, there might have been cash and fame, but there is none of this now.

There is instead a legacy of two men's hands touching, high above their heads.

Michael Grumley, 1979

tenderness more fiercer than torture

Will Inman

i was waitin
                          shouldna waited
couldn help it
                          could ef you had any backbone
i *love* you
                          no   you jes *wants* me
judge me by yourself
                          maybe   what else *is* there?
i'm not you
you're not me
                          no   i'm shadow and you're sun
                          you're stars and i'm night sky
we create each other
                          in our own heads, our own ribs
i love *you*
                          you love your hang-up with me . . . you
                          think of me, get a hard on . . .
                          you like *that*
no, it's more
your dark skin is like sand dunes
                          i'm a lost island   you discovered me
                          you wants to plant your flag
you judge me by all whites
                          you ain' got no neon sign 'round your head
                          sayin you different
if you'd listen to me
you could tell i'm different
                          you different   you the same   you both
                          i got to love all both of you
                          tear my soul apart
yes . . . does that to me, too
                          then hi come we cain't jes let go?

135

'slike you and i are man and woman
to each other, one black, one white
        yeah   i'm a man, you a woman
        you a man, i'm a woman   no, it ain't
        that, neither: it's jes, we the
        secret sides of each other
yes . . . shadow and sun
        good thing you put it like that
        some folks don'know darkness creates
        light
i love you
        you love the you you lost
        you find in me
narcissus leaning into a dark pool
        lazarus in love with jesus' shadow
raise me, brother
        i'll raise you
we'll raise each other
        that the way it got to be
you're beautiful
        if all you white folks could learn to
        love your own darkness, y'all wouldn
        hate us so
you're teachin me night vision
        you always had it   you was jes
        scared to use it
i thought dark was evil
        y'all the ones separated god and devil—
        got to put'em back together
        to be really you
you and me together—
we're god
        we really *us* . . .and if we could jes
        live that
i love you
        you keeps sayin that
i'm teaching it to myself
        you don't *know* it?
i know it and i don't know it
        tha's what scare me so . . . yet and still
        you knows it (*kisses him*)
you're so beautiful . . .

i love the way you taste
                    i loves the way you tastes me
(laughs, reaches again)
                    ni i breakin the law of gravity
gravity don't apply to us
                    no   i reckon it don't   jesus—look!
what goes up—
                    got to *come!*
(laughs)
                    what go up
got to be done down on
                    we nasty
we're wonderful
                    sometimes i feels like god bein devil
sometimes i feel like devil bein god
                    when we holds each other, i feels like
                    i'm all they is
oh, man, you *are!*
                    you, too
then hi come you don' say
you love me?
                    i got to *say* it?
well—
                    don't i *show* it?
yes
                    den—?
i love you
                    you likes to heah yourself sayin it
yes . . . i guess i have to hear it
keep on hearin it
really to believe it
                    you crazy, white boy
if lovin you is crazy,
i'm glad i'm crazy
                    yeah   you right   me, too
you *said* it! you *said* it!
                    say what?
said you love me
                    i sayed i glad i'm crazy
—if lovin me means you're crazy
                    well——i didn right out and *say* it
you love to torture me

                       i'll torture you all right
no—hey!—stop that!
no—that—oh my god
                     you see?
oh my god
                     you better be careful what you says to me
you never did that before
                     no   i helt it back
but—why now?
                     tenderness mo' fiercer than torture
you speak with your whole body
                     words don'mean nothin noway
god—oh you—oh my god
                     ni   hi you like that?
you're so beautiful
                     but i ain'no sand dunes
                     i a whole ocean
drown me
                     you already got tears in your eyes
                     i wash you up on shore
                     for the firs' time you kin see
                     i licks your feet with my surf
look—it's—you—here—
                     we bof of us ocean
                     we both land
i can't stand it
                     yes you kin   you *better!*
                     come on, ni!
                     ni you be the wind

                     17, 18 August, 1982
                     Tucson, AZ.

PEANUTS AND THE OLD SPICE KID

A Short Story

Larry Duplechan

I DISTINCTLY REMEMBER the first time I fell in love. He was seventeen years old. I was seven.

Barry was a big, handsome boy of a complexion that used to be called "high yellow." I don't know what they'd call it now. "Light Black," I guess (for all the contradiction inherent in that). Barry had green eyes—the first green eyes I had ever seen—and a reddish-brown crew-cut that felt prickly to my fingers, like a new-mowed lawn. He called me "Peanuts," after the comic strip, in honor of my round full-moon face. Barry was as good-looking as Ricky Nelson, and he had bigger muscles than Beaver's big brother, Wally. Barry was my hero.

He was also my aunt Theodosia's boyfriend. Theo lived with my mother, Clara, and me while she finished high school. Theo was a pretty girl, brown and sweet as a Hershey's with almonds. I remember how beautiful I thought she looked in her cheerleader uniform, with her freshly-straightened hair in shiny, wet-looking curls against her head, framing her pretty, heart-shaped face like a cap, and the expanse of legs, glossy and smooth between her short-short skirt and bobbysocks. Theo painted her toenails red. She thought the Ronettes were "the most." When Theo liked something—anything, really—she said it was "the most."

Barry and Theo were to be married as soon as they graduated from Fremont High. Theo loved Barry—she told me so herself. Once, when I caught her writing Barry's name, over and over, in diffferent kinds of lettering all over one of the book covers she'd made out of a Food Giant grocery gab, Theo smiled her wide, slightly crooked smile and said, "I love Barry. You'll understand when you're older."

I already understood. I loved Barry, too.

Every time Barry came to see Theo—and he came to see her almost every day—I'd run up to him and say, "Barry, pick me up!" And he always would. "Whoa!" he'd say, lifting me into his arms, "you're getting heavy." Then he'd press me a few times, like a barbell—Barry lifted weights. I knew I wasn't really heavy to him. I figured Barry could probably lift Clara's car if he wanted to.

I loved being up in Barry's arms more than anything. More than hot chocolate or Kukla Fran 'n' Ollie or my two-wheeler. I still remember the warmth of Barry's big hands, the cool leatherette of the sleeves on his letterman's jacket—Barry played football. And I remember Barry's smell, clean boysweat and Old Spice. Many was the time Barry kissed Theo hello with me in his arms, and if it ever bothered Theo, she had the remarkable good taste not to show it.

Barry and Theo didn't go out much. I don't think Barry had much spending money—I know Theo didn't—so, as often as not, they'd stay at our house. They'd study together with the radio on. Or watch T.V. holding hands. Or play records for hours on our big Magnavox cabinet-model stereo, replaying their favorites over and over: "Having A Party," and "Hit the Road, Jack," and "Baby Work Out." They'd kick off their sneakers and dance in my mother's living room. Or Barry would sit on the Danish modern sofa and laugh while Theo taught me the Soul Twist and the Monkey Time and Walkin' the Dog and the Bristol Stomp.

Sometimes, Barry and Theo babysat for me to give Clara the evening off for her church meetings or PTA or a Tupperware party. They didn't seem to mind—they probably would have been there anyway. Clara liked for Barry to spend time with me—"It's not right for a boy to be cooped up with just womenfolk all the time," she'd say. And, of course, the more time Barry spent with us, the better I liked it.

Often during those babysitting evenings, Barry would have me read for him. (At the age of seven, I was tested as reading past sixth- grade level, and while I feigned ignorance of this distinction, I was secretly quite proud of myself.) "C'mere, Peanuts," Barry would say. "Come read for me." Theo would be in the kitchen, steaming tamales or slapping hamburger into patties. And Barry would sit me in his lap and listen with obvious amusement as I read from one of his schoolbooks, or the TV Guide, or the list of in-gredients on a bottle of ginger ale.

"Good greasy gravy!" Barry would exclaim. "Theo, this kid's a lit-tle genius!" Then he'd tickle my terribly ticklish little belly with his strong fingers, and I'd fall, squealing with helpless laughter, into Barry's arms, collapsing against the hard muscles of his Old Spice-scented, tee-shirted chest.

"A little smart-aleck, you ask me." Theo would call from the kitchen. But she'd be smiling.

Barry liked to bring presents for Theo and for me. He'd bring Theo bunches of flowers purloined from his mother's garden, or Whitman chocolates — which Theo would walk a mile for — or some new album or other. For me, a bag of peanut M&M's — "peanuts for Peanuts" — or a comic book he'd finished with. Once, he gave me an old football jersey of his. It was nearly floor-length on me, and I wore it to bed for over a year. Even after repeated washings, it smelled just like him.

On one of the evenings Theo and Barry sat with me, Barry brought me an old portable record player he'd had since he was little. I couldn't have been more excited if it had been Christmas day, and Santa himself had strolled in with reindeer in tow — a record player of my very own! I jumped up and down like a puppy, screaming, "Is it mine? Is it really mine? For keeps? For real?"

"For keeps, for real," Barry assured me.

"Pick me up, pick me up!" I almost ordered. I hugged Barry's thick neck and kissed his beard-stubbly cheeks, and thanked and thanked and thanked him.

"Boy, cut that out!" Theo said, slapping me sharply on the behind. "Boys don't kiss boys."

I could barely contain myself while Barry showed me how to work the machine, how to replace a worn-out needle with one from the little brownpaper envelope of replacements that he'd brought.

He had even brought me some records. Later, in my room, I would listen to them time and again, until I had memorized every word and every song. One of them was the story of Peter Pan. I played it tirelessly; I saved Tinkerbelle's life countless times with the strength of my belief in fairies, clapping my hands and never once doubting that she would perish without me.

Another record featured children's dance songs, the Hokey Pokey and Go in and Out the Window. I'd spend hours alone, singing along with the lady singer's sweet, high voice, and performing the movements in front of my mirror as if to an attentive audience:

"I bring my left hand in,
I put my left hand out,
I give my left hand

Shake-shake-shake,
And turn myself about."

My favorite record of all was made of translucent red plastic, nearly as much fun to look at as to hear. I'd amuse myself first by closing one eye and peering through the disc, coloring my little world a hazy rose; then I'd hold the record up to my bedroom window, allowing the sunlight to shine through it and create flickering red ghosts to dance across my ceiling and walls. Then I'd finally put the record onto the turntable, and listen to "Slim Jim, the Singing Cowboy."

I'd listen in rapt attention to Slim Jim's stories of shootin' and ropin' and a-ridin' the range. I'd sing along in my biggest, loudest cowboy voice,

"Yippy-i-ay
Yippy-i-o
Git along to the big cor-ral,"

as often as not causing Theo to holler from the next room, "Boy, shut up! I'm tryin' to study in here!"

I couldn't wait for Theo and Barry to get married, so Barry could come and live with us. When, after the wedding, they both went to live with Barry's parents, I was heartsick for weeks, disconsolate, carrying the torch at seven and a half. For the first time since acquiring the power of speech, I was given to long silences. I'd sit in a corner in my room and listen to my records in silence, while Clara took my temperature and clucked her tongue in puzzlement.

As it turned out, Theo and Barry lasted less than a year of married life. They were just kids, really, neither of them even remotely ready for marriage. And, from what I managed to overhear of Theo and Clara's conversations, Barry's mother and Theo got along like two cats in a sack. And so they parted, Theo for secretarial school and, later, three more husbands; Barry to—well, actually, I couldn't say. I never saw Barry again.

Of course, I recovered from my heartbreak relatively quickly— the seven year old heart possesses the resilience of a Wham-o superball. I soon found myself quite infatuated with Joel Brechtschneider—a new boy in the third grade with the bluest eyes I'd ever seen—and actively campaigning to make him my best friend. And so life went on, as it does.

Still, I do think of Barry, quite fondly, from time to time. And I can't help but think it significant that, to this day, I still have something of a weakness for cowboy songs. And letterman's jackets. And Old Spice.

BEYOND THE BINARY: RACE AND SEX

Charley Shively

I GREW UP in rural Ohio. Clermont County had only a sprinkling of Black people segregated in the county seat (Batavia). I don't recall ever seeing a Black person even in Batavia. Although I remember people saying that Batavia always won the county basketball championship because they had Black players. (I never attended any games: lack of interest, lack of money, lack of a way to the games.) I went to the Williamsburg Township School which had no Black students.

The first Black people I ever remember seeing were two students who tried to enter Williamsburg School. (I don't exactly recall their sex—although I think they were female.) Their family had evidently moved into the township, but I'm not sure of the details. I was only in the second grade in October, 1943. I remember the Brown Twins (who I had played around with sexually) were sort of gang leaders in our class. They led the playground in taunting and stoning the two Black children (who were not in my class). It wasn't physically brutal (small sticks and stones). I don't remember what I did exactly: did I shove? yell? (if so, what did I say?) did I throw something? Only the feeling of wrong lingers. I can remember precisely the school door, the corner of the building where it happened, the undergarments of the Brown Twins. Certainly, I did not say, "Stop! No! Don't!" I feared the ostracism of the Twins. (Later I associated their conformity with all heterosexuality.) The two Black students withdrew from Williamsburg and went elsewhere (Batavia I would guess).

My next vivid memory more definitely associates Blackness with sexuality. I was then around thirteen and had begun a semi-affair with another boy, who worked with me setting up pins in the bowling alley. He was the toughest boy in our neighborhood (Bobbler's

Knob); arrested several times, he was eventually given a stiff sentence for armed robbery. Earl was a little (but not much) older than me; still, at thirteen one or two years means a lot. He was certainly more experienced than me—the shy, quiet, studious, good-boy type. We had our first sex in a pig pen and he fucked me—rather gracefully. Earl told me things about the world—like Cincinnati. He confided in somewhat hushed and warning tones about Black men on Central Avenue in Cincinnati. They had such big cocks they would run a hole right through me. I guess he was projecting what he wanted (but because of his butchness couldn't even entertain) onto me. My feeling was one of intrigue and desire. I suppose my relations with any Black man will always be touched by the things Earl said.

Of course, coming to Harvard in 1955 from rural Ohio changed a lot of things. On the racial side, I discovered who and what Jews were. In my high school we had not learned about the concentration camps or Hitler's anti-Semitism. I knew nothing about Judaism as a religion, although Cincinnati is one of the country's centers of Jewish theology. And although my roommate for two years was Jewish and I generally socialized with all the non-WASPSs in my dormitory, I remained very much a country bumpkin as far as grasping the Eastern subtleties of ethnicity. Even with a Korean and a Chinese-American friend, I maintained a rather fraudulent idea of equality—that everyone was the same (i.e. potentially "American"), homogeneous. My college friends were all studious, hard working, poor and very much out of the social elite of Harvard. We all despised the "Clubbies." As far as sex goes, I don't think anyone did much of anything but masturbate. Certainly, if they were like me—busy in the tea rooms and bushes—they kept it totally closeted.

At the end of my sophomore year in the summer of 1957, I met a man who fell passionately in love with me. He said he was a direct descendant of Sitting Bull—although I'm never too sure of such genealogies (my father always said he was part Indian). We made out in the little town library and exchanged phone numbers. I still have the passionate letters he sent me (after our first meeting) saying, "I love you with all my heart, and no one will ever take your place." After our second meeting, he said, "I would be forever content just to wait for you." We rendezvoused a few times and I felt very uncomfortable not being able to return his passion. I think I was a bit snobbish about his taste in music (Frank Sinatra), his religion (Pentecostal) or literature (he gave me a Norman Mailer book, which was then considered "vulgar"). I felt very relieved when he moved to Indiana and I never heard from him again.

I did not know any Black students at Harvard (there were few if any in those days). Since I generally scored in the undergraduate library (Lamont) tearoom, I didn't meet many Black partners. My sophomore year was one of the busiest in my life, making it with something like three men a day every day of the semester, I was intrigued with the varieties of bodies, penises, personalities (whenever I could get into that) and generally going to bed with any man that was willing.

One night, going home from the library (it closed at ten then), I caught a Black man's eye by a camera store on Massachusetts Avenue, the main drag. He went down a side street and stepped into an unlighted doorway. Fearing assault or robbery, I nonetheless followed. We kissed and groped each other and he invited me back to his place, which, as we walked, seemed miles into East Cambridge. He lived with his elderly mother and we made it together, alone on the living room couch. He was tall and thin, built like a dancer, short hair, mocha skin; his family was from the French West Indies. Those were the 50's and I was very much into playing a passive role: getting fucked or doing some stud. After he had fucked me wildly, Norman asked if I had ever fucked anyone and I said (quite honestly) no I never had. He said, "O.K. I've always said that if I ever met a virgin like you, I'd want them to fuck me since I've never been fucked myself." So I did it, very easy and gentle, nonetheless he found it a little hard (I remember his back stretching and straining—sweating a bit down the spine). Whether his being a "virgin," was a line or not, he deeply impressed me. After I had breakfast in the morning with him and his mother, we exchanged addresses.

The next time we met, he gave me a pink shirt. Pink was then considered very wild as a color—somehow associated unfavorably in my mind with Elvis Presley, whom I considered hopelessly vulgar. I was totally floored by the idea of a gift: no sexual partner had ever treated me so nice in all my life. I was also worried. At the time I remained a totally dedicated, industrious student. I had never had a love affair and—sad to recall—I looked on such things as a great waste of time. My relationship never developed further with Norman. I suppose I saw it as the career girl torn between love and promotion, and in my mind there was no question of not going for the sweepstakes. I later saw Norman from time to time and, in fact, moved into a house just around the corner from him.

In the meantime he'd moved on to New York: I once met him and
his new lover, a Columbia professor. In retrospect now it all seems
like an episode out of Langston Hughes' *The Ways of White Folks.* I
was even then against the middle class, against the empire war and
the state, but I was more against the body, against the animal
myself, and dedicated to what I thought was pure thought.

In pursuit of "pure" history, I went to Madison, Wisconsin for a
year (1959-60). There I came upon the twentieth century, beat
poetry, radicalism and other now-familiar things. I remember only
one Black man in Madison. He was a law student from Alabama—
paid by the state to study in the North if he would stay there.
William B. Hesseltine, a professor in the history department, said
Whites were beginning to make pets or teddy bears out of the few
Blacks they ran into. Pete may have suffered from such saccharine
attention as a member of the Blue Lantern Cooperative, where we
ate together. The Lantern was then the small center of student
radicals in Madison. We managed to get a good-sized crowd out to
demonstrate against the local Woolworth's (whose lunch counters
were the center of protests against segregation), and in April we
had a large march from the university to the State Capitol
Building. I wore a red and black lumber jacket and felt very
righteous when I saw myself on TV that evening.

In Madison, my sexual life remained very underground: library
tea room by day, the Capitol grounds at night or occasionally the
one gay bar. I don't think I even saw a Black man in any of the
cruising areas. I did meet a Mexican-American from the Southwest;
he was a graduate student in Spanish literature. I had done him
nine or ten times in the tea room (a marble altar he called it, as he
went down on his knees under the stall partition, and I went down
on his penis). Finally he invited me home to his room and we went
to bed together. I liked him a lot, but he was deeply afraid of any
emotional attachment: he was married and had two children at
home. He showed me pictures of his family and told me how difficult it was being gay at home.

Back at Harvard in the fall of 1960, I passed notes in the Lamont
tea room with a Black man making arrangements to meet outside.
Lester was tall, thin, still in his teens; he lived in Cambridge with
his mother. He was slightly wild and outrageous to my sober,
scholarly outlook but also immensely talented, charming and spectacular. Through Lester I met Edmund, who was much quieter,
winsome, sweet and affectionate. The three of us formed an almost
inseparable circle for a couple of years; we didn't have much sex

with each other, but we were "sisters in the night."

Harvard graduate students are totally isolated; they lack the charm and attraction of the undergraduates (who include jocks, poets and thespians) to either the school or to each other. They are supposed to be dedicated entirely to cultivating their minds, reading everything and committing themselves to nothing. Edmund and Lester kept me alive through those dry years of torturous study: in a way they were wives to me: absorbing the psychic shocks I was suffering, strengthening me to survive in the straight world, keeping me going with friendship. Whatever else, they were my family, the only people I talked to; the only people I loved.

Ours was not, of course, a traditional family by any reckoning. They each lived at home with their parents, and I lived in a furnished room, later a small apartment. Above all else we shared our love of sexual adventure. New Year's Eve 1961 we picked up a pack of soldiers home on leave (Fort Dix basic training). Three, four, maybe more of them were hanging around the Hayes Bickford all-night restaurant in Harvard Square. They wore neat khaki uniforms. We all went to my room and turned off the lights; arrangements were a bit awkward. One of the boys was shy and couldn't do anything with the others around: so I took him into the closet and even there he was absolutely trembling, could barely get it up and was happy to get away. He returned later and stole some of Lester's records and got to enjoy homosexuality more. One of the soldiers—"Johnny" was his name (and we used to sing "When Johnny comes marching home again" in memory of the night) wanted a woman and decided to check out the landlady who was between sixty and seventy years old. The soldiers were all White and she was Black; either age, race or her motherly demeanor turned Johnny away.

We all three tricked regularly in Lamont. I remember a husky Santa Barbara freshman cruised me in the library and gave me what he said was his name and address to call for a later rendevous. I then gave the note to Lester; he called the number and went over and made it with the other party, who it turned out had also cruised the freshman and had been given my number. (I eventually made it with that mischievous trickster.) Another time, Edmund brought a married friend along—partly I think just to shock him with our wicked talk. Then secretly the friend would come around to see me for a blow job; in fact, he almost became a nuisance.

Not all my contacts were Black and White. I remember seeing *Hiroshima Mon Amour* and on my way home meeting a Japanese man, who looked like the star in the movie. He was a Harvard student, a swimmer with a perfect samurai body. I couldn't believe it: almost fantasy fulfillment. Physically he gave himself totally to me; emotionally it was as though I did not exist. The experience was strangely unnerving: all those years not sleeping with a Japanese man; then suddenly there he was, almost a total fantasy fulfillment. Was I the creature of random media stimulation — a sexual consumer always in the market for novelty?

Certainly Lester, Edmund and myself pursued novelty and variety in our sexuality. I wonder now that we got away with all we did. One evening Lester came by with a carload of Irish teenagers in a remade Mercury that was painted with the mouth of a dragon on the front and shooting flames all over the car. This was sort of a *Rebel Without A Cause* fantasy.

We decided to go to the country to give the boys blow jobs. When we got out to Waltham, they saw some young woman walking along the street and started to follow her. Then a gang of Watertown/Waltham boys challenged and started chasing our car. Perhaps they were outraged that one of us was Black or maybe just pissed that we were operating in their territory. We began a high speed drive to get away.

Hoping to lose them, we managed to hide in a suburban driveway (the car was hard to hide), but the people living there yelled for us to get away and the pursuers found us. They had pikes and chains; the Cambridge boys told Lester and me that we would have to help fight or else. Luckily we got the car started and away (a few chunks of filling were knocked off the headlight).

As we streamed down the main drag in Waltham going fifty or sixty miles an hour pursued by the other car, we attracted a lot of attention. Two police cars began chasing. We approached a red light but shot around the other waiting cars, crossed the island and went through the intersection. The cop car pulled alongside and then in front of us; the pursuing car made a safe getaway.

On the way to the police station I coached everyone on a story that we had come to study the architecture of Brandeis and were chased by these hoods. Whether the police bought that story or not, we all stuck to it and they let us go with a speeding ticket for the driver. I was all for continuing on our way to the country for the blow jobs, but the teenagers would have none of that.

I think Lester, Edmund and myself had become enough of a family that we began to find lovers a bit like each other (though we didn't have sex much between us). That must certainly have something to do with my first full-time lover (that is, we got a place for living together). I met Lou in 1961 late one night in back of the Club 47; Joan Baez still sang there along with other jazz and folk musicians. I had never been inside, because I didn't have the money; I was passing by that night on my way to cruise the Charles River bank. Lou was very spaced out, pissing, cursing, holding a broken beer bottle in his hand, crying. I asked him if he needed anything, and he put his arm around me and we walked to his place. We took our clothes off, and he fucked me with enormous passion and enthusiasm; he was very large, but at the time I was totally loose, relaxed and happy to have him inside me. He went asleep and I left a note and went along on home.

I actually didn't expect to hear from him at all, but in a couple of weeks he called and wanted to see me. We met and he said he remembered nothing of the night and wondered who I was and what the note meant. I explained that I was a faggot and we had fucked together. He said that was the first time for him, and I said well, I was always pretty much available. Lou was at the time a cult figure around the Club 47 crowd; he was an extraordinary piano player and had a whole act of being a wasted jazz star. He also dealt and used a lot of different drugs, of which there was also a cult at the time. Lou had been officially deported for narcotics violations from Canada.

We made an unusual couple. While I may have been a faggot, I was still very academic, serious, disdainful of most pleasures — drugs, drink, music, smoke. Hardly a likely companion for a sophisticated jazz pianist; yet something clicked between us. My poetry perhaps: I wrote poems for him, and he would play for me alone at night wearing only jockey shorts. I wrote a friend of my love for Lou: "The experience is a real one. It brings out my being and carries me to the limits of human experience — something I've never had before."

We got two baby kittens together from the Animal Rescue League. We would go to Cape Anne for sunrise on the rocks. We took pictures of each other by the sea. We walked along the Charles River, Easter morning sunrise. Lou was vomiting Sweet and Sour chicken, thanking me for being there. And when I had to take a Spanish test, he made love to me and gave me some speed to keep me awake (the two most helpful things he could have done). I was deeply touched that he knew what I needed.

Our relationship came to a rather dramatic end in Ohio. Lou, a drummer in his group, and myself, were going to Mexico on some dope business in this rich suburban woman's car. We got to Cincinnati and were stalled at my family's house, mainly because we were quite out of money. We went into Cincinnati to audition for a job in a downtown club. On the way home, Lou drove even though he could scarcely stand up. In Cincinnati he ran a red light and just missed hitting a Cadillac by a microsecond. Nonetheless, the drummer and I went on with him driving; outside of town he ran the car out of control.

I was sitting next to him in the front seat and could see us moving off the road through the air. We hit a utility pole just six inches in front of me; I saw it coming like a rerun on a football movie. I was thrown out of the car and landed in the mud relatively unhurt. Lou and the drummer were also unscratched but still a little drunk. I was nearly sober and vomited quickly so as to have no alcohol on my breath and said I was driving when the police arrived. The woman whose car was totaled flew out and took him back (they were later married). I think Lou resented my keeping him out of jail or at least trouble. As he said, it was as though I had something on him. The drummer and I returned by Greyhound.

Back in Massachusetts, I could cry on Lester's and Eddie's shoulders, but they were relieved to see that adventure ended. Lester wandered on into Cambridge nightlife as he grew older and I saw less of him. Edmund and I grew closer. I shared the tribulations of an Irish lover with him; we went cruising a lot together and kept up an endless stream of gossip, tricks and cups of coffee. In 1965 I met my present lover who was very jealous of my friends, and after that I didn't see a lot of Edmund. Later he moved out of town and we only get in touch with each other like old family cousins. I've since wondered if I shouldn't have stuck with my friends and forgot about lovers.

*   *

One of the common charges against those engaging in interracial sex/love/marriage/life is that the experience is self-destructive, pathological. The case of my liaison with Lou certainly contains elements of that. I could see that Lou was a homosexual— physically attracted to Black men, while he had all his sex with White women and me. That among other things led to his destruction. He married the wealthy suburban lady for her car and money; she went insane; he went to Florida and (as informed sources report) shot himself.

For myself, I think I was not destroying myself but trying to destroy what Harvard-Conformity-Western Civilization would make for me. There was always in the middle class intellectual life enormous lures: the quiet harmony, soft chairs, fine offices, sociability and order. Whenever I left home in Ohio, I breathed easier in the relaxed atmosphere of school where nobody seemed to be scrounging for grocery money or rent, where there was no weekly crisis of injury, unemployment, conviction, car wreck, breakdown, pregnancy, fights or disease. Harvard (and the middle class values it preserves) is quiet, total self-destruction. What is really pathological is trying to hang on to that security while trying to escape it: the conflict and tension tear people apart. You must cut the umbilical cord in your heart to Western Civilization.

I think the issue is not the self-destructiveness of miscegenation, nor by extension the self-destructiveness of homosexuality, masturbation or sexuality in general. The issue is rather the destruction of capitalism, middle class culture and Western Civilization. Bakunin said, "Let us have confidence in the eternal spirit which destroys and annihilates only because it is the unfathomable and eternally creative source of life. The urge of destruction is at the same time a creative urge." Do not cry/Let Western Civilization die.

The issue of Western Civilization and interracial sexuality are intimately linked: these were the two questions Malcolm X found White people most often asking about. The two issues are intrinsically tied together because Western Civilization is in itself a system of sexism and racism. The "Western Tradition" begins by dividing everything into two parts: Adam/Eve, Male/Female, God/Devil, Good/Evil, Sex/Love, Mind/Body, and by extension White/Black. These dichotomies do not correspond with any reality, but they do have a devastating effect on believers in the system.

Race or skin color, for instance, can not be divided into *only* two parts. The Supreme Court can only deal with Black/White segregation; when they face multiple groups as in Corpus Christi (Chicano, Black and White), their language cannot function. In Boston, Spanish-speaking students must by law be designated either Black or White by the individual teacher; under this system one identical twin was categorized White, the other Black. In writing this article, I have tried to think multiply—not only of my sexual contact with Black men but with all Third World men (American Indian, Japanese or Mexican-American). The effort is obviously somewhat

152 / CHARLEY SHIVELY

strained: the mind focuses almost automatically Black/White.

The conceiving of race grows out of the conceiving of sexuality. Racism or fascism or imperialism originate in the heterosexual world view in which everyone is divided through a binary system of male and female (plus and minus)—daddy and mommy (master and servant). Following the binary line requires everything to be divided into two with one part being designated inferior by the other. Homosexuals should know better but cannot completely escape some contamination from the system. Obviously, White faggots carry a fantasy of Black men being more at home in their body (more animal, more thing). Good in music, dancing, basketball and bed. This grows out of a denigration not only of color but also of sexuality and humanity. Christians have long had a tradition of the "slavery of passion." That is, to submit to pleasure, desire, love, lust, the body—is to become a slave of something lower, inferior, less celestial—suicidal and self-destructive. To become MASTER of the self is to stop giving in to sex. (Any number of religions share this sick philosophy.)

I would say that interracial sex only highlights a wider contempt and fear for sex, the body, flesh, lust, animal or whatever you will call it. Cocksucking as an act of revolution would go against this system, would celebrate values of sex, desire, love, the animal in us all. If we fight the love, strength, humanity that is inside us we are self-destructive—we are suicidal. If we attempt to break down the tyranny of the binary system which would celebrate mind, mastery, power, authority, hierarchy and order—we can become truly creative, human, alive, beautiful.

PHOTOGRAPHY BY
SIERRA DOMINO
(Calvin Anderson)

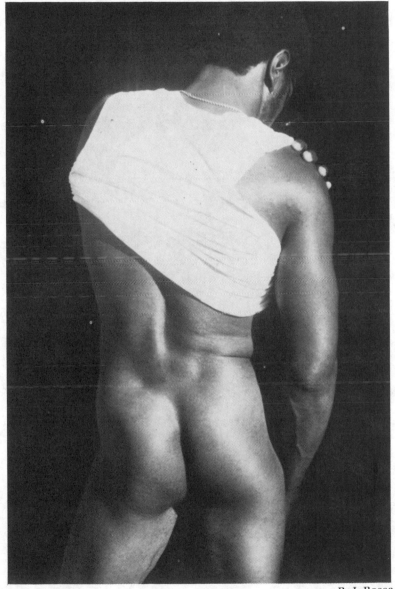

B. J. Bassa

Trucker

Fred Thompson

Cueler Rogers

Frank Smith

Carlis Sharp

"NO BLACKS"
Racism in the Gay Press

Michael J. Smith

IF I WERE A BIGOTED White person, fed us hearing about racism, I might write something clever to my local gay paper:

Dear Editor:
My friends and I just don't understand some people in this city. We wanna know what's going on. We are black and Gay and sometimes white Gays don't want to have nothing to do with us, but there is this black guy that seems to draw a lot of attention from white guys, but turns his nose up at us.

As you can see, I'd use phrases like "don't want to have nothing. . ." for color. You know how Blacks talk.

Then I'd continue:

Why don't he stick with his own kind. Me and my friend have tried to get his attention or we speak but he doesn't care to talk to us. He ain't all that hot but tries to act like it.

And then, just in case anyone missed the point:

We don't know his name, but he should know that he should be on our side of the fence, since white Gays don't like us.

Clever, eh?

If I weren't clever enough, however, I might not see that my "Black" English slips here and there, reverting to "regular" phrases such as "seems to draw a lot of attention." (Doesn't fit too well, does it?) And what about 'wanna.'? While some Blacks may speak that way, they sure don't *write* that way. And take 'Gay'. That word is capitalized, but 'black' isn't. That's suspicious too. Oh well, maybe you wouldn't catch on.

The gay press continues to slam Black people and no one seems to care. It's not so much the Whites-only message blared by the

159

commercial advertisers with their White young men peddling one thing or another—I've gotten used to that. (And, what the hell, you have to pay the bills, right?) I'm even getting used to the editorial end of things, the virtual, uh, . . . blackout of news about gay and lesbian people of color. That too has been going on so long I don't notice it much anymore. No, what's getting me down is the insensitivity, the plain stupidity.

Take the letter above. It appeared in a local paper not so long ago. When I called the editor and suggested it might be a fake, he alibied defensively that he couldn't authenticate every letter that comes in. He also steadfastly refused to pick up the phone to verify this particular one. (It would have taken him all of five minutes.) And it *had* been printed—who's going to admit such a mistake in this day and age? When I tried explaining the race-baiting nature of the letter, I might just as well have been speaking Greek—the man's social and professional sensibility was that dulled. Next week, the predictable responses poured in: how prejudiced that Black guy was! "Racism" was finally being discussed, but in terms of what Blacks were doing wrong! Suddenly I longed for the good old days when the issue was simply ignored.

Then there are the well-meaning liberals. Another local gay publication put a Black man on its cover. Good, I thought to myself as I turned to the inside. The article began promisingly enough. The publisher related how the cover man, a supervisor's aide at City Hall, had expressed surprise being featured in a White- dominated newspaper. Wow, I thought, it takes guts for a publisher to print something like that. But I should have known better. Having the last word, as all publishers do, he weaseled out of this one claiming simply, "Ethnic minorities have often appeared in . . . (our paper)." Wait a minute, I thought, recalling to mind past issues. No they haven't. Not by any definition of "often or appear." I guess, though, if you say in print that they have, somehow it'll seem true.

As I read further, things got worse. After listing some of the personal accomplishments of the politically ambitious Black man, the article added:

He is also a Regional Director for the Committee of Black Gay Men, a political organization that does both lobbying and provides an opportunity for its members to engage in introspective discussions. "The gay community needs to recognize that ethnic and racial prejudice among gays is counter-productive to our Human Rights goals," he says.

Oh, no. Never mind that there is no Committee of Black Gay Men in San Francisco 'lobbying' and 'providing opportunities,'—and that there hasn't been for two years (at least according to four Black men I know who belong*ed*)! Never mind that those pretty words about racism are just words, nothing more. (It isn't the first time a politician has padded his credentials at the expense of those who *are* active in a cause—in this case, anti-racism.) What's annoying is that the publisher who, just a few sentences before, crowed about his paper's ethnic pedigree, doesn't realize he's never printed Word One about this "political," "lobbying" Committee (how could he—there's been nothing to report!). The whole send-up is just so much hot air, packaged to give us what they think we'd like to hear. As for a simple journalistic exercize like verifying facts, why bother? If this upright, White-selected Black man says such a group exists and is engaged in all this activism, why, it must be true. Even if it isn't, it . . . helps the 'cause,' doesn't it? (One of them must have sensed they were pretty close to the edge, though. Specific information about the Committee—a contact phone or address, a meeting schedule—is conveniently omitted.)

Unfortunately, racism in the gay press isn't always that subtle. Take this employment ad from a Washington DC paper:

Help Wanted: GWM (Gay White male) for 3-4 days job, helper, home fix-up . . . Exp pref but not nec if good worker. Must be clean, dependable . . .

Or this from a San Francisco paper:

Jobs: Bartender, conservative GWM to work in straight establishment. Work into partnership. No exp required . . .

It works in reverse too. In Philadelphia:

Jobs Wanted: GWM painting student seeks weekend position in art gallery. Seriously interested in learning the gallery business . . .

Our GWM artist at least knows his colors. White is so much more . . . preferable for this kind of job. Or this kind (from a national publication):

Prof pilot—White male, 30, straight looking—seeks flight crew position . . .

Or, for that matter, just about any kind. From Memphis:

GWM seeking any type of employment . . . All offers considered.

He sounds desperate, doesn't he? But he *does* have one thing going for him and he knows it. He has another too: a gay press that's perfectly willing to help him trade on his Whiteness and the system's preference for it. And, well, why not? Freedom of the press and all that. If Whites are somehow more employable— and, let's face it, they are—who are we to buck the system? Besides, there's nothing illegal about describing your race when looking for a job. There's also nothing relevant about it. Or is there?

Whites are also more "houseable." From coast to coast, North, South, East, and West, gay newspapers carry hundreds of discriminatory housing ads. In Denver:

Responsible roommate(s) to share large 3-bedroom Victorian. Quiet area near City Park. Must be GWM, neat, clean, with stable employment . . .

And Washington DC—with a twist:

GWM/F to share NW townhouse w/3 M and pets; must be stable, neat. . . .

This last one in a city where the population is 70% Black! (There were twenty such ads in the one issue of this paper I examined. Just what kind of message are they trying to convey?)

Wait a minute, you say? There's a difference between refusing to rent to Blacks—Fair Housing and all that—and refusing to *live* with one. Sure there is. One is overt racism, the other's more subtle.

Subtle too is this:

GWM, prof, quiet, clean, seeking apt for Sept 1. . . .

Someone else out to trade on a system which favors Whites. The Boston paper which printed that one advises ironically:

Dear Advertiser, if race is not a crucial issue for you, why put it in your ad? It is not a required formula: GWM, GWF are not necessary. GM, GF would do as well, unless you really want it otherwise.

I'm tempted to respond:

Dear Editor, it's your fucking newspaper. If race is a crucial issue for you, why run the ad? . . . Unless you really want it otherwise.

Do we really want it otherwise? Is it our intention to continue promoting Whiteness by shutting out people of color? Well, maybe not. Maybe we want them to have the same freedom and privileges we have. Maybe it's just that we don't think about it. Maybe.

AT EBENEZER
BAPTIST CHURCH

Leonard Patterson

IN SEPTEMBER of 1972 when I arrived in Atlanta, Georgia, to begin my career as a medical student at Emory University, like many young people of the post-Vietnam and civil rights era, I had many idealistic views of what Atlanta, Ebenezer Baptist Church, Martin Luther King, Jr., and Morehouse College represented. For me, these institutions symbolized honesty, integrity, tolerance, and compassion. As the years passed, though, I came to the realization that in these places being a conformist was more important than being compassionate. I found that if I did not play the political and social games, my lifestyle would not be accepted.

For one year I attended Ebenezer as a visitor every Sunday, not stopping to meet anyone, just enjoying the services, the singing of the choirs and preaching of the Rev. Martin Luther King, Sr. For a medical student away from home, these two hours on Sunday morning represented a time of peace and tranquility. Many of Rev. King's comforting messages seemed aimed directly at me. This year was an interesting time for me, and I decided to become a member. I joined the choir, met many of the other members and really enjoyed the fellowship. But because I have always been very active in church affairs, I began to get more and more involved with the life of the church. As the years went by, I became a Sunday School teacher and youth leader. In June 1974 I decided to end my medical training. I just felt that God wanted me to do something else with my life. Needless to say, this was a difficult period for me. For fifteen years I had prepared to become a physician. It wasn't easy to leave. But I did leave and soon found the pull of the ministry—the call of the ministry—was the answer to many of the questions that had filled my life.

Two wonderful things happened to me that year: I started a new life and met a wonderful person, Jim. He and I have been together ever since. Feeling a special sensitivity to the problems of America's disenfranchised, I felt that I was in a unique position at Ebenezer to help the image of "the homosexual" in America since this church represents liberation and stands as an oasis for the downtrodden in a desert of persecution. After all, the son of this church, Martin Luther King, Jr., had given his life marching for the rights of garbage workers in Memphis who had been mistreated and oppressed by an insensitive society. What a wonderful opportunity, I thought, to worship as myself with a people who I thought would be sensitive to oppression, they themselves having been touched so often by society's cruelties. Jim became a member of Ebenezer the following year, and we both became active in organizing the youth of the church. I found that this aspect of the church's life—youthful development—had been severely neglected over the years. We led Bible studies with them and took them on retreats. We had cookouts and swimming parties. We listened to their problems and became their friends. We made them feel a part of the life of the church. Soon, what had been a handful of young people attending services became a large crowd. Jim and I were sensitive to their needs, and they trusted us with their feelings.

I plunged into every phase of Ebenezer's life: Children's Chapel ministry, prison ministry, sick and shut-in ministry and organization of the Young Adult Fellowship. Up to this time, my acceptance at Ebenezer was high as long as Jim and I were discreet about our relationship. But I felt that in order for the myths about gay relationships to be dispelled and for them to be seen as healthy alternatives, we would have to invite church groups to our home. We did, and these invitations, combined with the retirement of the Rev. M. L. King, Sr. and the subsequent election of the Rev. Joseph Roberts as pastor, brought a radical change in attitudes toward me at the church.

Pastor Roberts felt very uncomfortable with my relationship with Jim. It was not so much that I was gay. It was not so much that I was involved in a relationship with another man. It was that this person was White. I was told, in effect, that as long as I played the political game and went with a person who was more easily passed off as a "cousin," I would be able to go far in the ministry. Perhaps I should even marry and have someone on the side. Apparently these arrangements would make me more "respectable." Well, there are many Black ministers in Atlanta who are gay. Most of them live double lives. I had decided not to do this; and for that, the new pastor decided to make my life miserable.

On Sundays I was attacked verbally from the pulpit, forbidden to enter the study for prayer with the other associate ministers, and had seeds of animosity planted against me in the minds of certain members so that in meetings with them the subject of homosexuality would inevitably be brought up. Once, in a Young Adult Fellowship meeting, a member looked directly at me and said, "If you lie down with dogs, you get up smelling like dirt." As time passed, I found that I had to resign my offices in the church. Going to Ebenezer on Sundays and participating in its many activities had once been a joy, and now it was a nightmare. The final straw came on a Sunday morning when I was scheduled to bring the message while the pastor was out ot town. I arrived at the church as did the congregation. The organist and choirs did not. I later found out that that morning the pastor had called the organist and told him that the service had been cancelled. This was obviously an attempt to sabotage the service. But in spite of these efforts, God blessed the message and the messenger.

What a disappointment! Here at the mecca of Black liberation, where busloads of pilgrims come to see where the prophet of non-violence and social change lived, here where all oppressed persons should feel compassion, it appeared the church was just another political and social club where, if you play the right games, you inherit the power and the prestige of an elite group. What racism! What hypocrisy! As was brought to my attention one evening by a "concerned" member of the church who "just happened to be passing" our house, everything would be all right with me if it were not for my "associations." The central problem was Jim. Be gay. But be our kind of gay—a hypocrite! Say one thing publicly, and do the opposite privately. In effect, hide Jim, or better yet, get rid of him altogether. Either conform or get out. I chose the latter. God loves me. God loves Jim. God loves Jim and me together. It has been eleven years now, and our relationship has grown. It has outlasted many "straight" marriages that began when ours did. We are loved. No one can convince me otherwise.

The church, and especially Ebenezer, should be a gauge measuring how society treats its oppressed groups. Ebenezer has prestige, it has power, it has respect in the worldwide community. It is internationally known as a place of compassion for the downtrodden. Yet, it is afraid to take controversial stands for righteousness.

There is a story in church history in which Thomas Aquinas

visited Rome and was shown the luxury and affluence of the Eternal City. The Pope, it is said, was in a jovial mood and said to him, "Thomas, you see no longer can the church say, 'Silver and gold have I none'." Thomas replied, "Yes, Father, and no longer can the church say, 'Rise up and walk'." Gays are an oppressed group in our society and in many other societies in the world. I am told that if he had lived, Martin Luther King, Jr. planned to take a leadership position in the gay rights movement. He was sensitive to the needs of others. Therein lies the difference between the man and the institution, between Christ and the Pharisees, between truth and falsehood. The people of God (and especially a people who know what it means to be oppressed) should serve a prophetic function in our society. When injustice raises its ugly head over any group, the church should tell the world that someone is being mistreated. It should take a leadership role in changing prejudiced attitudes. Instead, it has become a co-conspirator in the persecution; it establishes rules of conduct that conform to the status quo.

Jim and I are better persons for having gone through this experience. It served to bring us closer. It has given us more strength to love each other and others. We now realize that our common fate is not bound by the four walls of a building that sits on a corner, but is determined by the fact that we love our brothers and sisters whether gay or straight, Black or White, male or female.

STRUGGLES OF A BLACK PENTECOSTAL

James S. Tinney

I AM A BLACK. I am gay. I am Pentecostal. Talk about a multiple frame of reference, or about a multiple sense of oppression, and you will have a pretty good ideal of what I have felt and experienced in my 30-some years.

Let no one feel pity, however. The purpose of this article is not to cause sympathy, but to share some of the creative tensions which these identities represent, and to try to locate those particular strengths which have made it possible to say, at last, I am also proud of all that I am. In addition, it seems important to take a look at the mutual and disparate facets of each of these personal elements of identity.

The road to the present feeling of assurance has not been an easy one. I have not always felt good about who I am; and I have sometimes, in the past, attempted to deny myself as myself. But I am constantly reminded of a woman evangelist I often heard say, "Be what you is; 'cause if you ain't what you is, you can't be what you ain't."

It would be hard to say which of the points of reference were impressed upon my psyche the earliest. Certainly, none of them came easily or automatically. I struggled with my Blackness because I was so light-skinned I could have "passed" for White, were it not for the sense of history and heritage which my grandmother (a proud Black woman who had taught school when no one else was available, just to keep the doors of a one-room Black schoolhouse open) passed on to me.

I could also have "passed" for straight because my appearance and mannerisms have never been pronouncedly feminine (at least not to those who were unfamiliar with the subtle signals gays send out). And I was married for a time and am the father of two children. But as early as I can remember, even at the age of four, I

167

was emotively and sexually drawn to men.

I could also have been something other than Pentecostal. After all, I was neither dark-skinned, poorly educated, nor religiously deprived—characteristics often believed typical of "us sanctified folk." And I was a frequent visitor at churches of all types, a student leader of an interdenominational fellowship group, and later an enrollee at a non-Pentecostal theological seminary. While a revisionist in some senses, I was by nature also mystically inclined, ardent in my zeal for God, and most content and happy when in the middle of a deeply moving spiritual ecstasy.

I could also have been swept away by non-intellectual pursuits. It was true, from the first, that few, if any, of my friends shared the academic interests I did. No different from them in other respects, I too was prone to waste my time with play, sex, "getting high," and other less-lofty concerns. But I was also physically challenged in that my feet didn't work right (I had barely any ankle movement), so while others played ball or ran the streets, I stayed in the house and read books. They were saturated in interests of pursuing women, money and sports—three things that did not especially interest me. Instead I developed an interior life, a heightened curiosity of mind, and a habit of reflecting on the serious problems of life.

To say all this, however, is not to say that I never tried to be anything other than myself. As perhaps most of us do at times, I too wondered what it would be like to be *not* Black, *not* gay, *not* Pentecostal. Sometimes I played games with other people (and sometimes, confessedly, with myself) which were intended to let me escape from these things which seemingly set me off from everybody else and haunted me with a sense of "differentness."

There were times when I just listened to White folks talk about us "Colored folks," and dared not open my mouth. There were times when I let them write down "White male" on my driver's license application, and when I attended a predominantly White school, and when I visited White churches—always wondering if anyone knew, or if anyone could tell I was Black. If they found out, I hauntingly questioned, what would they do to me? How would they react?

Similarly, there were a lot of years when I kept my gayness to myself, never sharing it with anyone except those with whom I went to bed or a few close friends I also knew to be gay. Even now, while I have become very self-assured about taking my stand on political rights for gay people, I still find myself asking, "Do they all really know I am making a personal statement by doing this?" It is easy to be gay (even to try to act gay) when I am cruising someone I want to have sex with, or when I am a stranger in an unknown city, or when I am in gay environs; but I find it harder to express my gayness on my job, when I am in the company of business or professional friends, and especially when I am at church. I believe that my job was once in jeopardy because everyone knew I was gay (I soon left on my own course); and I have already experienced the total rejection and the object-of-concern relationship which developed when it became known at one church that I was gay.

Curiously, perhaps, I have never been ashamed of being Pentecostal, although I often hasten to let others know that I am a revised or reconstructed edition—that I am free to drink or dance, yet still adamantly proclaim that I do go to church every Sunday, do "get my step in" when I worship, and do speak in tongues. In fact, there is a certain "safety" about religious rebellion (in the sense of being a proud member of an alternative religion): it does not have the same risks about it as do the facts of Blackness or gayness.

One of the most important things about my identity is the way in which one characteristic modifies or enhances another characteristic.

Take church, for example. It is probably no accident that I am a member of a Pentecostal church. After all, that is reputed to be the "Blackest" form of religion, as well as the "gayest." Historians of religion are pretty well agreed that there are more surviving Africanisms (the drums, the dance, the state of possession, the emphasis on spirits, the ecstatic speech known as tongues, the healing magic, the use of inanimate objects which are blessed and transmit blessing) in Pentecostalism than in any other religion in the diaspora. My faith, then, certainly reinforced that sense of historical continuity with the Africanity in my heritage, as well as compensated for my lack of melanin.

Pentecostalism is the "earthly heaven" for sissies (and closeted homosexuals) of all types. Estimates of the percentage of Pentecostal members who are gay run as high as 70 percent. Who can know for sure? Certainly, there is no quarrel about the fact that obviously gay, flamboyant and queenly males and masculine-type females exist in abounding numbers in Pentecostal churches—more so than in other faiths. If our churches were to instantly get rid of the homosexuals in them, they would cease to remain "Pentecostalist." For the gospel choirs and musicians (the mainstay and pivot of our "liturgy") would certainly disappear.

There was a sense, of course, in which the "holiness or hell" judgment was continually applied to homosexuals. Cognitive dissonance was painful, as a result, for most of my earliest years.

But there was another side to it all. I could not grow up in a religious environment wherein a majority of my spiritual teachers and preachers and shouters and other liturgical actors were known to me to be gay (sometimes also being my own bedmates), without feeling that, despite their disclaimers, homosexuality could not be altogether wrong.

Despite the anti-sexual theme which characterizes much of Pentecostal preaching, a certain practical tolerance of variant sexual activities (including both hetero- and homosexual acts) exuded itself. The conscious way in which the presence of homosexuality was recognized (whether approved or not) contributed to a feeling that it was really no worse than women wearing open-toe shoes or saints missing a mid-week prayer meeting. In such an atmosphere the mind easily reaches its own conclusions: either the church doesn't take seriously its own preachments or else homosexuality is as culturally and temporally conditioned as the stricture against wearing red (which also fell into abuse and then disuse and finally joyful change).

Two other things about the interrelationship between my religion and my gayness should also be mentioned. One is negative; the other positive.

First, the negative. My reconciliation of faith and sexuality did not occur without some trauma. Sometimes this took the form of fear. I early learned to beware of the guest evangelist who was a closeted gay and who delighted in prophesying over me about my homosexuality. While (to their credit) this type rarely exposed my "problem" aloud to the congregation, but rather prophesied quietly in my ear, the easy way in which this elicited a penitent response was useful in convincing the audience of that evangelist's "gift." Few realized that it was the fellow-gay's "sixth sense" (really a mutual recognition of discreet signals of mannerisms and speech and dress) that had brought the accurate reading.

There was also the breakup of my marriage which, because it occurred within the church family, was accompanied by unusually stressful incidents. After three years and two children, I announced to my wife that I was gay. She immediately called the pastor and his wife and other close confidants to pray for me. Pray and talk and counsel they did. Because this whole sequence really marked my own "coming out," it happened at a time when my own reconciling of faith and sex was unfinished. Thus I was once a subject of an attempted exorcism. That in itself was extremely painful to my own sense of worth and well-being. It was an experience I would not wish upon anyone ever.

But there were also positives. Most important, it was the Pentecostal church which furnished me with the only two lovers I ever had—one a minister and one a laymember. Each of these relationships involved a monogamous living together; and each lasted about two years.

These relationships took place within the context of full church life. Two separate churches in two different cities were involved—neither of which was the same congregation my wife and I had formerly belonged to. In each instance my lover was already an active part of the congregation. As was I. And in each case, we both continued very active roles in the church. I, for example, served as an adult church teacher.

The members, of course, knew what was going on. But if they talked about it, they did not approach us with it. Perhaps because we did not flaunt our relationship by displaying overt affection at church meetings, we were able to feel accepted, loved, and even honored for our faithfulness to the church. We always attended all church-related functions together; and we were invited as a pair to dinner nearly every Sunday at someone's home. The unintended lesson which became obvious to us was that the Black Pentecostal church reacted negatively when a social construct within the church was broken (as in the exorcism-attended divorce from my wife), but reacted positively when no such marital contract was threatened. The key seems to have been the orderly life of the church, which could be maintained when my lover and I "did our own thing" at home but continued to work and testify within the church in a way in which internal social networks were not disrupted. Curiously though, while this practice of homosexuality between the two of us church members was tolerated, the presence of visiting open gays who were not regular attendants or members would nearly always elicit negative remarks in sermons or post-meeting conversations among the "saints."

So for me, the story has a pleasant ending. I have found within the church an affirmation of my Blackness and my faith; and I have been able to reconcile my sexual orientation and my religion. It has not been easy, however, and others without the internal stimulation that intellectual inquiry occasions, have found it easier to leave the church than to arrive at affirmation of Blackness or reconciliation of faith with sexuality. For them, I am sure, the testimony of what it means to be gay and Pentecostal is quite different.

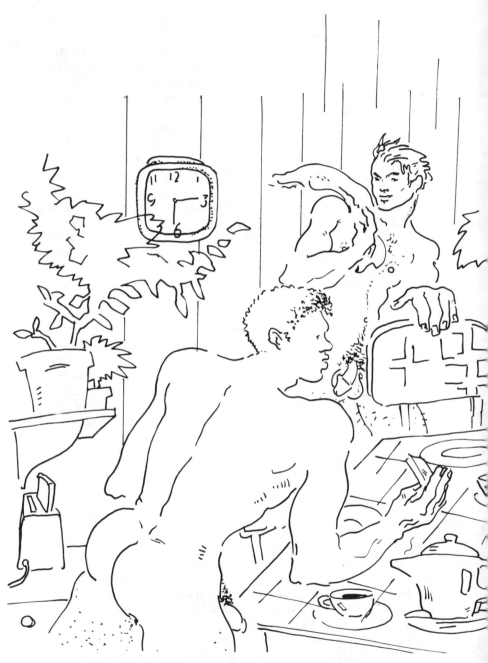

Drawing: Ross Paxton, 1983

THE REUNION
A Short Story

Paul Thomas Cahill

Julius Griffin pulled the patio drapes open and revealed a morning shrouded in fog. "Just another beautiful summer day in San Francisco," he mused. How he longed for a smoggy but sunny-bright L.A. "Perhaps," he said aloud to himself, "the day will improve with a cup of coffee." The ringing of the phone interrupted him.

"Hello," he yawned into the receiver. "David Madison, you tired queen. What are you doing up at this ungodly hour?—Is it nine o'clock already?—I was just this minute gonna put on a pot of coffee.—Well, just let yourself in when you get here. I'll probably still be in the shower."

After Mr. Coffee had been set to do his thing, Julius stepped into the black marble-tiled shower. The pulsating spray from the cyclomassage slowly brought him to consciousness. If only he hadn't had that last gin before closing, his head wouldn't be throbbing so much. At least his stomach was in good shape. He suddenly became aware, as he soaked up the warmth from the water, that he'd lost track of the time. He shut off the stream and grabbed a towel, dabbing at enough of the wetness to keep from dripping all over the apartment. He walked to the dining room and found David sitting at the table with two steaming cups of coffee poured.

"What's cookin' sweet thing?", David purred. He was thirty-two, but looked to be a well-preserved twenty-five. His piercing blue eyes sparkled beneath his straw-thatched curls.

"Nothin' but hot Julius Griffin," Julius fired back. He flipped his towel in David's direction, snapping the end for punctuation.— "Even at ten o'clock in the morning on a foggy Saturday in San Francisco." Water droplets fell from his still wet hair and rolled down his firm, ebony bicep. "Did you happen to think to call George and Dan before you left home?"

"Is the Pope a Pollack?...I spoke to George. Dan was still in the sack. Poor girl needs all the beauty sleep she can get. They're gonna meet us at the 'Gardens' at eleven-thirty."

"Shit, it's almost ten-fifteen, now! I'd better get some rags on. Have I got time for this cup?" Julius wrapped the towel around his head, turban-style, and sat down at the table.

"You'd better get it into gear." David shook his head, accusingly. "You know about your well-developed sense of...what do you people call it...uh...CP time?"

"Was that an ethnic slur, paddy?" Julius flashed a pearly grin. "I'll be ready in two shakes of...a big, black dick. Hmmm, you wouldn't by any chance want to shake mine, would ya?" He smiled again and winked.

"I'm no fucking' pervert," David intoned in mock innocence. "I think you ought to be reported to the N. Double A. C. P. — the "National Association for the Abandonment of Cute People." Julius had moved to the bed room. "Besides, it ain't that big!" David shouted after him.

Julius appeared in the doorway, tugging on his tightest jeans. David couldn't resist one more swipe.

"How're you gonna get ALL THAT into those tiny, little pants? Be careful you don't bruise nothin'."

"I ain't had no bruises," Julius protested, "since the last one I got from you, sissy."

He should have been a GQ model, the way he looked in jeans and a t-shirt. His one hundred ninety pounds were economically hung on his six-foot frame. When Julius F. Griffin walked into a room, everyone took notice, not the least of which was David Madison. He had "had the hots" for Julius for several months, but for some unconscious reason, he couldn't find the courage to approach Julius in any serious way. They had developed a solid friendship over the past two years, but Julius seemed to steer clear of conversations regarding love and relationships. Especially as the idea applied to him. He rarely spoke of his past, and David assumed that he wasn't interested, in him or in a relationship— period.

When Julius returned to the table, he was fully dressed, including a pair of suede western-style boots. They were his favorite pair, given to him as a birthday gift by his former lover, Rodger, whom he hadn't seen in over five years. They had met shortly after Julius' twenty-fourth birthday and had been together for six years. The light glistened on a drop of moisture in the corner of his right eye. He gulped some cold coffee. "What," he asked David, "did you do, or should I say *who?* after the bar threw you out last night?"

"Honey, your sister was so fucked up, she nearly fell out into a trash bin. How I made it home in one piece is a miracle known only to Jesus, Mary and What's-his-name. A devilish smile spread between his dimpled cheeks.

"Queen, you were sucking dick in the schoolyard again—don't lie!"

"If I was, I sure don't remember it. Say," he said, looking at his watch, "we better get moving—it's after eleven."

"All right, already. You White folks never have gotten over cracking that ole plantation whip."

"I was only tr—"

"Jus' funnin' wit ya, massuh. I's right behin' ya. Y'all jus' go an' stahts de cah, an' I goes an' locks de doah."

David tried to force a laugh. He always felt uncomfortable when Julius went into his Stepin Fechit routine. He didn't understand why. It seemed to gnaw away at some secret corner of his unconscious. He dismissed it as evidence of any latent racist feelings. David had always found Black men attractive, and that couldn't be if he were a closet Klansman. He'd have to think about it some more.

Julius opened the passenger door just as David turned the key in the ignition.

"All set," he asssured.

They were soon in motion. It was a ten to fifteen minute ride from Julius' place in the Sunset, over Twin Peaks, to the Castro. At the crest of the hill on Portola, the fog could already be seen burning off over the bay. David was unusually quiet.

"Something on your mind, young man?" Julius inquired.

"Nothing of any earth-shaking importance," he replied.

As they pulled onto Eighteenth Street, David spotted a parking place in front of the Pendulum, the popular interracial bar in the Castro.

"This is just great!" Julius whined. "You know how much I like this toilet. Can't you find another space?"

"We're almost late as it is," David responded. "Put a bag over your head, and no one will notice."

Julius threw him a glance that would have withered Joan Crawford and got out of the car. He dropped three hours' worth of change into the meter as David joined him at the curb. Together, they walked the block and a half to the 'Gardens'.

It was a new restaurant on Castro, quite pleasant in atmosphere, and reasonably-priced. Or, at least, as reasonable as you could expect in the 'Village'. George and Dan were waiting at the front door. Dan made a big show of looking at his watch.

"Don't start, Miss Perfection," David said with a hint of exasperation. "It's only eleven-thirty-five—that's on time in San Francisco."

"It's eleven-forty-five," Dan replied, "and you're late for anywhere." Dan Watson was about five foot three, with the temperament of a banty rooster, and a quick wit to match.

"Shall we go in?" George interjected. He was almost a full head taller than Dan, and looked as though he had once lifted weights.

By San Francisco standards, their three year relationship was long-lasting. They were rarely found "hanging out", and spent most of their time at home or going out together. They were quite comfortable in their monogamy, though they took quite a little disbelieving comments from some of their friends.

The four of them were seated out on the patio. The sun was nearly completely out. The waiter brought coffee.

"I'll have the Eggs Benedict," David began.

"I think I'll try the Spinach Omelette," Julius added. "Greens keep me lookin' young...and *good!*"

"What do you think, Dan? George asked. "You feel up to a Crab and Shrimp Omelette?"

"Why not," Dan replied. "As long as that was not one of your 'short people' jokes!" George winked at Julius.

"What did you two do last night," David asked, "as if I didn't know?"

"We stayed in," Dan said. "I had a bitch of a day at work, and George had a day off, so he spent it painting the den. Neither of us felt like going out. I suppose you closed the Pendulum?"

"That's what I've been told, but I don't honestly remember much beyond twelve-thirty. It all seems to run together," David explained.

Dan shook his head. "When are you gonna settle down? What you need is a good husband. You, too, Julius. You know, it's been some time since Rodger split. You can't remain a widow forever."

David smiled. Julius pretended not to hear. The conversation droned on, but Julius was paying only partial attention. He excused himself to go to the restroom.

The entrance to the men's room was not well-lit, and someone was coming out just as he was about to go in. The figure was silhouetted against the interior light, but a familiar shape is only slightly dimmed by the passage of five years.

"Rodger?" Julius said, catching a lump in his throat. "Is that you, Rodger?"

"I beg your pardon, but you must have me mistaken for someone else," the stranger said.

He turned abruptly and hurried from the restaurant. Julius stood in the doorway of the men's room, staring after the vanished figure.

Julius lay back on the sofa, one hand cradling the back of his head. Except for the faint hum of the refrigerator and the ticking of the mantle clock, the apartment was filled with silence. It had been exactly two weeks since the brunch at the 'Gardens'. Sleep had not come easy, and he had kept the telephone unplugged. He hadn't gone out. He wanted to be alone.

Memories of happier times were everywhere. A crystal decanter and matching glasses were set up on the buffet. They were a gift from Rodger on their first anniversary. A bronze replica of Rodin's Thinker, Rodger's thirtieth birthday present, sat on the desk. A painting of the Golden Gate bridge was hung on the wall over the mantle clock; it had been a fifth anniversary gift from Rodger's mother. Julius had not been able to part with any of the reminders.

On the cocktail table lay a small wrinkled five-by-seven piece of paper with a few short sentences written on it in Rodger's unmistakable scrawl.

"My dearest love," the note began, *"the last thing on earth I want to do is hurt you. I cannot continue this way any more. I can't deal with the pressure. It's tearing me apart inside. You will be much better without me. All my never-ending love, Rodger."*

Rodger had packed a suitcase and had gone by the time Julius had returned from work. There had been no outward signs of problems. No serious arguments. No infidelities. Nothing that Julius could put his finger on. But, Rodger had been acting somewhat distant the few weeks before he had left. In fact, just the day before, Julius had asked him what was wrong, but Rodger had put him off with the usual "nothing" and had refused to comment further. The ache in Julius' heart was as intense today as it had been that day five years earlier.

The image of the man in the restroom doorway still haunted him. Was it Rodger? Of course it was — it had to be. But then perhaps the feeling was more wishful thinking than from certain knowledge. Julius got up from the sofa and went to the wall and plugged in the disconnected phone. He stabbed a finger at a remembered sequence of buttons.

"David," he said, when he heard a familiar greeting. "What are you doing?—I'm sorry," he apologized. "I should have first asked *how* you were doing?"

"Well, it's about time, Miss Disappearance," David scolded. "Where have you been?" No one has seen or heard from you in two weeks. There's been no answer when I've phoned. I've worn my dialing finger down to the knuckle. 'Fraid you might have been taken by jungle rot. What was it? Some fantastic out-of-towner?"

"Don't I wish, but hardly," Julius replied. "I've been staying in. Uh, mind if I come over?" I...need to...talk to someone, and, uh, I can't think of anyone else."

"That doesn't exactly sound like a vote of confidence, but I'll let it slide. This time only. What's the problem?"

"I'll tell you when I see you. About half an hour?"

"I'll be here, waiting. With balls on."

"Don't you ever stop? 'Bye."

Julius replaced the receiver in its cradle and thought of unplugging the phone again, then decided against the idea. He walked over to the patio door and observed the plants and flowers basking in the sunlight. Rodger had bought and planted most of them. He opened the door, and took a breath of warm, sweet-scented air. He turned away from the patio and headed toward the bedroom to change clothes when the phone rang.

"Damn!" he said out loud. "I should have unplugged the bitch!" He thought of not answering, but then thought that it might be David calling back.

"Hello," he said, his voice cracking from dry mouth.

"Julius?" the voice on the other end inquired after a brief pause. Julius froze. The voice was as unmistakable and unforgettable as was the handwriting or the silhouette. "Julius, is that you?—Are you there?—Hello!"

"I...I'm...uh...here," he said, his voice slowly dropping to a whisper. "It's...uh...me. Where...a-are...you?"

"I'm here, in San Francisco. It was me you ran into in the restaurant two weeks ago. I wasn't expecting to see you, not so soon. I just panicked. I wasn't ready. Wanted to get settled in and then call you, but, well, life plays its little tricks. How have you been?"

"I've been...fine...just...fine," Julius lied. He was beginning to regain some control over his voice. Sweat had broken out on his forehead. A zillion thoughts raced through his brain, all screaming to express themselves. He sensed that if he tried to speak about any of them, he would end up babbling, so he forced out a weak "how have you been?"

"I have been doing about as well as I could, in light of the fact that I have been...well...I'd rather not go into that just now. I was wondering, uh, could I, maybe, like, drop over this afternoon? I'd really like to see you and talk to you. That is, if you can spare the time?"

Julius was thinking quickly now. He didn't want to see Rodger, not after five years' absence, in the same environment that they had shared together. That would be too much to bear.

"I'm...uh...right in the middle...of...uh...painting the apartment, and...the...uh...place is a holy mess." Julius hated lying, and he had never lied to Rodger. In the eleven years he had known him, this was the first. But he had to get the situation in proper perspective, and he needed some time. Time away from home base. "Maybe I could meet you somewhere?"

"Well, I was really looking forward to coming by the apartment, but I do understand. How about the 'Gardens', in...say...an hour?"

"Sounds okay by me. In an hour, then. 'Bye."

Julius stood in the middle of the room, holding the phone until the wail of the off-the-hook signal reminded him to hang up. Though tears were streaming down both cheeks, he fought to maintain control. He couldn't afford to lose it, not now. He phoned David.

"Something's come up, and I won't be able to make it this afternoon. I'll call you tomorrow."

He changed clothes. He picked up the wrinkled note and carefully folded it and put it into his wallet. He closed the patio door and turned on a lamp, just in case he was gone past sundown. He looked around the room—at the decanter, the statue and the painting. He wiped his face and blew his nose. He grabbed a jacket and went out to the garage. He started his car and backed out into the street, forgetting to close the garage door. It had been five minutes since he had spoken to Rodger, and five years since he had seen him. The zillion thoughts kept coming, but one stood out from all the rest. He was going to get the answer to at least one question: Why?

Foot traffic on Castro was light for a Saturday afternoon. Julius sat at a window table in the 'Gardens' and waited for Rodger's arrival. He glanced at his watch. It had been twenty minutes since he had spoken to Rodger. He hadn't planned to be quite so early, but momentum had taken charge and Julius found himself sitting at the table, nursing a gin and tonic and watching the passing parade.

The thoughts, questions and feelings were beginning to form themselves into some order. The last thing he wanted to do when Rodger arrived was to lose control. He was not a weak person emotionally, but he had always believed that giving expression to true feelings was proper and necessary. He had always been open and honest with Rodger and believed that Rodger had been the same with him. That is, until the few weeks prior to his departure.

As he sat and thought, his feelings alternated between anger and hurt. He thought that he would have been able to better deal with it if only he knew why. There had been no indication, other than Rodger's growing withdrawal, of any problems. Certainly nothing tangible. The one thing which was certain was that there was a problem—people don't usually run away from happiness. He ordered another drink.

"Julius! Julius Griffin!" a voice called from behind. Julius turned his head, and his heart sank. It was Artie Maxwell, an acquaintance of long standing. "I haven't seen you in an age—where ya been keeping yourself these days?"

"Oh, I've been around. Nothin' special. And you?"

"Same ol' same ol', you know. You married yet?" Julius shook his head. He wasn't in the mood for small talk. Artie made a few more trivial comments and excused himself. Julius turned back to the window and his drink.

Another voice came from behind.

"Mind if I sit down?" the familiar voice for which Julius had been waiting inquired.

"By all means. Certainly. I mean, that's why we're here, isn't it?" Rodger pulled the chair back and sat down. An awkward silence followed. Finally, when it seemed as thought the whole world were about to explode, Julius spoke.

"You're looking well. These past five years have been kind to you." He wished now that he hadn't agreed to meet Rodger. Not under these circumstances. He fingered the folded piece of wrinkled paper. He unfolded it and laid it on the table, smoothing it out deliberately. Then, slowly picking it up, he looked Rodger in the eye and held it out to him.

"It's been five years since we've seen each other," Julius continued. A lot has happened since, and apparently a lot had happened just before. This note you left me marks the turning point. It might be a good point to begin." He was steady now, in full control. He had Rodger pinned to the wall, and nothing short of a full explanation would do.

Rodger took the note and read it, or at least appeared to. "You're right about a lot having happened. Both before and after I wrote this. I was going through unbearable pressures and I couldn't find any—"

"I must be mistaken, but I thought, after six years together, we could talk—that communication was not a problem. What happened? Did you stop loving me?"

"Hell, no!" Rodger shot back. "I have never loved you less than when we first met, and never more than I do now. It's just that...well...it's a long story."

"I've got the time. After all these years, I'm all ears."

"Do you remember when I got that promotion at the office and a small increase in salary along with it?" Julius nodded. "Three weeks later, you got a promotion and a larger increase. Then my Aunt Lillian died and left me six thousand dollars. A couple of months later, when we went to Reno, you won a big jackpot. Then one of my poems was selected to be published in an anthology, and you received that award for your community work. Every time something good happened in my life, you came along and topped me. I couldn't win."

Julius shook his head. "I didn't realize our relationship was based on...competition. If anyone should have been competitive, it should have been me. Remember, *I* grew up with the nine brothers and four sisters. *I* had to fight for everything—and we didn't have much to fight over. Besides, I know you are an intelligent man, and what you have just described are situations based largely on chance. You'll forgive me, but I think I smell some bullshit here. I think the problem is more basic than that."

Rodger played with his moustache. "I've spent the past five years living in New York, working part time and writing a lot. During that time, I had seven lovers—er, well, long-term boy friends, I guess you'd say. When Timothy, the last one, and I called it quits a few weeks ago, well, it was very upsetting. I decided to take some time off and do some serious re-evaluating."

"'Bout time, I should think. Tell me—something I'm curious about—were they...all...Black?"

"As a matter of fact, no! I met Arthur when I first hit New York. He was English and we lasted six months. Then came Julio, who was Puerto Rican—Julio is Spanish for Julius, I suppose you know. The rest were...Black—George, Richard, Michael, Jeffrey and Timothy."

"Do you detect a slight trend?" Julius asked.

Rodger shifted in his chair and looked out the window. "It was just that realization that prompted me to reflect. I had never before been involved with a Black man until I met you. I had never had any Black friends—hell, my home town was ninety-nine and forty-four one hundredths percent Ivory Snow. I was attracted to Black men for as long as I can remember. It just took me a long time to finally admit it openly to myself. I'm still not sure I understand why. I guess it's just because I am—like some prefer blonds with blue eyes." He paused. "Never having come into contact with Black people in a personal way, I simply didn't understand the environment. I had years of stereotypes and preconceptions of how Blacks behaved, believed, and loved. During our five years together, I loved you, but I never really got to know you, because you failed to live up to what I expected of you."

"Which was...?" Julius looked into Rodger's eyes.

"I'm not sure that I can put it into words, exactly."

"Why not try—you might learn something from the experience, as well as me."

Rodger excused himself to order a drink. Julius could see that he was having a difficult time. He didn't want to be too hard on Rodger, but five years of frustration and pain had worn his patience thin. When Rodger returned, he had bought a drink for Julius.

"I still remember your drink at least," he said, pulling the chair closer to the table. "My understanding of what was happening in our relationship, and in my own thoughts and feelings, didn't begin to crystalize until after Timothy and I parted. You know how 'in charge' I always was. I'd been on my own—taken control of my own destiny, so to speak, since I was fifteen."

"Yeah, you were a little impossible. I gave in to you and let you handle things like the finances only because it seemed so important to you."

"It was life and habit with me, and I...didn't think...must not have thought...that it was something you had any concern for."

"You mean, the ignorant colored boy, refugee from the ghetto, never had none, wouldn't never get none, and if he ever did, by accident, get some, he'd jus' piss it all away—is that it?"

"I never thought that. At least, not in those words. I mean, I knew you were educated. Had a good job. Were stable—I knew all that, consciously. It just didn't fit in with my preconceptions. I loved you, but I was threatened by your successes. I couldn't be in charge, couldn't take care of you as I thought I was expected to, not when we were...equals."

Julius turned these words over in his mind carefully, uncovering things in his own thoughts he had not been aware of before. "You took our relationship for granted because you had never questioned your beliefs. You couldn't communicate your fears and discomforts because the reasons were not conscious to you. And since I believed that our communication was open and honest, I never questioned you about your growing withdrawal. In that respect, I guess I must bear some share of the responsibility."

"I don't blame you. How could you know when I didn't know myself? After I left and time passed, and one broken affair followed on the heels of another, only then did I begin to get a sense that I might be doing something wrong. I spent several weeks thinking. I even wrote down descriptions of each of my relationships and tried to find common threads. Then I remembered something Timothy said to me just before we broke up. He said, 'Your problem, Rodger, is that you can't deal with a Black man who is as successful as you are, successful in life. God forbid you should ever tangle with one who's way ahead.' It was like the wall of ignorance that had been built around my life had suddenly been blown down, allowing fresh light in from the outside world. I could see things so clearly, for the first time. I cried for a long time, because I now realized I had run from the wrong problem. I thought I was runing from you, when it was me I was running from, and damn!, I had taken the problem with me to New York."

It was getting dark now. The ice had nearly melted in the untouched drinks. Rodger fell silent. He was holding Julius' hand. Julius could tell there was little strength left in him to continue. He had his answer. He knew and understood why Rodger had written the note and left. He felt sorrow, anger and a little pity; but he also felt relief, as though a slab of granite had fallen from his shoulders. Funny, he thought, Rodger had to tear down an entire wall, while he had had to deal with only one block, but both were gone now, the wall and block.

Julius' living room was bathed in total darkness. The ticking of the mantle clock was the only sound to be heard. Julius had been sitting alone and quiet since he had returned from the 'Gardens' two hours before. All during their meeting, he had feared Rodger would get around to asking in some way, if they could...if it were possible to consider...their getting back together. When Rodger had finally suggested it, Julius had prepared himself. He needed time to adjust, to sort out the remaining conflicts. Julius had said that he would have to think about it, that it was too soon to give an answer just like that, but that he would call soon.

Julius became aware of light. He had fallen asleep in the chair. He got up and showered. He fixed some coffee, and puttered around the apartment. His mind kept turning over the conversation with Rodger. He picked his way through eleven years of peaks and valleys. He savored the pleasures and cried over the pains. And now he understood. After all that had happened. After all that had been said. The decision was actually quite simple. He picked up the phone.

"Hello!" the voice said.

"Hi! It's Julius. I've finally gotten a few things in perspective, and I was wondering if you'd like to have dinner with me tonight?"

"Love to," the voice responded. "What time?"

"How 'bout if I pick you up around nine?"

"Sounds great? I'll be ready."

"See ya then. 'Bye."

Julius smiled. He carefully replaced the phone in its cradle. He took a leisurely shower. He went through his wardrobe and picked out his tightest pair of Levi's, a clean white t-shirt and his favorite suede boots. He slipped on his matching suede jacket with the fringe. He checked himself out in the mirror and nodded approval. He glanced at his watch and noted the time. It was almost eight-thirty. "Got to get moving," he said aloud. He paused in front of the hall mirror and looked at himself hard in the eyes. "Julius, my boy," he spoke to the reflection, "it is most definitely true—you can't go back, only forward, and you've stood still long enough! Now, let's not keep David Madison waiting."

"A FINE WHITE BOY"
A True Story

Gabe Sims

IT WAS ANOTHER typical night in My Way, a gay bar in Shreveport. I was the only Black in the club. As I was sitting there, in walked a White dude. He was wearing a short-sleeved shirt, his bow legs clad in faded Levis and boots. The way he walked in and stood by the bar seemed natural to me, not clonish at all. Matter of fact he looked like some redneck from a small town near Shreveport. The hour grew late and I got up to go home. As I left, his eyes followed me out. I spoke to him, but he didn't answer which pissed me off. "At least he could've spoke!" I said angrily to myself, promising never to even look at him next time I saw him.

Thursday, to someone in Shreveport, is like the dawn to the day, for Thursday night is the beginning to the weekend and partying. At the My Way bar it's show night, and I'm there in the crowded bar, in the midst of the Black gays, partying, dancing, and clowning with the drags on stage. Shreveport is prejudiced by custom, and this prejudice extends to the gay ghetto. In the gay bars, there is a Black section and a White section where the Black and White gays gather respectively. For a Black to go to the White Section or a White to go to the Black Section is a climactic event only for the daring. Even I, liberal as I consider myself, rarely cross that line. If I see a White friend, I usually wait until he passes our section, and *if* he speaks, I speak.

In walked again this White dude. He looks at me and merely walks to the Black section, through my surprised Black friends, introduces himself as Bob, and asks me to dance! Amazed, I dance with him feeling everybody's eyes on us. After the dance, Bob fades into the Whites, and I return to my seat.

When the second show starts, Bob comes over and sits with me. We talk about each other, our jobs, interests. We also talk about the Rainbow Connection, a gay bar in Longview, Texas that is open on Sundays. Bob stated that he has never been there. I told Bob that if he ever wanted to go, he can go with me, for I go there every Sunday. He said okay and we traded numbers.

Friday afternoon, I just arrived from classes at LSU. The phone rang, I answered it, and it was Bob! He invited me to come to his home in Sibley, a town 20 miles from Shreveport and spend the evening.

I knocked on his door. He answered, clad only in some tight- fitting gym shorts, a fine White boy! He offered me some wine "to take the cold out." I stripped to my running shorts and laid on him, on the couch, my head resting on his crotch. There I was, a 6' 3½" nigger cuddling on the couch with a short, muscular White redneck with my feet sticking over the couch! I smiled at this to myself. In response to my smile, he smiled and began to kiss me. I felt his hard stomach against my ear and my mouth, my tongue tasting his tongue which was tinged with wine, my brown eyes looking into his blue eyes. Then Bob lit a joint which we both smoked. Afterwards we started kissing again, both high off the wine, the dope and each other. I felt his cock hardening under my head and my cock enlarging spread down my leg out of my running shorts.

He got up, taking me by hand to his bed, a low bed. I laid down and he lit a large candle by the bed and joined me. I started first, biting his neck working down to his tits, sucking them. I then started licking his stomach, his muscular legs and blowing his cock, as slow and intense as I can. I enter Bob, thrusting slow and hard, kissing him all over again until I climax, afterward laying down beside him still hot.

He then starts to make love to me, his short body climbing all over me. He bites into my neck, my tits and begins to play mouth music with my cock. Then, as silent as the burning candle, he turns me on my stomach, placing a pillow under me. He enters me, screwing me as loving and hard and gentle as I did him, and licking me softly across my back. He climaxes and I turn over to look at him. Again we look eye to eye at each other, blue eyes into brown eyes. He lays closer to me and I allow him to sleep in my arms. We softly talk to each other until we fall asleep in the candlelight.

INTERVIEW: BWMT
FOUNDER—MIKE SMITH

Thom Beame

I'D RATHER TALK about the movement and what I've learned," says Mike Smith, who seems to consider the other accomplishments of his life "not all that important." The 'movement' is Black and White Men Together (which he founded) and 'what he's learned' about minority concerns could fill a book. In fact, it will: Gay Sunshine Press is publishing the first anthology of Gay Black and Black/White writings, in which this interview is being printed, and Smith is the editor. This follows close on the heels of his news-making story of Glenn Burke ("The Dodger Who was Gay," *Inside Sports*, October, 1982). And all this in addition to his occupation— and pre-occupation—the *Quarterly*, a magazine "which promotes the interests of the more than 100 interracial and Third World gay and lesbian groups." So that's what the mysterious little *Advocate* ad—"Black/White, Asian, Latin."—is all about.

Something of an individualist, though not a glory-seeker, Smith downplays praise and kudos. Defarge-like in meetings, Smith is a handsome, no-nonsense activist. Yet he's philosophical, idealistic— and humorous ("when you get to know me"). Smith also is a successful businessman, published composer, lecturer, and Woodrow Wilson Fellow from Harvard. Most importantly, he's put four full years of his time, his energy—and his money—where his lifestyle is: into his brainchild, Black and White Men Together. One wonders, how did a "pretty White boy" from Harvard get himself mixed up in all this.

"Like most people, I guess, I come from a lily-White background. I'm lucky, though, to have had parents who wouldn't tolerate prejudice of any kind. And yet it was years before I realized that that's barely a beginning."

How so? "To disparage racism is one thing. To resist is another. I've been gay all my life, but it wasn't until minorites began appearing in the gay community that I realized I was attracted to Black men."

Sexuality came first? "Yes, but even then I had no idea of the subtlety of racism. Contrary to popular belief, bedding down with Blacks doesn't necessarily make one less racist."

The reverse can be true. "Absolutely."

When did you consciously face the issue? "I'm still facing it! My racism—and sexism and ageism. Actually, real consciousness- raising began when I read the *Autobiography of Malcolm X*. I then read his speeches and everything else I could lay my hands on. What a mind! I even wrote a play about him. But, you know, it's a continuing education. On Thursday I gave a workshop, "Unlearning Racism", and Friday, caught myself being racist."

What happened? "I was having lunch with two friends, one Black, one White. Suddenly I was talking to the White person as if the Black person weren't there. When I realized it, I stopped and owned up to it."

Then and there? "Yes. It's tough sometimes—and awkward. The action had passed unnoticed, so I ran the risk of unnecessarily opening old wounds. But it's part of the 'cure'."

You don't seem to be the "guilty White liberal" type. "Oh, I'm far from that. First of all, I'm not liberal, politically speaking—a fact which annoys some of my friends. Breast-beating just isn't my style. Owning up to racism can be as simple a matter as acknowledging one's limited education. And privilege. If real racism is understood as prejudice that *effects*, prejudice with *power* behind it; and if we recognize that that power—especially economic power—is in the hands of White people, then we can begin putting things in perspective. Racism becomes a White problem, not a Black one. Just as sexism, for example, is a man's problem, not a woman's. We White men have been *taught* an awful lot of crap. But once we realize we don't have to *own* that crap, we're free to become better people. Disowning racism is like coming out all over again—it's that liberating."

That's a logical way of looking at it, but let's get down to the nitty-gritty. What about racism in the gay/lesbian community? "Well, in a word, it's pervasive. In most cities I've visited, people of color are routinely denied admission to, and/or common courtesy in, some bars, baths, and other businesses. In San Francisco, where I live, even though the carding has pretty much stopped, the problem is still what I'd call serious."

How is it manifested? "In employment, for example. BWMT-SF recently surveyed 99 men's bars and found that only about 10% of the employees were people of color. This in a city where more than half its inhabitants are minorities! And, of course, you're aware of the Whites-only image projected by the gay media."

Yes, even the non-gay community has a better record than that. I remember once, as past president of BWMT-SF, trying to get a local gay paper to re-think a racist article they ran and print a letter in response—they ignored me. Why some gay and lesbian people, themselves victims of homophobia, are so insensitive to the oppression of others is incomprehensible. "Well, the silence of the gay men's press *in toto* is deafening. There are papers running discriminatory housing ads, discriminatory employment ads, and nobody seems to care. The *Advocate* is an exception—and I hope you'll put this in. They should know that someone appreciates that they've devoted considerable space to minority concerns. And what's remarkable about this isn't so much the fact that they're the largest gay paper and could easily thumb their nose at the whole issue. No, what's meaningful for me is that, unlike local gay papers, they don't have a vocal constituency to worry about. Yet they've provided forums like this. That kind of sensitivity is uncommon. In discussing a racial issue the other day with the publisher of a San Francisco paper, he suddenly became angry and said, "Everything with you is racism!" Now here's a man who's been involved in the gay movement for twenty years, yet he's never seriously analyzed why there are no Black people employed in the bars—or for that matter, in his office. You can see him grip his desk when the subject comes up. Yet, he's a good person, obviously committed to gay rights. Given the illogic of his stance, I wonder where the problem lies. Maybe I'm just not approaching him correctly."

It's the ego thing. Don't we occasionally run into it with straight people and their attitudes toward gays? Their first instinct is to defend—even if something's indefensible. "Yes, when sometimes it would be so much easier to say 'Maybe you're right—where do we go from here?' "

Why do you think things seem 'better' in the non-gay community? "Well, of course, it would be a mistake to think that gay and lesbian people are somehow worse in this regard. I think rather it's the system. In the 'outside' world, the personnel director of, say, a large corporation can hire a Black person and 'stick him somewhere.' It's impersonal. He doesn't have to deal with the 'hiree' on any personal level. The other employees can't say anything, and the Black person is at least happy to get a foot in the door. Gay/lesbian businesses are much smaller, often owner-operated. Hiring someone usually means working personally with that someone, accepting him or her as a peer."

And Whites, gay or non-gay, aren't ready for that? "Don't get me wrong. I believe Whites when they tell me they have no ill-will toward Blacks—I've been there. They're just unaware of how a racist system is perpetuated. We Whites live and work—and play—among other Whites. We also hold all the cards. The bars, for example, owned almost entirely by Whites, are little more than an Ol' Boy network. Jobs are passed around from one White person to another. There's no open hiring—I mean, when was the last time you saw an ad for bartending in a gay bar?"

Then there are the stories of the qualified Blacks who found out about the jobs—and weren't hired anyway. "Sure. Then racism is overt, vicious. I recall a related incident. BWMT-SF, in coalition with the Third World Lesbian Caucus and the Gay/Lesbian Latinos, had written our gay supervisor concerning a gay sculpture he was attempting to acquire for the City. We argued that the work, depicting four young White people, served only to reinforce the racist (and ageist) imagery which dominates our community, and we asked him to reconsider. While sharing our concern, he nonetheless replied he would continue to pursue the sculpture. In a follow-up conversation with another local figure, I was personally accused of being a spoiler, of dividing the community. When I asked him point blank about racism, he offered the same lip service: 'We appreciate the problem, but it will simply have to wait.' Now, again, I believe these two White men are sincere in their feelings. What they don't comprehend is institutional racism—or they simply don't care. Who created the 'division' in the first place? Whose power perpetuates it?"

You're either part of the solution or you're part of the problem. "Yes. Again, I believe Whites in general don't intend to be part of the problem. But every time we buy a drink in an exclusively-White gay bar, we are. Each time we cash in on our White skin, we reinforce the system. While I'm proud of the gay institutions that have blossomed in the last ten years, my eyes can't help but notice how 'colorless' they are. For example, the gay World Series was held here a few weeks ago and only one of the 12 teams was what I'd call well-integrated. A Southern team, from a city where the population is two-thirds Black, had no Black players! Statistically speaking, that's a real oddity—one in a million—yet no one seemed to notice. 'Business as usual.' Don't we Whites who run the show ever stop to wonder why people of color seem to be missing?"

I know what you mean. There's a bar here in San Francisco which exists on Black gay money, but seems to employ only Whites. What do you think should be done about employment? "Well, we can either await the inevitable, the crisis that comes when people of color have had enough. Or we Whites can exercise our privilege and resolve *our* problem ourselves. We could, for example, establish open-hiring policies, and even offer job training for those interested. After all, how many young White men came to their first bartending job skilled in the trade? Some interested White person took them aside and helped them out. Couldn't we make the same minimal gesture to those we've victimized so long? Imagine too the example we could set for the 'outside' world. Think of the possibilities for coalition-building: gay/lesbian people of color could be our cultural link to other minority groups. When the S.F. bar survey was released, I was approached informally by a few members of the Tavern Guild and the Golden Gate Business Association. These are the two largest groups in the city, yet both are virtually all-White. They asked what could be done, and I suggested starting with a workshop to share ideas. I'd like to think White people would take the initiative. We're capable of it."

And what do you say to people who accuse you of living in a dream world? "I say they are probably right. But rage, no matter how justified, doesn't win allies—it only buries resentment further. I don't have much time for angry people who won't channel their anger constructively. And believe me, ever since I bit all this off, I've gotten it from all sides."

From both Blacks and Whites? "Sure. Some activists seem more interested in expressing their superior knowledge of racism than in sharing that knowledge with others. Indeed, some of the most divisive people have been Whites who've suddenly 'got religion' and hurl hell and damnation on those who haven't. Lord, I'm sure my own impatience has alienated some uninformed, sincere people."

Likewise. But you know, it's hard to tell who's worse—those who, as you put it, 'got religion' or those who don't consider the consequences of their ignorance.—Or those who won't even get involved at all. "That last one's the classic, isn't it—apathetic people, both Black and White, who 'can't be bothered.' Now that it's become chic to be 'out', all the middle-class closet doors are suddenly swinging open. I suppose we'll eventually see that in the BWMT movement too."

Let's talk about BWMT. How did it come about? "It was an intuitive decision. I stood on the corner of Castro and 18th, looked around at all those bars, and thought to myself, There's got to be a better way. So I ran an ad in the *Advocate* and that's where it began. White men who are into Black men are isolated in the gay community. The only time we recognized each other before was when we'd lock horns over a trick in the bar. And for Black men BWMT offered a safe environment where they knew they weren't going to be rejected because of their race."

What was the response? "There was an informal newsletter for three or four months, then groups began forming. The first four were organized Summer, 1980 in San Francisco, Chicago, Boston, and New York. A year later there were thirty groups and we held our first convention in San Francisco, Out of that came the International Association, more groups, and the second convention in Washington D.C. Columbus, Ohio was 1983's site, and Atlanta/Memphis will co-host in 1984. Not bad, eh?"

How do the chapters differ? "They range from activist-minded groups to purely social ones. And there are both big- and small-city groups, all fairly independent."

What do you see as BWMT's main strength? "Well, of course, I'm not a formal spokesperson for BWMT. I can only speak as a member of one local group."

You're too modest. Some would say you've put your own personal stamp on gay history in having founded BWMT. "Thank you for saying that, but there are many men, organizers in every major city, who've guided BWMT. Billy Jones of the National Coalition of Black Gays was an early influence. And, in a sense, the conscience of the women's movement helped too. To answer your original question, the strength of BWMT lies in its diversity and the varied ideas that come from that."

Do you find the activists in conflict with those who want to stress the social side? "We're each unique, and as such, we have potential conflict in a variety of ways. It's funny, I've wondered occasionally why some BWMTers feel the need to hide conflicts that arise. Isn't it the open sharing of conflict that brings growth? Just as the vigor of the gay movement has led gay people to take stock of the quality of their environment, so too BWMT has provided a space for Black and White men to re-evaluate the White world around them. Particularly revealing are the varying levels of consciousness in interracial relationships."

There may be an issue of two separate cultures to consider here. Don't you find that some Black men get swallowed up by the more dominant White culture? "Sure. And, of course, 'dominance' is the key word. It's only human, I suppose, to seek acceptance in the mainstream. There aren't only cultural disparities, but more importantly, economic ones. The White partner in a relationship will often have a greater income than the Black one and, like it or not, that's going to affect them. And sometimes that will lead to a consciousness gap. I've heard Black men lament that their White lovers don't seem to give a damn about racial issues—they won't even come to a BWMT rap."

What do you say to Blacks in that situation? "Close your legs and open your eyes."

And 'open your mind.' "Amen! The reverse occurs as well. More caring White men are getting involved. And even though Black men live with this issue every day of their lives—not just when they think about it—some of them aren't as aware or as assertive as they could be. Yet who am I to intrude if they're happy with their lives? A related issue too is that virtual invisibility of Black-on-Black couples. Most of us assume that the Blacks we meet are automatically attracted to Whites."

Of course, Whites don't see Black-identified Black gay men. And all too often they see only what they want to see. If they want a sex- fix, then they see that; if they want an economic, social, and cultural peer, they should open their eyes and realize that that kind of person is available too. Can you characterize the class, social, and economic spectrum of BWMT members? "We're a microsm of the gay community at large—generally middle class. Some regret the fact that we don't seem to reach the poverty level class of Blacks. That's a complex concern."

What about the racial breakdown? "Some of the groups are 50-50, I'd say. Others have more White members than Black, the ratio sometimes approaching 70-30."

And age? "From 18 to 80, I guess, though the common age runs between 30 and 40. Leadership tends to come from this latter group."

Do the groups have a problem with ageism? "On a personal level, probably. Unless one's consciously confronted his or her feelings about age, about older people and younger people, there's usually something to be worked out. Just because we're sensitive to racial issues doesn't mean that we've worked out our ageism—or sexism, for that matter. I'm a great believer in the wisdom and experience of older gay people, and I've harped on the subject more than a few times. Occasionally I'll get a letter from a *Quarterly* subscriber who'll say I must be 50 or 60 because I promote older people so much. I think too older people need to confront their own ageist treatment of each other, just as Blacks sometimes need to examine their own feelings about Blacks. Personally, my problem is learning to take younger people more seriously. I've been called on it a couple of times by some sharp youths."

How do you handle objections from the outside? "I think most people who criticize BWMT don't know BWMT. First and foremost, the groups belong to those who care enough to participate. If they want to be activist-minded, fine. If they choose to make it a fuck-club, hey, that's their business. If people who denigrate BWMT don't care enough to roll up their sleeves and work for improvement, how important can their concerns be in the first place?

What about the more personal objection? How do you answer someone who asks why you prefer Black men? "If the person is non- gay, I'll start by asking why he prefers women? If he's gay, I'll ask him why he prefers Whites—or why he doesn't like Blacks? The point's obvious if one takes the time to think it through. I've come to learn there are varying degrees of interracial attraction, as there are varying degrees of gender attraction. I've even run into people who prefer other races regardless of gender! Surely people have better things to worry about than the color of the consenting adult I'm sleeping with.

"But, if I may turn this defensive stance into something more prideful, let me state that we interracialists are an entity as real and sincere as any other. We hurt when White—and Black—non-interracialists poke at us. And we resent their assigning us their racial hangups—we have enough to deal with. We also have our special joys. Any person who's come to grips with his own minority—be it racial or sexual—is, in one sense, grateful for the 'affliction'. For it gives him or her the opportunity to become a better human being. Gay and lesbian interracialists are dealt an even greater 'affliction', and those of us who weather it take a special pride in the accomplishment. When you ask me if I'm glad I'm an interracialist, I'll ask you if you're glad you're gay. And if you say 'yes', I'll tell you to double that feeling."

Readers interested in further information can contact: *The Quarterly*, 279 Collingwood St., San Francisco, CA 94114. (415) 431-0458. The International Association of Black and White Men Together (IABWMT), Box 42257, Philadelphia, PA 19101. The National Coalition of Black Gays (NCBG), 1311 W. Pratt Blvd., Chicago, IL 60626. Gay Sunshine Press will send a free list of books available, including some material by Black writers: P.O. Box 40397, San Francisco, CA 94140 (415) 824-3184

MOUNT MORRIS BATHS, NEW YORK

Past it all
to the dirges of winds mourning
through the smashed glass and empty
rows of bitter brick, my head yanks
back as a taxi matter of facts along
a life I've thought I might have lived in.
Silence. The meter ticks a time off
beat, while early ghosts begin to float
on swollen sidewalks: swaggering, in groups,
alone, tempting up and
down. Broken above all,
the outside seems to misunderstand
all that's behind it, making me
rush faster for the chance to immerse
my rising blood in a hidden shelter
where love denied in every other place
is touched like dispensation
over every waiting tongue.

Without choice then, some
of them are still here now, but mostly
they appear as nocturnal apparitions
hauling into Harlem from the seven oceans
and the sewers to pace the porcelain tiles.
Cracked by the passage of years, they pound
out the same heated pleas, pleas:
"Allow me to follow;
I offer you sweat in these hot rooms."

What hath man rotted, that this
could happen only here,
kissed in misty steam and smoke
where the hungry cluster
in blind corners waiting for the
hungry. I watch the old men, hour fathers
to lithe hustlers, the young visions, confident,
the disconsolate, the deceased,
all released for a night.

Soaking them each inside of me,
I drench with them in the salt of
decades of dignity getting by
on these ancient, loving rooms.
For hours surrounded by that
furtive heritage, a way of life has survived
to bless some of its suffering
with their safest moments.

G. S. Weinerman

*The Mt. Morris Baths are the oldest Black
bath in the country. For decades, when the
downtown gay establishments were either
underground and unknown or otherwise not
open to Blacks, Mt. Morris served as an international meeting place for gay Black men.
Today, it is old and faded, but if you look
hard, you can feel and see the lost elegance
which somehow remains.*

PASSERBY

This dark-skinned street boy
may be young but already
he broods proud and grim,

like a hot southern climate
in search of
colder northern skin,

penetrating easily
whatever engages him in passing,
uncoiling down

his leg an instinct
destined by nature
to touch the tongue of a stranger.

Richard Royal

Michael Grumley, 1979

Four Poems by Prince Eusi-Ndugu

BLACK MEN (WE LOVE EACH OTHER)

Oh, how good it would be to love you,
Beautiful creature like me,
with a badd afro to complement your
smooth ebony colour.
Wishing to hold your body until we
both rejoice with moans and cries.
Loving you Black man in brotherhood
and a love that only you and I understand.

IMPERIAL QUEEN AND THE BOY

Hey, Mister,
Ain't my jeans hugging my truck-load
tight enough?
Only fifteen dollars and your fine room;
And he says, "it sure is big,
ten dollars now and five when you leave."

SOMETHING LAW CAN'T STOP

Standing in the window
After my bath, rainy Spring.
He stands in the park . . . wet, as I was.
He sees and I see,
He's seventeen, I am thirty
and we both know code 69a.
But he likes my wetness and I like his.
Code or no code . . . 69 we did.

PAST HISTORY

On the horizon the Sun rises,
Bringing with it two warriors . . .
Zulu warriors of old . . .
They loved in the coolness of night.

BLACK MARINE

for Réné

We had gone to the Esplanade
where it was cool and currents
of the Charles glinted under blue
electrical advertising. You carried
flowers stolen that night from
the Victory Gardens. A thin
representation of queers prowled
the promenade. You liked the legs
of a rider on an English lightweight.
But he didn't come back. I had spotted
a black Marine. I liked the way he
seemed to have just returned from
the Asian jungle, fatigued in his
fatigues. He was practically dumb,
shell shocked I thought. You talked,
in your effortless way.

We took him to Joy Street. In the odd
little room we tried to open the convertible
sofa. He wouldn't say anything. The
mattress looked desperate. The spine
and rusted ribs underneath screamed.
He took off his shirt, his pants,
his shoes. There were no scars, no
tracks, and very little hair; his skin
was a uniform, matte black. He wore
sleek blue nylon boxers. He lay down
on the bent mattress. We were on either side.

We began to touch him as if examining an object
of great antiquity. He lay absolutely still,
frozen. There was no expression on his face.
We took off his shorts.
It was like unwrapping the Maltese falcon,
the fake one.
The sound of his breathing filled the room.

When he had gone, you marveled at his manners,
and went to sleep. I lay awake all night,
as in a billet, watching the gunfire
illuminate the sky.

Peter Barrett

BRAZIL

Brazil is like its bananas;
　　blooming wild with color;
　　transcending into vertical spikes,
　　　　hard and green like Amazonia
　　　　where they're cut;
　　assuming the tawniness
　　　　of Rio's beach—warm bodies
　　　　and yellowed cocoa-softness
　　　　of Afro-Latin curls;
and
　　　　rotting to the *favela* shades of mud,
　　　　the *favela* scents of musk.

On a darkened Copacabana
the spawn of Brazil pressed to me
one,
　　just overripe,
the skin peeled slightly back.
As I swallowed Brazil,
the nectar tasted sweetly black.

Troop

THICK VEGETARIAN CUM

Roosevelt Williamson

Dear Mike,

Hope that this missive of peace, love and much respect will reach you safely and that it'll find you in the best of health as well as high spirits. Received your warm, considerate and deeply comprehensive (undated) letter and you know I was delighted to hear from you. And it was also most rewarding to receive the much needed books and magazines you so beautifully sent me. The mag is very delicious, such beautiful photos! and the ass got me going mad with horniness. To me, Mike, White gays got me going mad with horniness! To me, Mike, White gays got to be the sexiest and lovliest people in the universe! And I'm very much attracted to them. Yes, I love the contrast, as well as the highly concentrated and stimulating sexual magnetism I get from such purely over-abundant, organic relationships. Once I'm in bed I just can't seem to get enough, and the more I get the more I want! I can go for hours and hours and hours! I'm very aggressive in bed and love to dominate, and once I get deeply inside a nice firm, round, meaty, White hot ass, I love to fuck it real good, vigorously, deeply, roughly, and longlastingly! As I'm very well-hung, thick, muscled, long, sturdy, strong, very potent, energetic, full of clean, thick, healthy, vegetarian cum. And I'm handsome, slim-muscled, athletic, yogic, a track runner, swimmer, dancer, poet, singer, artist, ceramic sculpture maker etc. etc! And I'm tannish, keen features, magnetic and comprehensive! I love gay men and boys of a gay consciousness, of all shades, colors, ethnicity. Most of all I love feminine, gay White men as they're the most appreciative of my dominant sexual penetration and aggressive loving expression, and how I love to mount them, ride them across the milky ways of gay nebular galactic cosmic amoebic love! I love to fuck a guy real good and longlastingly, as I'm quite able to cum again and again and again. I'm oversexed and love to explore and express it all! What a boring world this would be (for me) without your White body (and mind and soul). I love to cast my large, black Greek olive eyes upon you and I thank you so much for sending me this sexy gay magazine (which I constantly stare hotly at) which only makes me want you more. And the book *Meat* is a gay literary masterpiece! I can't put it down! It's got to be one of the most realistic, down to earth, straight-forward (in sexual approach), open-minded, and covers many fields of sexual day dimensions. It's mature in scope, expressions and articulations! I'm still reading it. Haven't seen such good gay literature in years!! Very rare here, within this repressive hall of mass depravity! Whenever you come across such good sexy gay literature, keep me in mind, ok? And the book *In Search of Common Ground*, I'll return it as soon as I'm done with it, ok? I know it'll be a great book as I've read a good deal of comrade Huey's stuff and I'm very much into the struggle against all forms of oppression, repression, sexism, ageism, racism, etc. etc. I truly believe in a multi-ethnic, multi- cultured, and strong unified solidarity of the progressive, militant elements within various molds of sexual identities, expressions etc.! As we're living in a time when all avenues of basic needs and support for life's elements to sustain us in our cultural sexual health and growth etc. is being cut off by the fascist racist right-wing neonazi, Reaganistic type of oppression that's cancerously spreading across the trails of our struggles, we must unite to cut them off. Before they cut us off! We must strive to reach out to those of love, courage, true solidarity, concrete realness, and a true dedicated heart-mind and soul towards the true liberation of all oppressed people!! Let's remain for real with ourselves and with others and the struggle will continue to carry on! We are one people—one defiant militant fist by which to smash oppression, racism, sexism and all that which is contrary to true goals. You and I must keep in contact with each other, and I certainly would like you and I to become more than the best of friends! I want to get to know you more and I want you to get to know me real well also! Please don't hide your gayness from me, because I love the quintessence of your genetic makeup and your gay existence! You generate my strength, masculinity, sexuality—and I want to make love to your body-mind and soul! If you're not the feminine type of gay, that's kool with me. As long as you don't mind me desiring you and craving you hotly and madly!! I promise to more than please, Mike! And I'd love to bring our sexual contrast into actuality some day! I bet it's good and tight for me!! And I'd love to get deep inside your wet hot-tight contracting-succulent meaty gay love flower and to plant my abun-

204 / R<small>OOSEVELT</small> W<small>ILLIAMSON</small>

dant potent hot creamy seed deep within your firm fruit of ultimate pleasure and inner freedom!! I'd love to spread my black muscled beauty upon your white firm extremely magnetic inviting sexuality! Please share with me something about you! Let's loosen up together! If I was there with you maybe you'd loosen up a bit! (?) I wish I could taste your sweet lips, bite gently on your neck and earlobes, and caress that hot ass of yours. One of these days I'll get a photo to send you and hope you'll do the same. I don't really know what to put in an ad except I think you know me pretty well already!! If I'm intruding on a nice relationship you already have and if you know of someone that's feminine, nice and sexy, keep me in mind. ok? That still doesn't have to rule you out at all!! As this is only the beginning with us! And I should hope not the end! You seem mature, open-minded, well-read progressive, intelligent and experienced etc. And you're the type I'm mostly attracted towards. Plus I love that which is hard to get! Once I mount you I'll be there for a while! Until you're well pleased and fulfilled! This I promise you! We can melt into oneness and I can feel your vibrations and hope you feel mine, as I'm sincere, for real, been through much shit behind these grey walls of hostage status! I'm still in the struggle!! I appreciate the stamps very much! Wish I was there to prove to you how much I appreciate you!!! Write me back soon!! Get to know me! Explain your sexiness to me bodywise, ok? I miss your gayness!
                                    Roosevelt

LETTERS COME TO PRISON

From the cold hands of guards
Flocks of white doves
Handed to us through the bars.
Our hands like nests hold them
As we unfold the wings
They crash upward through
Layers of ice around our hearts.
Cracking crisply
As we leave our shells
And fly over the waves of fresh words.
Gliding softly on top of the world
Flapping our wings for the last horizon,
High in the blue sky someone's Gay Love.

Shahid (Roosevelt Williamson)

LIFE IN A RURAL TWO-STORY FAGGOTRY

Louie Crew

"GOD MUST LIKE sex, since God made it," W. H. Auden is supposed to have said. God must really like me then, because I really enjoy the sex that God made.

I was not a nester when I entered the Atlanta YMCA for a Labor Day Weekend. I liked sex with lots of folks, especially with strangers who wouldn't know me back at work. I didn't keep score, but I didn't head for a line marked "finish" either. All Friday and Saturday I had a holiday of semen.

Then about 2 a.m. on Sunday, I heard someone step off the elevator. I stepped out of the tearoom to inspect. He smiled and invited me to visit his room in 15 minutes. Although I waited, I was sure that the stranger would not open up when I knocked. I was wrong. We courted every weekend for the next six months, then married. That was nine years ago.

I didn't like myself very much before I met my lover, although I thought I did. I divided my sex and my intellect. When I was at work, I resented my sexual enthusiasms. I reserved sex for special weekends out of town. Then I made up for lost time, sometimes frantically. Later I punished myself with great doses of guilt.

I was a spermaholic. Cum was delicious going down but caused wretched hangovers. Only more cum seemed to provide relief.

In our marriage sex integrates with everything else. My lover loves all of me. I am a whole person. Dick and mind war no more. My lover and I are not stupid enough to look back with guilt on any of the sex we share. It affirms us. I repent, not for earlier sex, but for having devalued it and for having devalued myself.

From the begining my lover and I were very conspicuous. He is dark pecan, I am pale peach. We integrated our White neighborhood and the Black college campus where I taught when we first set up house together in rural Middle Georgia. We are still just as conspicuous in our small town in rural Central Wisconsin, where we moved four years ago. My lover is one of only 23 American Blacks in the community, and he is active politically. I clarify gay issues on local radio stations about 4 hours each year and in classes outside my English Department about 55 more hours each year. I told the hiring committee here that I would bring my lover with me to any occasion where spouses are expected, as I did in Georgia. They still felt I was the best of the 150 applicants for the job.

The town is often less liberal. We can't buy milk without a 1 in 25 chance of hearing "Nigger!" or "Faggot!" Still, things are better. Four years ago those odds were more like 1 in 5. People do change. Even living 60 miles from Plains, Georgia, we found that we got to be only old gossip. We have staying power. Many already can't remember when we weren't here.

Gay people look at us a lot too, especially since I'm a writer by trade and an activist in my church and profession. People always ask what it's like to survive openly in rural America, what interracial sex is like, what keeps our relationship going so long after the honeymoon.

A marriage that is still alive, not just a show-piece, is a fragile, delicate thing. It can die. I'm not impressed by how long any two people have been together, but by the quality of that time. Some folks have more quality, more kindness, in a 2-minute blowjob in a smelly restroom than some others have in 40 years of bad marriage.

My lover and I don't expect our marriage to end at just any moment. We can relax together. We can trust each other to stick around in hard times. But we don't assume that we are guaranteed forever either. I respect his fragileness, he mine. We both respect the grim reaper.

We have to be a bit cagey, to know when to agree to be on camera, when to be alone. Many gays tell us that they want models. I personally think people need to be their own models. Fragile relationships don't thrive best in overexposure. Still, some of us have a talent for exhibitionism. I have earned my living as a professional actor in the past. Perhaps in an earlier life I was a flasher. In this life, I sometimes think my public discussions make me a "flasher for truth." That is, I'll tell more secrets than anyone should have to, but I preserve large areas of privacy.

While I have learned to welcome the challenges of being gay, I spend much more time deviating in other ways. I'm amused that when I jog past hecklers, they never shout, "Poet!" or "Reader!" or "Seamster!" or "Pianist!" or "Rhetorician!" or "Christian!" or.... Surely they know far more gays than they know poets, readers, seamsters, pianists, rhetoricians, or Christians. Heterosexuals just aren't very logical, at least the mean ones aren't.

Being an announced sex deviant does have advantages. I don't have to waste lots of time on insecure people. The friends I do have are very well grounded. They have to be, to live next to a lightning rod.

I am increasingly ignorant about race. I have to be aware of why people all around me are reacting so strangely to the two of us, but otherwise I notice color less and less all along. I like color when I see it, White and Black alike. I am not one of those Whites turned on only by Blacks. I don't think White people worse or better than Blacks. I do dislike Whites who think that Whites are superior.

The Black culture nurtures me extensively. Black writers challenge me. Black colleagues encourage me. My Black family sustains me. Black people give me a fuller community than I ever knew growing up in a segregated South. I have gained access to another half of the world just by crossing the street. I have not had to sacrifice any of the culture I brought with me either.

Still, much of the time I debate the relevance of color. When we have just had three breathing calls or murder threats on the phone, I can as easily celebrate or ignore the Blackness of the arms I fall asleep in or the Blackness of my lover's face as he prays calmly, "God, help those kids to do their algebra and us to get some sleep."

I'm glad that my lover doesn't think my gentleness comes just from my Whiteness. I'm glad that he enjoys equal access to any privileges I can control.

I enjoy the way my lover's Blackness reflects a cloud moving above us as we sit on the grass. He seems to like the way summer freckles and reddens me. I enjoy imitating him, he me. We both had similar Black models when we were under 5. My mother's maid taught me the same low-level ways to fuss that he and I use together—"Child, I ain't studying you" or "You best be doin that!"....

People sound sick to me when they talk about how long Black dicks are, about how much hotter Black men are than White men.

Some Black men sound just as misinformed when they talk about White men. Several have told me that they like White men because White men are kinder or more generous than Black men. Some tell me that Black men too readily trash other Black men.

Any man who hasn't seen a fair share of long White dicks and a fair share of short Black ones is simply inexperienced. Any man who still thinks that size alone packs the punch is hopelessly unrealistic. Any person who thinks that any race has a monopoly on a specific virtue—be it kindness, sexiness, or whatever—is ultimately as racist as those who think any race has a monopoly on a specific vice.

Love is as economic as it is sexual, much more so if one compares the time spent in commercial versus sexual intercourse. Fairness doesn't just happen because we have good intentions. We believe that we each should own property equally. We try to share equally in shitwork and in leisure. For a time we tried a joint checking account, quite successfuly for several years. Now we prefer separate accounts. We keep better records and buy more efficiently, still finding alternate ways to resolve any imbalance. We respect our separateness as much as our togetherness. We have some friends in common, some separately. We have common interests and separate interests. We do lots together, lots separately.

We try not to adulterate our strong wine. You can ruin even the best wine by sneaking water into it or by mixing it with other good wines. But by the same token, I do not aspire to be Sister Monogamy. Nor am I concerned with Adultery with a capital "A." I am thankful that I don't have to be.

I did try to be cool earlier on. I frequently said, "What happens when I'm not here is none of my business if I'm not required to know about it." I didn't know myself. I'd have to put my soul in the deepfreeze to make that bull come true.

I now see that I was really trying to give myself permission to be cheap. Rather than see what I was trying, I claimed to give my lover this permission. I found, however, that I do not want to be cheap or sneaky. My lover never has needed such permission from me: he sets his own character.

We avoid several other tests. We don't play divorce. We never ask, "What would you do if we split up?" or say "Well, I suppose if we can't work this out, we'll just have to go our separate ways." We also don't risk the fire of temper. We probably could survive a loud shouting match, but we don't see much sense to using anger destructively.

We even avoid name-calling. Before I met my lover, I thought that speaking my anger was healthy. I felt that saying "Bastard!" or "Bitch!" was infinitely more honest than bottling up those feelings. I remember well the first time that I called my spouse one of those names. It was even half in jest, as he knew, but he didn't speak to me for about three days. He didn't sulk either. Non-verbally he was kinder than ever before. Finally he broke his silence: "Look, I love you very much," he said, "more than I have ever loved anybody. But I don't love you enough to hate myself. If you ever talk that way to me again, I will have to leave you. And I surely don't want to."

At the beginning, neither of us was seeking a relationship. That weekend at the Y, I was three months out of a heterosexual divorce from a marriage of five years. He had earlier ended a long relationship. We both knew that we were strong enough not only to make it alone, but to be happy doing so. We don't have to have each other. We come together freely, not out of frantic compulsion or overwhelming need.

The truth is that many people would think us pretty dull if they got behind the gossip. We spend most hours working. We're incurably domestic. We haven't even bothered to drive the 30 miles to our one gay bar in about 2 years now. We like to read. He cooks. I sew. He practices ballet. I jog or swim. He spends hours each week helping people through the tenants association which he organized when we were evicted from our apartment three years ago. I teach an adult Sunday School class at the parish where they discussed excommunicating me three years ago.

Our life is far blander than the hecklers credit us with. We do not swing from the chandelier or operate a local brothel.

Sometimes I enjoy being all that scandalous, especially since I don't have to get worn out by activities to deserve it. I also like some of their attention, though I wish I could control their timetable. Still, I am sane enough to recognize what our real adventure is.

Growing up as a sissy, I thought that courage belonged only to everybody else. I certainly thought that a sissy would have to stop being a sissy to have any. I still am surprised less by my enormous supply of courage than I am by the secret that courage is not what most people think courage is. How nice to discover that courage is simply a by-product of risking to be oneself.

WET CLOTHES
A Short Story

Will Inman

R AIN BEATS ON the shingle roof, sweeps in bursts of wind across the front porch, strives with angry fingers at the windows on the south side of the house. For awhile, Darius stands at the open door watching, but then spray begins to build a puddle along the rug. He shuts the door, stares thru the foggy window briefly, then turns abruptly, stands, listening, in the middle of the living room floor.

He switches on the table radio. An hourly news report of the war's progress is on. Too much static. He turns it off.

A noise at the kitchen door. Hammering.

Darius strides barefoot thru the small house swiftly, opens the back door. A very wet figure with leaping dark eyes stands there.

"Anybody home with you?"

"No. I'm by myself. Come on in, quick! Mother's gone to Wake Forest, and Dad's in Norfolk. Ain' nobody here to bother us."

A very wet figure. Soaked clothes drip a small lake on the kitchen linoleum.

"You're all wet. Huh. Look—take off your clothes, I'll try to find something of mine to fit you."

Clothes in a dark pile. Smooth body, long good limbs, questioning eyes, expressionless mouth. Firm fine mat of wiry wet hair. Loins serene in strong thighs.

"Here's a towel. Then try these."

Sweatshirt, loose khaki trousers.

"Thanks," Then: "Surprised to see me?"

"No. Yeah. Well, I don' know."

Self-conscious laughter between them.

"How'd you get here?"

"Tuk the bus to the Beach Hotel. Den walked in the rain."

211

"What if my mother'd been here?"

"Huh. I'dha' said I left something th'other day when we finished paintin'."

"You didn't leave anything. Did you?"

"Yeah."

"You did? What?"

"You."

"Me?"

Eyes mate with eyes. Purple surges of knowing rush like waves under the skin of the one. Cardinal flowers beat, inly, the flesh of the other, like wings of trapped birds.

Towel swathes face and hair for a long instant. The other stands trembling, watching.

A nervous laugh.

'You couldn'ha'told my mother that."

"Well, she ain't here, is she?"

"No."

"Then..?"

"Then what?"

"Boy, you don't know nothin?"

"You got to tell me."

"Hi come I the one got to tell you?"

*   *

Darius has never learned to swim. He can float, between breakers, when the sea is momentarily calm. He will not dive into the breakers, but he will jump them.

This one sweeps in higher than the others. He's frozen, afraid to try to jump so high, yet unable to move fast enough to prevent its catching him before he reaches shallower water.

As he turns to run away, his feet and legs are trapped in undertow, thick as gelatin, churning. The wave takes him, thrashes him under.

I'm down in here. No foothold, no sand under me. No breath in me. I got to get out of this. Got to put my foot down. This current's too fierce. Got to fasten my feet in sand...have to stand up...breathe...

Flung, limbs flailing, hurled, churned, no purchase in sand under, air over.

In all that fury, suddenly there are quiet arms and legs around him, strange hair harsh as sand bruises his cheek, cuts and caresses him like dune grass, ocean touches his body, tenderly, all over, whispering him back into her body, his mouth filled with her flesh, he reaches to take those currents to him.

Sun when it flashes thru surf, when his head breaks from those sullen churning black currents, curses him with waking, laughs in his spuming nostrils.

He sits on dry sand, stroked by wind and sun; he neither welcomes nor resists them. He is not apart from their strokings. He is entirely worn down, numb. His chest cracks full of broken glass. He spits and drools mother. He gasps god.

*   *

A dark dune rises from beside him. The bed creaks. Mouths bruise each other against hungry teeth. Tongues speak with writhing silences of deepwater eels. Air is precious to come up to. Rain breaks thru the roof in sounds of torn sky.

Nearer Wilmington, along Burnt Mill Creek, earth is swamp black. It works between bare toes like sacred offal of long-departed reptiles and amphibians. Here beside him, dark earth wears pale leaves on the undersides of hands and feet, here are raw red openings inside dark puckered rosettes, here are purple swellings, set in hills and glades and smooth brownleaf rises, here are eyes and lips that demand and are not passive, here are hands that now push and hold and press, now caress and stroke and reassure. Darius feels his own pale dunes stir and wrestle, winds and tides discover themselves in him he suddenly knows entirely, has never not known their brotherness working in his limbs, directing his responses with wordless language sown how many aeons ago in his tongue and throat.

He has wrestled his lion.

But this is no beast. Though jungle wise and cage wary, this one has long been the secret brother. You can throw him a slab of meat and stay, watching, outside certain iron bars. Or you can enter yourself into his arena, equal and alien, daring, naked, whole.

His breath comes hard. He has broken all the expectations bred into him by his family, his church, his teachers, his peers.

He turns and studies the body of the one with whom he has shared his own. That face is watching him, now that death has been evaded, now that the wave has brought him back to the beach.

Those eyes do not ask, they observe. Wait.

A tenderness rises in Darius' chest like a flow of clear golden water down the heart of a swamp. It carries dace and gambusias swimming among anacharis and eelgrass. He smiles. The dark arms reach for him and he folds into them with his own.

"I—this—can you come back soon?" Darius asks.

"No. I got my draft call. I go to Fo't Bragg day after tomorrow."

Darius stares. He feels sharp makings of tears edging out of his eyes. He looks down, but salt drops fall on dark dunes already moist with sweat.

"Hey—man! You ain't!"

Darius buries his face in the other's shoulder.

"Hey, look. When I git out of service, I'll come see you. I promise. Maybe things'll be different then—"

"Will you write me?"

"I ain' much on writin letters."

"Jus' once in awhile?"

"A'right. But whut kin I say?"

"Jus' tell me about boot camp. Don' say nothin about—"

"Naw. Ain' nobody never go'n know nothing 'bout that."

"We'll know."

"Yeah. You'n'me'll know. F'sure."

Eyes fall into each other. Distances are terrifying.

"Look. I better be goin."

"It's still rainin."

"Got to catch the las'bus back to town."

"Wait a minute. I think I got a raincoat you can take. And a bag for these wet clothes."

*   *

Several days later, a newspaper blows along the already dry beach. It turns and slides, twists, rattles. Darius sees himself under that high wave. Terror works behind his eyes like a snake caught in a grass fire. He lies down behind a dune and cries.

After awhile, he falls asleep.

He dreams he has a secret sister in a distant city. She is about to tell him his true name, but he wakes up just as she opens her mouth to speak. He sits up and looks around, bewildered. *But you didn't tell me who I am*, he says aloud, then laughs at himself, runs back to the cottage. The white paint is all dry.

AT VERITY HIGH
A Short Story

Robert Thorpe

IT FINALLY HIT him. After all those years.

"Hurry up. You know Frank and Jerry—eight o'clock sharp." Chuck didn't like to keep his friends waiting. They weren't what you'd call close friends, more like friends of convenience. The three of them had played Wednesday night bridge for some time, but there was still a certain aloofness. In fact, Chuck thought, they seemed even more aloof the last few months. Was it Darryl, he wondered.

"Okay, I'm ready," Darryl responded, giving Chuck a hug. They'd been together exactly three months. While Darryl appreciated Chuck's making room for him in his circle of friends, he didn't really care for Frank and Jerry. If Chuck had asked outright, Darryl might have gone into it. He knew what the problem was: his being Black. He'd gone through this before with another White lover's friends: the double take when first meeting, the involuntary shock (their friend taking up with a Negro!). And the aftershock, the attempt to act as if there was nothing wrong, when everyone knew there was. Then, like a road into the wood, the encounter could take a variety of directions: to talk about it or not talk about it; to act 'liberal,' or, even better, to act 'beyond liberal'—that could really get crazy. Darryl was tired of adjusting to Whites adjusting; but what could he do? Over the years, a few meaningful friendships had made their way to a clearing. Only a few, though. And the friendship with Frank and Jerry would never reach such a space. But since Chuck was so fond of bridge, Darryl bore up. When the little racial remarks were fired, especially when Frank and Jerry were losing, Darryl would stare benignly at Chuck and wait them out. Sometimes Chuck would notice Darryl's stare and smile back—a balm of sorts. If Chuck's consciousness was not quite all it could be, Darryl could overlook it. That's love.

"Oh, anything in the mail?" Chuck asked.

"Not much. Just my old high school bulletin." Darryl opened it without enthusiasm. "I guess the change of address reached them."

"Did you tell them to address it to 'Darryl Johnson and lover'?"

"Of course," Darryl laughed. "I even sent them a picture of us in bed."

"Let's see," Chuck said, going along with the gag. But Darryl held onto the bulletin, his eye drawn to an item. Chuck paused. "What's up?" Chuck was attentive that way. Darryl couldn't help but yield.

"It's Gary Robertson, an old friend. Well, he wasn't really a friend." Darryl paused, searching for the right word.

"Is there a picture?" Chuck leaned in. "Hmm, quite a hunk. That kind of 'friend,' eh?" He smiled and gave Darryl a reassuring hug.

"God, I sure had a thing for him!"

"Well, what's it say?"

"Oh, he's become President of something or other. He always was a winner."

Chuck looked at the picture again. "I see you liked White guys then, too."

Ordinarily, the remark wouldn't have bothered Darryl, for he and Chuck had reached that level of frankness in their relationship. And it wasn't that he was bothered now, but he'd honestly forgotten that Gary Robertson had been White and that he had been Black. He remembered only that he'd been very attractive and unattainable. He offered his standard defense. "There wasn't much else to like. In those days 'upwardly mobile blacks' were a prep school rarity."

Chuck fell quiet, taking in the lesson. "C'mon, we better go. Your friends will pitch a fit."

"Okay. I'll drive."

On the way over, the memory of Gary Robertson and Verity High tugged at Darryl. "I hope we do better tonight," Chuck broke in.

"I'm not sure I'm ready for Frank and Jerry this evening."

"Oh, c'mon. They're not so bad," he lied. (Maybe saying it would make it seem that way.) "You know I don't like their salt and pepper cracks either, but, well, these things take time. You gotta understand." He stopped. "Huh, listen to me telling you!"

Darryl was quiet a moment. Chuck had noticed more than he realized. "What really gets me, though, is when they start talking as if I weren't there."

"Oh, come on now. Be fair. Old friends are bound to reminisce. It's not a racial thing." 'Not a racial thing.' The eternal question. It was never a racial thing, but it was always a racial thing. And was it a racial thing back at good old Verity with Gary? Maybe Chuck was right. Maybe Darryl was being too sensitive. Chuck continued talking. Right at the moment, though, Darryl couldn't hear. He'd slipped back to Verity.

I first noticed him—really noticed him—our senior year. We were assigned the same home room and sat across the aisle from each other. What a goodlooking guy he'd become: 6'1", blonde, well-built. Captain, yes, of the football team and student body president; but nobody thought of him that way, least of all me. High school politics was bullshit as far as I was concerned. The kind of people who seek cardboard homage never impressed me. But Gary was different. Actually he was a sort of wallflower his freshman and sophomore years. More striking faces had led the student council, dated the pretty girls—been the 'boys most likely.' But they'd lost their luster somewhere along the way, and Gary arose like some populist figure, embodying something of each of us. For me, isolationist that I'd become—increasingly aware of my differentness, my Blackness, my sexuality—Gary held out a last hope of belonging. His all-American-ness was that irresistible.

For the first few weeks of the term I stared across the aisle at him, exchanging pleasantries—"God, this homework!" and "How'd you do on the quiz?"—fantasizing when he smiled. Then one day an opportunity for real contact came up. Veritas, our monthly paper, needed a feature about the football team, and I, as associate editor, had suggested one of those first-person 'afternoon before the big game' pieces.

"How about it, Gary?"

"I'm no writer."

"I'll help you. C'mon."

"Ohh, okay.—If you'll help."

He had football practice every day till 6:00, so I'd wait. We'd meet afterwards and work on the article an hour or so. Never before had I put so much energy into a project. This must be love, I thought. Gary was right. He was no writer, but his ingenuous ramblings, held in check by my editor's pencil, began to gel. It seemed a fair tradeoff. He was White and not especially smart; I was Black and clever. I suppose I could have felt a certain power, or racial irony, or God-knows-what, but I didn't. We were two guys with complementary talents showing everyone, or ourselves at least—or maybe just myself—that we could make it: Black and White, jock and scholar, straight and not so straight.

Gary was one of those lucky people with a car. Since it was after 7:00 the first day we worked, he offered me a lift. It was a blue '54 Ford, and riding alongside him was a thrill. My imagination flew free while he talked of nothing in particular, as if it were perfectly ordinary for us to be together, as if we'd be together forever thereafter. The 'flight' was brief, though. When we reached Lake, I got out to catch the bus to Borden Hills (Gary lived the other direction). As I continued home, it occurred to me that I was probably the first Black person ever to ride in his car. I felt vaguely proud about that, though I'm not sure why.

The fourth afternoon Gary's car was in the shop, and we had to find another way home. "That's okay," I said. "Why don't we hitchhike?" Gary balked, and I guess if I'd thought about it, I wouldn't have made the suggestion. By the time you were a junior at Verity, if you didn't have a car you surely had a friend who had one. Only the 'outsiders,' those who lacked entree to a car, hitchhiked. Was I an outsider? I could see the question in Gary's eyes, so I quickly assured him that I'd suggested hitchhiking as a lark, an adventure. I didn't let on that I didn't have a friend with a car and that *I* could be seen regularly on Vine Boulevard, hitchhiking alone — or, worse, with Raymond, the other Black senior, with whom I had absolutely nothing in common but the unmentionable stigmata. (How pathetic we were, the two of us in prep school uniforms, hoping some White liberal in a nice car would offer us a lift, but knowing, like as not, we'd have to settle for a brother in something dingy and rattly; and that we'd have to listen to his sincere but stale encouragement to strive. It was crushing, 'striving,' packaging nappy thoughts and thick-lipped words into something acceptable, something White.)

Gary sensed something of my earnestness, I guess, for he shrugged his shoulders and agreed. Fortunately, it being so late, there were no other students out. It was an awkward time, though. Traffic consisted mostly of people running late from work, not the regulars accustomed to the Verity hitchhikers. After some time without a nibble, Gary suggested we go a block down to Newcombe where there was a traffic signal and where we'd have a better chance. I agreed, glad for a sign of interest on his part.

As we walked, I saw in the distance two Black women waiting at the signal. When we reached the corner, I realized they were prostitutes, also 'working' the traffic. Ordinarily I wouldn't pay them much mind except to recall my parents' stern admonition to avoid such people. When I'd bump into them, particularly at Walton and Vine, the next big intersection, I'd distance myself comfortably so passing motorists wouldn't associate me with them. But here they were at Newcombe (I guess Walton was too crowded), and here I was with a White boy.

"Hey, Daddy, where you headin'?" one called out. I stopped cold. Never before had one addressed me. Surely she realized I was a kid. Hadn't my prep school appearance put her off? Her next remark explained. "And who's your good-looking friend?" Of course! This tall, beefy, White guy was a potential trick, and since he was with me, why, it must be okay. I was mortified. I tried ignoring them and dared not look at Gary who also remained silent. I hoped they'd take the hint and the moment would pass. But they walked over. God, what would Gary think? "Hi, sugar," the same one said to Gary, as she approached. "I'm Shirelle." She looked toward me and remarked sarcastically, "I guess the brother here's forgotten his manners."

"Don't call me 'brother'," I hissed.

"Well now, get you and your dicty clothes," she hissed back.

"C'mon Shirl," the other one called out. "You're wasting your time."

The woman turned to leave. I snarled, "Yeah, beat it, 'ho'." She looked back, a forlorn expression on her face. The late afternoon wind had come up, and the dirt and grime stirred up by traffic on Vine piteously exposed her: raw features exaggerated by too much makeup, scanty clothes whipped against her thin frame, a ridiculously blonde wig askew. As the women sidled away to look elsewhere, I felt sick, terribly sick. All my efforts to bring Gary and me closer, to unite Blackness with Whiteness—wiped out.

Gary was looking at me now, I could tell. I returned his gaze reluctantly. "Gee," he guffawed, embarrassed. He looked down the block after them. "You call them chippies, don't you?"

"How should I know?" I snapped, hating his linking me with them.

He stood silent a moment. Perhaps he realized he'd offended me. Or perhaps he didn't and was just bewildered. He was right, though—I did know they were called chippies. He spoke again. "I heard a couple of Black guys call them that on the bus one time."

"Yeah," I said finally. There was a pause. He chuckled. I chuckled too, but it wasn't funny. We stood there a bit longer, our thumbs extended, until a car pulled over and offered us a ride. Gary did the talking during the brief ride to Lake. I was sullen. If I was to have a friendship, a relationship perhaps, with a White boy, it wasn't going to be one built on the gutter. Why the hell had I been sent to Verity anyway? To act as some sort of go-between for Black hookers and pampered White boys? Gary's laughter resounded in my mind. And again and again, his remark, "You call them chippies..."

That night the incident returned to me in a dream. The two women were pulling at me while Gary stood by watching. It was fearful. I awoke, feeling sorry for myself, for my Blackness.

The next afternoon we finished the football article, and this time it was I who was the talkative one. I'd resolved to forget the incident, to forge ahead, but every mending step seemed for naught. I spent the evening in the bleachers watching him, and as his hundreds of fans cheered, I realized how unlikely it was we'd ever become close.

Football season came to an end, and I became more involved in journalism. There was a yearbook to get together, and I was chosen editor. I found a new hero, Daniel Sullivan, who'd been awarded a prestigious science scholarship, but I decided not to try getting close to him. It was safer admiring him from afar. Besides, I think my occasional stares were arousing suspicion. I resolved to dedicate myself to the work at hand. The yearbook would be the best ever. As the weeks passed and articles and layouts took shape, I began to feel good again. A book was coming to life, the progeny of my talent. A personal love life no longer seemed important. I ceased looking at Gary or Daniel so longingly. There were just a few weeks of school left. Why risk my secret? Some of the guys may have wondered—I never talked about girls, or dated—but nothing was said.

When the book was ready for the printer, I felt a great release. It had been exhilarating, but also plain, hard work. It was mid-May now, a few weeks before graduation. Despite my personal trials, I felt melancholy about leaving: Verity had been my life. Gary's extracurricular activities had slowed too, and when we saw each other in class, we exchanged small talk. This I handled well. There were other times, though, when he'd appear unexpectedly and my imagination would take off. I'd see him hurrying down the hall, asking me to join him in his blue Ford, and off we'd go. But I didn't get too carried away. I was resigned to my status, my Blackness in a White school, my gayness. Yet at times, knowing that something better awaited me on the outside, I'd become unusually confident, almost cocky. I'd cruise a classmate or two, dropping comments here and there, staring lingeringly. But classmates don't want to believe a rumor so close to the uncomfortable truth, so my gay manner was assigned to my 'racial nature.'

There were now two weeks to go. In assessing my career at Verity, I felt, all in all, I'd behaved honorably. I'd never raised a racial fuss, and though I'd become gay, I'd kept that well in check too. I'd associated for a time with the school hero and, well, we'd liked each other. And then, of course, there was the editorship of the yearbook, my greatest triumph. It was still to be acknowledged.

Finally, two days before graduation, the books arrived. I raced through the first one out of the box, scanning each page proudly, praying the printer hadn't committed some grave error. Upon reaching the end, I closed the book quietly against my chest and announced, "It's perfect." An excited staff cheered, and we all celebrated. Within hours every student on campus had a copy and half of them, it seemed, came by to congratulate me. The afternoon wore on, and it was almost six by the time I thought about going home. I stopped by my locker on the way out, and as I crouched down in the dim hallway, I saw someone approaching. It was Gary. Gary! In the excitement I'd forgotten him. I stood up eagerly. His congratulations would mean the most. And here he was, waving at me.

"Great yearbook, guy," he enthused. "Great yearbook."

"Thanks," I said as modestly as I could. "Thanks a lot. I'm glad you like it." I emphasized the 'you.' There was a pause. I swallowed. "Say, Gary, I guess we probably won't be seeing much of each other." I'd conceded that long before, but now suddenly found myself wanting one last, small...something.

"I guess you're right. Things come to an end faster than we know."

"Yeah, that was the fastest slow four years ever," I quipped.

"Yeah," he chuckled. There was a pause.

"Well, say, write something in my yearbook, will you?" I held it out to him.

"Uh, okay," he said. He took the book. "What should I say?"

What should he say! That he thought of me often (as I did of him), that knowing me was a 'uniquely enriching experience.' That it was too bad 'things' kept us apart—ships passing in the night and all that. Something! I swallowed again. "Oh, I don't know. But make it special, will you? Something special." I looked up at him eagerly.

"Uh, let's see," he said, thinking aloud. He stared out into space and twirled his pen a second, "Hmm, something funny maybe." He thought another second then wrote with a flourish and handed the book back.

"Thanks!" I said, dying to look, yet not daring to do so.

He stared a second. I stared back. 'Well...?" he said expectantly. He wanted me to look. What could he have written? My heart pounding, I fumbled with the book till I found it. I froze. 'To the cutest chippie at Verity.'

He chuckled. "Remember?"

"Yeah," I said softly. "Yeah, I remember." Still numb, I stood there, rooted. He looked at me. For a long moment, we didn't say a word. He laughed again, nervously. I had to escape. "Well, I'll see you!"

"See you!" he called as I raced out of the building. I rounded the corner and stopped to catch my breath. It was dark outside now. I leaned against the building and felt myself sliding toward the ground. There was something strange on my face. Tears. Tears of a stranger. Myself, a stranger. "You dumb nigger. You dumb nigger," I said softly.

"You seemed quiet tonight," Chuck said as he pulled the car into the driveway.

"Huh?" Darryl stared a second, holding a thought. "Oh. Yeah, I guess so."

"Anything wrong?"

Darryl didn't really know. He sat there a second as Chuck got out of the car, not waiting for his answer. Was something wrong? He was tired, he knew that. More tired than he'd felt in a long time. Frank and Jerry had gone through their recital, a crack here, a stale joke there — Darryl could repeat the evening's 'program' from memory. But there'd been something different this time (or was it just him?) When they reached the kitchen, they sat down for a late snack. Finally Darryl answered Chuck's question. He tried to be light and clever. "Nothing a new set of friends wouldn't help."

"What?"

Darryl paused, then repeated the answer, but Chuck interrupted. "I heard what you said. You mean Frank and Jerry? Did you let them get to you?"

"Yes, I 'let them get to me,' " Darryl replied angrily. He stopped, as if to add something else, but it wouldn't come to him.

Chuck reached over and placed his hand on Darryl's shoulder. "Come on, it's not worth it. People make stupid comments all the time." He paused. "Look, maybe it's not for me to say, but I think you should ignore them. That's what I do—makes things a lot easier. I've known Frank and Jerry some time," he went on, "and, believe me, that's just the way they are." He paused again, waiting for agreement, then patted Darryl's hand. "After awhile, you'll get so you won't even notice it." He went to the refrigerator. "We have to get some milk tomorrow, we're running low." He looked back to Darryl once more. "Come on now, let's see a smile." Darryl smiled absently. "Good. Now let's go to bed and get some sleep. I have a presentation tomorrow, and it's going to be a bear!"

That night Darryl had a dream. The two Chippies returned. They were dressed as they were that day so many years before. Only this time, instead of pulling at him, they were standing at a distance, watching. There was a stranger between them. No, it wasn't a stranger—it was himself. Himself saying, "you dumb nigger, you dumb nigger." The three of them turned to walk away. He called out after them. They stopped and one of them beckoned. Darryl awoke suddenly. He sat up in bed. Chuck was asleep next to him. Without a sound, Darryl arose and went with them. He never returned.

A PERSONAL TESTIMONY

"Benjamin James"

L ET ME BEGIN by saying that I am a man of African-American de-
scent and that I have not always been racist. It developed after
my coming out and from living in Chicago.

I was born in Arkansas into a working class family who had the
good sense to move to Dallas where I grew up. We were poor but
didn't know it. We grew our own food, used wood-burning stoves
for cooking and heating, lived in a four-room house without
electricity or running water, and never went hungry a day in our
lives. I attended an all Black grade school that had four rooms,
four teachers, and grades one through seven. High school was all
Black too, and we were bused forty miles a day through White
neighborhoods before busing became fashionable. I was the oldest
of four brothers and a sister. We grew up in rural North Dallas surrounded by beautiful grain fields and farm houses, all of which is
now solid concrete and asphalt shopping malls and parking lots.
Much of this land which belonged to Black folk was bought up
from my people who were ignorant of the building boom to come in
the 1970's. A lot of fat-bellied, smiling racists stole back more than
forty acres and a mule. But this is a song as old as the wind and
twice as funky. For my part, though, my contact with White folks
was through my parents' employers and an occasional chorus of
the word, 'Niggers,' that would echo from a passing carload of
White boys on our walk from the bus stop. I did not develop deep
hatred from this. We were church-going folk and taught to love our
enemies. This period is known as my blind faith period.

During the early sixties there still existed White and Colored
water fountains, bathrooms, and other such hallmarks of a United
States. It was the time of Martin Luther King's marches and of the
great Black Muslim, Malcolm X, and it was the time I began to experience discrimination. My first and most vivid moment came as a
result of my first job as a bright-eyed enthusiastic teenager. I was a
busboy in a restaurant and proud of it and never felt inferior for a

moment—in fact, I always thought there was something very special about me. But it bugged me when it came time for employee meals that Black folk had to sit in the back, in noise, filth, and confusion, while the White folk were allowed to go out into the cool, quiet, clean dining area. Well, I had been listening to King and had had enough of this mess and decided I was going to sit down in comfort and eat like a civilized human being. No one else had the nerve. I did not understand then that when one has mouths to feed, a car payment, a mortgage, clothes in the lay-away, and is trying to keep a little left over to get that bottle of Thunderbird for the weekend, one can ill afford to get pushy with management. I had none of this to worry about so I pushed and was immediately fired. The next day, to the utter shock and disbelief of the management and my former fellow employees, I returned, bought me a meal like a respectable gentleman, and sat there and ate it—daring them to kick out what was the first dark face to soil their sacred dining room. It was a wonderful feeling of triumph and freedom! I experienced similar discrimination in other eating establishments in Dallas. It was just not popular for 'colored' people to come through the front door of anything. Most places either had a little hole of a window in the back where they could serve us like some dog, or we were just not allowed inside. And I remember several times as a passenger on the city buses White folk would get up and move if a Black person sat near them—and similar incidents in churches, of of all places. I could write a chapter alone on White churches and born-again Christians.

Upon graduation from high school, I was eager to go to college with White folk because segregation had taught us, in a subliminal fashion, that we were just too dumb to mix with them—and definitely too Black and dirty to ever think of having sex with one. Looking at a White girl was like John Henry lusting after the master's wife or daughter and both parties knowing they wanted it—and did it—but one does not copulate with an animal and talk about it. In college I was popular because I played a pretty mean piano, and I was a showcase Black at a time when everybody was trying to have one. And since I was friendly, non-violent Sagittarian, smiling with pearly whites from ear to ear, trying to make White folk at ease in a climate that was growing more hostile by the day, I was liked and possibly loved. It seems I attracted the finest looking White boys in America, but nothing sexual ever came up. Most of my non-study time was spent attending White Christian campus groups, lusting after pretty White boys (and sometimes, girls), and talking about how Jesus could unite the races. I really believed this and refer to this period as my White-blight period. It was during this time of searching for a Black identity that I became the first one allowed to join the lily-White Greek system at SMU. Oh, if only it had been Greek I would not have been so frustrated sexually. But with these straight dudes it was all suppressed because religious good guys just don't have sex with each other, not to mention even playing with oneself, which was my only release and for which I just knew I was going to go blind or mad or both, and I was surely the only pervert doing it. (I just happened to develop a wart on my hand—I was sure God was punishing me for my sexual solitaire.) With some of these guys I actually think we became soulmates and religion was the adhesive binding. It was at this time I had two other significant racial experiences.

The first had to do with a 'fine, upstanding, born-again' family who went to great lengths to take the Bible and explain to me why I could not be the groomsman to my fraternity brother who was about to marry their daughter. But if I could be an usher (a servant position), I could participate! (My friend and I had justice a few years later when they named their first-born after me and made me his godfather.)

The second experience had to do with my chosen profession, music. The Metropolitan Opera of New York came to Dallas on tour. An announcement had been placed on the music school bulletin board soliciting students who would like to usher at the performances and see the operas free. All that was required was that one sign the posted list and arrive at the theater thirty minutes before curtain. When I arrived with one of my White friends, we learned that I could not be an usher because they had not yet integrated the ushering group. I was pissed as hell. They tried to appease me with a free ticket to see Mozart's *Magic Flute*. (The irony of it all is that a Black man, George Shirley, was singing the tenor lead—the Met's gesture of tokenism.) I was not appeased and was wondering how I could publicize this and thought of writing a letter of protest to the two major newspapers. I went to the chairman of the music department, a fine man named Bonelli, and told him of my experience. I'm not sure what he did, but the next day a story about the incident appeared in big bold type on the front pages of both papers. And because of this the segregated group was cleaned up. This was a personal triumph, but the experience made a skeptic of this naive country boy coming to grips with big and little city ways.

I continued my religious and Greek life and desperately wanted to be intimate with male friends, but a White cock had yet to touch my lips (though I managed to grab a few 'accidentally' during friendly wrestling matches.) It was only after my undergraduate days that I finally tasted the forbidden fruit of integrated sex. (The first time was no big thing, believe me. It occurred in a health spa steam room with some dude telling me I didn't really want to start doing 'this kind of thing.' Hell, I knew what I wanted!) About this time I also hit it off with a dude in a church choir I had joined. I managed to be in a White church choir, because by this time I had begun to sing and found out I could get paid for it. Black churches never paid. Talent was a gift of God and heaven knows nobody pays for it—though the preacher always drove a fancy car and passed the collection plate at the drop of a hat. (I could write another chapter on Black folks' Christianity.)

My fascination with the White body became all-consuming. After all, this is the age of consumerism. Every book, magazine, and T.V. show one saw had nothing but White folk as the ultimate in beauty and desirability. The only things Black were some old movies about Zulus standing around looking dumb, singing and dancing and beating a drum—and an occasional attempt at speech in the form of such brillant dialogue as, "Yassah, Bwana" or "Ooga mooga"! Don't even get me started on the great Black hope, Tarzan! I was hot for his body, but I cringed in shame seeing myself as the African. I was ashamed of Africa and my heritage, but I was too blind to see it at the time. I was completely brainwashed. Never mind the fact that my first sexual experiences had been with my brothers and that the first dude who screwed me was an older Black schoolmate. There was even a 'guy next door' or, I should say,...down the road. (It was exciting to sneak out at night and do it in the grain field under the moon. It seemed that my older cousins and everyone else had a bigger thing than me—though the biggest in the country had to be my friend's father's!)

After graduation I went off to West Texas to obtain my master's degree. I soon discovered the closet was invented in the West. There are no Marlboro men. No, nothing but pretty redneck White boys and chewing tobacco, both of which can be a bit messy.

I ended up in another White church choir, but this time I kept my act straight. I was not up to a lynching, and gay lib didn't mean a damn thing out in pick-up truck country. I made lots of friends, but none were giving out or giving in. I was even in love with two or three or four of them. One was an ex-marine, a 'real' man with whom I slept one night during his drunkenness. I tried everything but he would not give up his 'manhood,' though he was aching to.

There was one gay bar in Amarillo, but due to the conservative nature of West Texas and the racism, I never knew if I didn't score because I looked too anxious, too ugly, or too mean and Black. So I turned to straight White men, and most importantly, my physical education teacher.

He was an ex-gymnast with the body of life, and I first saw him sitting at the registration table. He was cool, calm, handsome – and bored to tears. I came over and brightened up his life with some witty comments, all the while thinking that I'd sing up for wrestling so I could get close to this blue-eyed cowboy. I fell head over feet for this dude and naively declared it to him in a letter and gift at the end of one semester. I even offered to play and sing a little program for our class. My voice teacher and fellow music students thought I was crazy to waste my time singing for a wrestling class full of hicks. They had no vision. I knew I had my man hooked on me as a friend – if not as a lover. Of course it never developed to physical expression, but we became very close friends and I knew there was something unspoken there, and so did he.

In the summer of 1979 I had graduated with my master's and took off for San Diego, San Francisco, and Chicago for some opera auditions. I was most taken with Chicago and decided to move there.

What a culture shock to come from Amarillo to Chicago! From the sticks to the bricks. From the crotch of the dust bowl to the enchanted fairy kingdom of the North Side. I lived North for two months and went to a few bars and quickly became aware of the smell of racism in the air. At Carol's it greeted me at the door like a wet dishrag – no, worse! I went back a few more times because anybody can have an off night, but again I was confronted with an unfriendly, condescending attitude. A letter of protest I wrote to the gay paper never appeared. It was the same thing at Broadway Limited and the Bistro: Black folk seemed to need five pieces of I.D. and a birth certificate for admittance. And here we were hearing that gay folk and Black folk were alike in our fight for civil rights. Hah!

The most positive beacon of light – White light, anyway – was Mattachine Midwest. This group of gay men were more real and, for the first time in my life, I could talk to someone about the problems and concerns of being gay. There were only about three Black men, though, and I soon began to suspect that gay Black men did not exist except in some secret social organization on the South side of Chicago. Fortunately, I began to hunger for some Black contact and quickly outgrew Mattachine. And I had decided that it was stupid to continue to patronize White bars that had quota systems and didn't want my Black face. So I move to the South Side.

The South Side hit me like a ton of bricks. The Black experience for once took on a new meaning for this country boy. I went to Black gay bars, and my whole sexual and social expression became totally Black. I became more and more anti-White and had no associations except at my job. During my three years in Chicago, I had only one White sexual encounter, and I regret that to this day. It happened out of loneliness and frustration after I had been in town for two months without job or friends. I had seen this dude twice on the street, and the second time I went to his home. After it was over we talked, and he invited me over many another day for food, talk, and sex; but I was not interested in the last and made it known. He soon developed the most annoying habit of using his two-bit psychology on me, and mothering me. Well, I hated to tell him, but I already had a mother, and one was entirely enough. And I let him know there were no romantic feelings for him, though I was most highly appreciateve of his groceries and his friendship, and offered my friendship in return—but not my body. Also, it seemed that his desire only for Black men was a bit pathological, and it made me suspicious of his motives. For I had already seen that Black and White relations was so much shit and sham. It appeared that Black men who chased after Whitey were just brainless snow queens looking for a sugar daddy. True or not was not the point. My attitude had become sour, and I could not see how an honest Black man, aware of the history of the fight for equality in this country could, in the words of the Bible-beaters, become 'unevenly yoked,' or have a deep love interracial relationship in racist America—particularly in Chicago where someone was likely to slip and call him nigger. I started going through my African stage, as I read for the first time the autobiography and speeches of the most brillant and misunderstood Malcolm X, and I regretted that I did not know the man and understand him while he was among us. The White press had made me close my ears to Malcolm. Then I discovered Chancellor Williams' moving book, *The Destruction of Black Civilization*; and I was convinced of his principal contention that the White power structure was, is, and always will be, bent on the total destruction of the Black man (though I was perplexed because Williams claimed to be a Christian, and my current view is that there exists no more foul tool of racism and colonialization on the African continent than the religions of Christianity, Islam, and greed.) My White-blight period had ended, and my Black period had begun. So I cut off all White social contact except for one man.

When I had first come to Chicago, I had stayed with a fraternity brother from SMU out in the dull suburbs of Oak Brook. There I met a friend who introduced me by phone to his brother who lived in the city. Gary invited me to visit, and he showed me around the North Side from a straight point of view. He was an exceptionally fine, handsome, and intelligent man, and very sensitive to the arts and the civil rights struggle. Just the kind of guy I needed during my White-blight period. When I returned from Dallas to move to Chicago, he offered to let me stay at his place until I got situated. I intended to stay only a few weeks, but the weeks turned into months, and Gary had the patience of Job. Even when my funds ran out he gave me money and fed me. This was the most depressing time of my life. Here I was with two degrees and could not find a decent job, and I was bumming off someone I hardly knew. I finally got work and moved to the South Side. Gary and I stayed in touch and would dine together every six months or so, and he would always attend any music program I gave. I grew to love this man very much, but not in a sexual way. I admit that if there had been the slightest suggestion on his part, I would have jumped on him like white on rice. We could easily have become lovers, blowing my racist views straight to hell. But we never discussed sex, so I suppose he did not know about me, or didn't care to. (I recently wrote him a long letter from Cologne to tell him.)

Getting out of Chicago has done wonders for my racist attitudes toward White folk in general and gay White folk in particular. Though racism exists in every corner of the world in a class or caste system, it does not appear to be as pathological in Western Europe as in America. But one can never forget that America was settled by transplanted Europeans (look what happened to the Native American Indians) and that Africa was colonized and is still being raped by Europeans. I will never forget South and West Side Chicago, the inner city. I grew to love and detest my own people and the system that perpetuated the negative elements in the Black community, particularly drugs, booze, welfare, and the mentality it spawns; and gang warfare—so similar to the tribal warfare that continues to keep African nations divided. I've known some of the finest Black men one would ever wish to know,...and then there were the fools. Regardless of the color, a fool is a fool. Black men have a lot to learn about loving one another, because for the most part it seems we are just into getting that nut. It is difficult to give love when one is struggling with a Black identity and a gay identity in a racist world that cares for neither. I was glad to become what I thought was more African. I like the way we looked, and was convinced that the Afro-American man was the hottest, the best hung,...that we had the best bodies—and I definitely knew we smelled better than Whites. And never would I let a White paw touch this ebony body again! (. . . have learned slowly but surely never to say 'never.')

Since coming to Germany and Austria in July of 1982 to study and audition for the opera theaters, I have met, of all things, a German man—and I do mean a man, not a child. He is one of the most sensitive friends and lovers I have had. But I must confess that I miss the abundant variety and energy of the Black brother in Chicago. Oh, there is variety, energy and beauty among Black men in Europe, but the Black man here has a totally different mentality, and tends to take on the characteristics of the country that colonized him; and at this point, I cannot detect the esprit de corps, the easy camaraderie, that American Blacks express among one another. The African seems even more alienated in Europe and seems to have nothing in common with the American Black man but skin. Certainly this is a topic for extensive study.

Racism and ignorant prejudice are the lowest of obscenities— poisonous attitudes I personally find loathsome, particularly when I see myself developing them in response to small-minded men. In Europe I am more aware than ever of the vast and wonderful array of humankind and its cultures. I have seen some of the most beautiful men in the world, particularly those of the Middle East, and it breaks my heart to see them killing each other instead of loving. How tragic that in this world, instead of marveling at the diversity of pigmentation and language and customs, we should separate ourselves by such superficialities as politics, religion, war, and other suspicions and ignorances too numerous to catalogue. How wonderful life would be if we could learn to love and respect those unlike ourselves.

BIOGRAPHICAL NOTES

WAYNE ALEXANDRE was born in 1952. He has traveled throughout the U.S. widely and currently resides in San Francisco. Wayne is a poet who "sometimes cooks to earn a living." He adds that the "Interview With a Black Homosexual Masochist" is a self-interview, and "my masochism is limited to the sexual."

MARK J. AMEEN was born in 1958 in Lowell, Massachusetts. In addition to "Transit House", which appears here in print for the first time, Ameen has been writing poetry, working on a play, and performing with The Front Line Improvisation Company in New York City—where he currently resides. He wonders "whether to follow in the footsteps of Bette Davis or Jack Kerouac."

CALVIN ANDERSON was born in Long Beach, Calif., 1946. He has a Ph.D. in biological sciences. He is the founder and director of Sierra Domino Publishing, the major U.S. firm dealing with the positive imagery of the nude Black male, and his photos have been published in most of the leading gay magazines. Calvin Anderson currently resides in a San Francisco Victorian with three room-mates, one cat and 29 goldfish.

PETER BARRETT, 37, has sung in two rock bands, lived on welfare, sold pornography to Yalies, worked in an inflatable chair factory, written for *Circus* Magazine, and has published two poems. "Black Marine" first appeared in *Gay Sunshine Journal* No. 40/41 (1979). Another poem appeared in an issue of *Little Caesar*, dedicated to John Wieners.

JEFFERY BEAM was born in Kannapolis, N.C., 1953 and moved to Chapel Hill in 1975—where he still lives—after graduating from U.N.C. with a Bachelor of Creative Writing. He is the author of *The Golden Legend* (Floating Island Pub., 1981), *Two Preludes for the Beautiful* (Universal Printing, 1981), and *Apostrophe to Stanley and other poems* (Catalyst, 1984). "Leave-Taking" and "You Go Off With My Life" are dedicated to Gene Philyaw.

THOM BEAME was born in 1944 in Nashville, Tn. A former chairman of BWMT—San Francisco, Thom has also served the community as Third World Co-Chair of the San Francisco Gay Pride Parade Committee and as interim Co-Chair of the Coalition for Human Rights. He has written and spoken extensively about racism. Both "Racism from a Black Perspective" and the interview with Michael Smith were first published in *The Advocate* (April 1, 1982 and December 23, 1982). The interview appears in the present anthology in its original form.

JIM BREWER JR. was born 1952 in Gallipolis, Ohio and currently lives in Wilkes-Barre, Pa. *Fantasy Man*, a collection of his gay poems, was published in 1984 by Cerred Books. "Imitation of Zebras" first appeared in *Quarterly* #19 (Fall 1983)

PAUL THOMAS CAHILL was born in Bay City, Michigan, 1944. He has had "several romances and affairs—with Black men mostly, and I will continue in that direction until I get it right." Tom, as he prefers to be called, currently lives in San Francisco, and "The Reunion" is his first published work.

LOUIE CREW was born in Anniston, Alabama, 1937. He founded Integrity, the organization of Gay Episcopalians and teaches writing at the University of Wisconsin, Stevens Point. He has published more than 400 items—poetry, essays, general fiction, non fiction. "Life in a Two-Story Faggotry" appeared originally in a longer version in *First Hand Magazine*, 1983.

JOE DeMARCO was born in Philadelphia in 1947. He has been active in Philadelphia gay groups since 1971 and still works with a number of community institutions. One of the founders of BWMT—Philadelphia, he continues to take part in their activities. Joe's journalistic work has appeared in many gay publications. In Philadelphia he edited *The Weekly Gazette* and was editor-in-chief of *New Gay Life*. His regular column appeared in *In Touch* and *Gaysweek*. Among his other publishing credits he lists poetry, fiction and photography. "Gay Racism" first appeared in Philadelphia's *Gay News*, October, 1982.

LAWRENCE DUPLECHAN was born in Los Angeles, 1956—of African, Cajun French, and American Indian ancestry. Larry has been a nightclub singer, a librarian, and a word processor, and currently works as a legal secretary. He is currently working on his first novel and "would like someday to write the way Aretha Franklin sings." His story "Peanuts and the Old Spice Kid" is his first published work.

JOEL ENSANA was born in New Brunswick, N.J., 1933. He is a graduate of California State College in San Francisco (where he currently resides) and is the winner of many playwriting awards— the Albee, the Shubert etc. His plays have been published in *The*

Best Short Plays and in *First Stage,* and his stories have appeared in *Quartet* and *Snake.* Some of his plays have been produced by CBS Television, the American Conservatory Theatre, the One-Act and Black Repertory theatres in Berkeley, and Trinity College in Ireland. "The Long Hard Runner" is previously unpublished.

SALIH MICHAEL FISHER was born in the Year of the Monkey, 1956, "in modern jazz Harlem." He began writing poetry in the third grade and was published in several school periodicals. His work also appeared in *Yemanja,* a Black gay men's journal. "Harlem Brown Baby" has been heard several times in group performances and is published in the present anthology for the first time.

ERIC GARBER was born in Pasadena, California, 1954. He is a member of the San Francisco Lesbian and Gay History Project and is the co-author, with Lyn Paleo, of *Uranian Worlds: A Reader's Guide to Alternative Sexuality in Science Fiction and Fantasy* (G.K. Hall, 1983). "T'ain't Nobody's Bizness" first appeared in a slightly different form in *The Advocate.*

LYLE GLAZIER was born in Leverett, Massachusetts, 1911. He has taught in Boston, Buffalo, Istanbul, Ankara and India, including courses in Black literature. He has had fiction and poetry published in *Gay Sunshine, The Alternate, Fag Rag,* and *Mouth of the Dragon.* He writes: "Since 1971 I have devoted myself to telling as honestly and vividly as possible what it means to be a married homosexual, out of the closet in 1956."

DAVID GREENE was born in Chicago, 1950, and currently lives there. He has enjoyed doing photographic portraits for more than ten years and has had exhibits of his work in various U.S. cities and overseas. The photos on the cover and frontispiece were done in Chicago especially for this anthology.

MICHAEL GRUMLEY was born in Bettendorf, Iowa, and attended Denver University, Mexico City College, the University of Wisconsin (B.S., Philosophy, 1964). He has done Graduate work at C.C.N.Y., the School of Visual Arts (NYC) and the University of Iowa Writers' Workshop. He has had one-man shows at Gallery 88, Rome (1968), Leslie-Lohman Gallery, N.Y.C. (1981). His books include: *Atlantis, The Autobiography of a Search* (with Robert Ferre), Doubleday, 1970; *There are Giants in the Earth,* Doubleday, 1974; *Hard Corps,* Dutton, 1977; and *After Midnight,* Scribners, 1978.

JAMIEL DAUD HASSIN was born in New York City in 1926 and still lives there. "Addicted to opium/heroin/alcohol at age 15. And my life was one abysmal hell. Jailing & failing were my constant companions, and I spent a total of 21 years imprisoned. However, some good came of my incarceration: very determined reading and writing were my pastimes. First published from Green Haven Correctional Facility, 1973. Received 70-odd credits for college level studies (Psychology). No narcotics since 1970." The poem "Freddi" appeared in *Quarterly* No. 18, San Francisco, 1983 and subsequently in the poet's book, *Main Street.*

LANGSTON HUGHES (1902-1967), American poet, was a major figure of the Harlem Renaissance. His poetry was brought to public attention by Vachel Lindsay in the mid 1920s. His work portrays American Black culture with the use of dialect and jazz rhythms. His published books of poetry include: *The Weary Blues* (1926); *Shakespeare in Harlem* (1942); and *Selected Poems* (1959). His other work includes plays (*Mulatto*, 1935), novels (*Not Without Laughter*, 1930), and autobiographies (*I Wonder As I Wander*, 1956).

WILL INMAN was born "White" in Wilmington, N.C., 1923. He grew up "with the usual racial biases, but was lucky enough" to work with Black people "who helped me see deeper than color." Editor of the literary magazine, *Kauri:* 1964-1971. His main books are: *I am the Snakehandler; 108 Verges Unto Now; 108 Prayers for J. Edgar*. His poems have appeared in *Gay Sunshine Journal* and many other publications. "Wet Clothes" is a fantasy built around "the wish that I'd known Black lovers at an earlier age." It was first published in *Bottomfish*, De Anza College, 1981.

"BENJAMIN JAMES" (a pen-name) was born in Arkansas, 1945, but now calls Dallas his hometown. He was schooled in Texas and later pursued vocal studies in Europe with the renowned Tito Gobbi and Thomas Carey. He has performed in opera, concerts, and recitals throughout the United States and Europe and is seeking his "big break" in West Germany where he currently resides.

PRINCE EUSI-NDUGU is a Black Canadian poet. The poems published in the present anthology appeared originally in *Fag Rag* #11 (1974) and are reprinted with their permission.

BRUCE NUGENT was born in Washington D.C., 1906. He is one of the original Harlem Renaissance writers. His short story "Smoke, Lilies and Jade" (printed here) first appeared in the November,

1926 issue of *Fire!!*, a little arts magazine put together by Nugent, Wallace Thurman, Langston Hughes and others to showcase younger black artists. The story was later reprinted in *Voices from the Harlem Renaissance*, edited by Nathan Irvin Huggins, 1976. Nugent also contributed to *The New Negro* (anthology), *Ebony and Topaz*, *Challenge* and *The Crisis*. He continues to write and paint from his home in Hoboken, N.J.

ROSS PAXTON was born in Oregon, 1931 and currently lives in Edgewater, New Jersey. He draws and paints male erotica as a "personal crusade for sexual freedom and acceptance of the homo sexual artist in the spirit of Shunga Pillow Books." None of the drawings included here have been published previously.

LEONARD PATTERSON was born in New York City, 1949, and lives now in Washington D.C. with Jim, his lover of eleven years. The experience related in "At Ebenezer Baptist Church" has left them both with a "strong distrust for organized religion." The article first appeared in *Insight* Magazine, December, 1981 and is Patterson's first published work.

RICHARD ROYAL was born in Glen Falls, N.Y., 1949. He is co-founder of *Central Park: A Journal of the Arts and Social Theory* (now publishing out of New York). His poetry and political essays have appeared in such publications as *Body Politic, Canadian Journal of Political and Social Theory, Fuse, Win, The Black Scholar*, and *Catalyst*. "Passerby" was first published in *Insight: A Quarterly of Lesbian/Gay Christian Opinion* (Spring/Summer, 1980). "Black Angel" is previously unpublished.

CHARLEY SHIVELY was born in 1937 in Ohio, and currently is a member of Boston's *Fag Rag* collective. He writes regularly for such gay publications as *Gay Community News, Fag Rag, Gay Sunshine Journal* and others. His first book of poetry, *Nuestra Senora de los Dolores*, was published in 1975 by the Good Gay Poets (Boston), and his book *Cocksucking as an Act of Revolution*, will appear in the near future. "Beyond the Binary" was published in slightly different form in *Fag Rag* #12 (Spring, 1975) and in *For Men Against Sexism: A Book of Readings*.

GABE SIMS was born in Shreveport, Louisiana in 1957. He's "a dreamer" and enjoys writing, "especially poetry." He also enjoys weightlifting, running, and reading, and is proud of "my Blackness and Gayness." "A Fine White Boy" is based on a personal incident and is Gabe's first published work.

MICHAEL J. SMITH, editor of the present anthology, is the founder of Black and White Men Together, which now has branches in most major American cities. He was born in 1944 in Culver City, California, and is the author of *Colorful People and Places*, a Gay/Lesbian interracial and Third World guidebook. He also edits and publishes the *Quarterly*, a similarly oriented periodical. "The Double Life of a Gay Dodger" first appeared in *Inside Sports*, October 1982, and "No Blacks: Racism in the Gay Press" appeared first in the *Quarterly* (#14 and #16, 1982). Mike is "still learning" and becomes "touchy when it gets too painful."

ADRIAN STANFORD was a Black gay poet living in Philadelphia. He was shot and killed in 1981. His poems appeared in *Fag Rag, The Philadelphia Tribune, Avanti, Mouth of the Dragon*, etc., and many of them were collected in the book *Black & Queer* (Good Gay Poets, Boston, 1981). The two poems printed here are taken from that volume.

JEROME THORNTON was born in Wellsville, Ohio, 1953. He writes, "I believe in poems speaking, thus I shy away from the 'poet as personality'." The poem "A Memory: Sana'a" is taken from an unpublished typescript, "City of Towers," which recounts the travels of this Black author throughout southern Arabia.

ROBERT THORPE was born in Southern California, 1945. He has published several small articles on a variety of subjects and has "a feeling that my greatest years of growth lie ahead." His story "At Verity High" first appeared in the *Quarterly* (#19, Fall 1983) Thorpe currently resides in the San Francisco Bay Area.

JAMES S. TINNEY was born in Kansas City, Mo., 1942. "Struggles of a Black Pentecostal" first appeared in *Insight* Magazine (December, 1981) in a special issue subtitled, "Black, Christian, and Gay", guest edited by Dr. Tinney. "Black, Christian, and Gay" are what James Tinney's life has been about. His extensive writings, lectures, and—perhaps most importantly—his spirited activism, have made him the foremost figure in his field. An anthology of his works is being published by the Quarterly Press.

DARRYL TOWLES was born in Pittsburgh, Pa. in 1959 but moved to Washington, D.C. as an infant. He writes: "There I was raised by strict nuns, later by hunky Jesuits. I attended Gonzaga College High School, an all-male prep school, with 500 gorgeous distractions." After graduation in 1977 he studied journalism. Turning to his true love, the theater, he moved to Boston to study drama at

Emerson College. He graduated in 1981 and moved to New York City, where he still lives. He has done several off-off Broadway shows as an actor, a little video, and some cable work. His autobiographical piece "Black and Gay" appeared originally in *First Hand Magazine*, April, 1983, under the pen-name "Boyd McNeill."

TROOP was born the 12th day of the 12th month at 12.12 a.m., 1941, in Lakewood, Ohio. He is an English teacher and has traveled widely. He and his lover have been together twelve and a half years and "are proud to be a Black and White man together." The poem "Brazil" is published here for the first time.

RON VERNON was a founding member of Chicago's Third World Gay Revolution, 1970. The article published in the present anthology is taken from a taped interview and appeared originally in *Gay Sunshine Journal* No. 6 (March 1971). It was later reprinted in a somewhat different version in *The Gay Liberation Book*.

C. S. WEINERMAN was born in Brookline, Massachusetts, 1946. His poetry has been published in several literary publications, including *The American Poetry Review, Partisan Review, Christopher Street, Bitterroot,* and *The New York Quarterly*. He is a practicing attorney in Boston and, in addition to having published several legal articles, is the author of *Practical Law* (Prentice Hall, 1978). The poem "Mt. Morris Baths" first appeared in *Poetry* (Nov. 1977).

ROOSEVELT WILLIAMSON was born in Atlanta, 1951. He's a vegetarian who is "loving, sharing, caring, and in true solidarity with all oppressed and progressive minded people." He is currently incarcerated in a penal institution in New York. "Thick Vegetarian Cum" appeared originally in *Fag Rag* (Twelfth Anniversary Issue, 1982) and his poem "Letters Come to Prison" in an earlier issue of the same publication. He has also had an article published in *Gay Community News* (Boston).

RICHARD WITHERSPOON is a Taurus, born in New York City, 1947. He describes himself as "very urban". The poem "A.R." appears in print here for the first time.

The anonymously-authored essay, "Far Away in South Africa" was previously published in the *Quarterly* (#16, Winter, 1982) and in *Mandate* (April, 1983).

ALSO AVAILABLE FROM GAY SUNSHINE PRESS

☐*BOM-CRIOULO: THE BLACK MAN & THE CABIN BOY.* A Novel by Adolfo Caminha. Translated by E.A. Lacey.
This controversial Brazilian novel relates in naturalistic style the overt sexual relationship between a mature black man (Amaro, or Bom-Crioulo) and a boy of 15 (Aleixo)—a relationship which develops during their service together in the Brazilian navy of the late 19th century. Cloth limited edition: $20.00; paperback: $8.95

☐*MY DEEP DARK PAIN IS LOVE* A Collection of Latin American Gay Fiction. Edited by Winston Leyland. Translated from Spanish & Portuguese by E.A. Lacey. 384 pp.
This is an in-depth anthology of fiction of gay themes by 24 writers from Mexico, Brazil, Cuba and Argentina. Paperback: $11

☐*PHYSIQUE:* A Pictorial History of the Athletic Model Guild. Photos by Bob Mizer.
The sexiest male models from the 1940s through the present (Black men/White men) in more than 120 magnificent nude photos, many in full color from America's oldest all-male physique studio. Regularly $20 ppd. Special price: $15

☐*MEAT/FLESH/SEX/CUM:* True Homosexual Experiences from S.T.H. Volumes 1,2,3,4. Edited by Boyd McDonald.
Men nationwide write "with no holds barred" about their true homosexual experiences—truck drivers, models, professors, workers, Third World homosexuals, Includes almost 200 pages of hot male-male sex stories illustrated with nude photos. Gay best sellers nationwide. $13 per volume postpaid (or $50 for all 4 books)

☐*UNZIPPED:* A Novella & 6 short stories by John Coriolan. Encompasses the explicitly detailed celebration of male-male sex: the excitement, the romance, the fun of it. With erotic drawings by Tom of Finland. $8.95

☐*MEN LOVING MEN: A GAY SEX GUIDE & CONSCIOUSNESS BOOK* by M. Walker. Illustrated. $11

☐*SEX BEHIND BARS* by Robert N. Boyd. A novella, short stories, true personal experiences on the gay prison experience. $11

☐Send me an additional copy of *BLACK MEN/WHITE MEN.* $10

TO ORDER: Check titles wanted and send check/m.o. to: G.S. Press, POB 40397, San Francisco, CA 94140 (Calif. residents add 6% sales tax). *Postage is included in prices quoted.* Complete illustrated catalog: $1

Published in paperback & limited trade cloth edition. A special edition of 26 lettered copies has been handbound in boards and signed by the editor.